PRAISE FOR
I'm Not Crazy, I'm Just Not You

"Differences matter. From the crib to the boardroom, from the golf course to the bedroom, differences matter. In […] *I'm Not Crazy, I'm Just Not You*, Pearman and Albritton bring up-to-date research to push our understanding of those differences to a new level. Their thinking challenges us to be proactive in our relationships and they give us the tools to be successful."

—*William W. Sternbergh, senior fellow, leadership education (ret.), Center for Creative Leadership*

"*I'm Not Crazy, I'm Just Not You* is invaluable in my role as leader of a multinational, multicultural team. Being able to understand my colleagues' type preferences—and explain my own—increased the levels of trust and support in the team. This book is essential reading for any leader attempting something new and challenging."

—*Malcolm Barnett, managing director (ret.), Corning Cable Systems*

"The acceptance of difference—a commitment to tolerance and listening to others without assumptions—is a theme for our times. This book is a guide for greater understanding in the next decade of rapid change across generations and different global cultures."

—*Dr. Sally Campbell, partner of S. A. Campbell Associates and former president of the British Association for Psychological Type*

"Individuals and managers who have taken the MBTI or use it for staff training will find this book a useful source for putting their knowledge of differing types to work toward communication with colleagues."

—*Library Journal*

"*I'm Not Crazy, I'm Just Not You* is a tool for the times. This book helps individuals and managers understand how to communicate through the differences among us, for swifter consensus, more dependable decision-making, with higher trust and understanding among the workgroup."

—*Charles C. Schroeder, vice chancellor for student affairs, University of Missouri-Columbia and past president, American College Personnel Association*

"Pearman and Albritton have created fresh insights into the 'fundamental threads of humanity' that weave through all of our lives. The reader will encounter a thought-provoking means of contemplating the courageous life and options for personal growth and will gain an understanding of the life tasks that are common to all mature human beings."

—*Gordon Patterson, president, Patterson Associates*

"This book should serve as a wake-up call for all to reevaluate how they behave and interact. I found *I'm Not Crazy, I'm Just Not You* personally and professionally enlightening and would recommend it to everyone with the desire to grow and improve."

—*Amanda Canavan, senior project administrator, Wachovia Bank & Trust*

I'm Not Crazy, I'm Just Not You

USING PERSONALITY INSIGHTS TO
WORK AND LIVE EFFECTIVELY WITH OTHERS

Third Edition

ROGER R. PEARMAN AND SARAH C. ALBRITTON

NICHOLAS BREALEY
PUBLISHING

BOSTON • LONDON

First edition published by Davies-Black in 1997
This edition published by Nicholas Brealey Publishing in 2020
An imprint of John Murray Press
An Hachette UK company

25 24 23 22 21 20   1 2 3 4 5 6 7 8 9 10

A CIP catalogue record for this title is available from the British Library

Library of Congress Control Number:2019957571

ISBN 978-15293-7829-0
U.S. eBook ISBN 978-1-8578-8470-8
U.K. eBook ISBN 978-1-4736-4387-1

Printed and bound in the United States of America.

John Murray Press policy is to use papers that are natural, renewable and recyclable products
and made from wood grown in sustainable forests. The logging and manufacturing processes are
expected to conform to the environmental regulations of the country of origin.

John Murray Press Ltd
Carmelite House
50 Victoria Embankment
London EC4Y 0DZ
Tel: 020 3122 6000

Nicholas Brealey Publishing
Hachette Book Group
53 State Street
Boston, MA 02109, USA
Tel: (617) 263 1834
www.nbuspublishing.com

For the next generation.
May you learn from our success and gain wisdom from our errors as you work to make a sustainable world.

"We read to know we're not alone."[1]

—William Nicholson

Grateful

Our families, friends, and colleagues have been instrumental in supporting the revision of this work. When the first edition was released in 1997 we could hardly imagine that the world would grow in such complexity and that type research would expand so dramatically as to make a third edition necessary. To acknowledge all those who have helped in the development of this new edition would require a book of lists. Without the publisher's commitment to our dream, this revision would not have made it into your hands. We are grateful for all the moments of care and intellectual questioning so many have offered, which ultimately enrich this work. Life is a type laboratory filled with many experiments and tests from which we gain insights, and we feel compelled to pay it forward.

Contents

Preface to the Third Edition

The constant before and after the inception of this book is that human beings are complex, have competing needs, are wired and socialized in different ways, and have at the core of our emotional lives the desire to be loved, competent, and significant in the world. We get most of these conditions addressed through our relationships with others. When those relationships are constructive and accepting, we thrive; when relationships are destructive and rejecting, we have no good outcomes in our health and overall well-being.

In the last decade, neuroscientists have shown that our whole body is a brain that perceives and acts on information, driven largely by sub-programs deep inside the organism. Given that neuroscientists inform us that our brain decides before we think we decide, that our emotions are the first reaction that colors our perceptions and judgments, and that the unconscious energies of our psyche are more in control than we are in control, we are invited to consider what Jung's "psychology of consciousness" has to say for guidance. At the heart of psychological types is a drive for adaptation and development. Human development has many vectors and these are universal.

There are no shortcuts in development, though there are many immunities to growth. The disquieting reality is that many don't turn on the psychic buttons to learn, many have insight but don't integrate the learning, and still many more choose to avoid development because the price of growth is perceived as too high. There are things we can do to develop our type of psychic system and inch toward greater clarity and discerning choices while overcoming those internal forces that like the comfort of where we are. With revisions to content, additions of illustrations, and enriching stories, our goal remains the same in this edition: to boost development by helping to "make your perceptions clearer and your judgments more sound" of your own self and in dealing with others.

—Roger R. Pearman and Sarah C. Albritton, 2020

Revised Preface to the Second Edition

We are bound together. And we now know that our bonds are genetic, economic, and social in ways we couldn't have imagined a decade ago: we all share a gene from our many-generations-removed ancestral mother in Ethiopia. The evidence of our common humanness has grown in volumes since the publication of the first edition of this book in 1997. Our interdependence as a global culture is an undeniable fact; we are connected at the most fundamental levels, yet we often see one another as aliens who must be approached with fear and defensiveness. The magic of psychological type is that, used well, it provides a way to enter a dialogue about our similarities and differences without the judgment and fear that divide, separate, and isolate us from one another.

We can make a reasonable hypothesis that most individual and cultural strife around the world—manifested at its worst in wars and human distress—is fundamentally driven by fear: fear that there aren't enough resources, that our ideals or religion are under attack, or that a way of life we cherish is in peril. In short, fear of differences—in individuals, communities, and cultures—leads to destructive behavior in the name of protecting what we are afraid we will lose. Yet the dynamic theory of personality known as psychological type invites a discussion about abundance and possibilities and about the potentials of mutual respect and goodwill. For this reason, the use of psychological type around the globe has grown exponentially in the last decade.

There seems to be an innate human response to reject or fear that which is different. It appears to be the way of the world today that the young distrust the old, and vice versa, that those of different races harbor suspicions about one another, and that entire cultures seem eager to go to war with others whose perspectives vary from their own. Since the first edition of this book, hundreds of wars and cultural battles have been waged, and untold numbers of communities and families have been torn apart because we do not learn from these events, nor do we talk about them in ways that have impact. The abundant evidence is that large numbers of people not only view others as crazy but also view them as being unworthy of life.

In the past decade, new research related to psychology and biology, growth in the complexity of human affairs, and ongoing interest in psychological type as a framework to make sense of the world mean that a revision is necessary if we are to stay true to the purpose of the model. Psychological type provides a pragmatic template for understanding the architecture and interplay of perception and judgment in human experience. When understood and applied properly, this architecture can accelerate and enrich creative solutions in human endeavors and increases our opportunities to make our corner of the world a better place. And, like any tool, if used incorrectly or under the wrong conditions, the power of type can be neutralized or may even cause harm.

No model, no system, no understanding of the architecture of human perception and judgment can help unless all parties accept three fundamental conditions:

1. An assumption of the positive intention of others. There must exist recognition that, while we may look different and live our lives quite differently from one another, those differences are neither inherently bad nor intended to be harmful or disrespectful.
2. Tolerance and use of "hypothesis testing." Rather than criticizing with certitude that we know the best method, best practice, or have the best perspective, we must stop to listen to other perspectives. It is a remarkable act of arrogance to assume that any one of us knows what another person is thinking in a given situation. We have to operate more like scientists: What is the evidence, what are the possible meanings, and how can we test our assumptions? A standard ground rule we use in teamwork settings is "offer your observations as perception rather than fact." No one person has a lock on the truth.
3. A commitment to dialogue and understanding, recognizing that empathy is the cornerstone of mutually satisfying connections. Empathy doesn't mean agreement; it means working toward a fuller understanding of the other person's point of view in a situation.

The goal of the second edition of *I'm Not Crazy, I'm Just Not You* is to provide you with insights and perspectives that encourage you to work with others in ways that promote the three conditions summarized above. We invite you, with this revision, to continue learning new strategies that will help you deal with interpersonal and intercultural strife wherever you see it: at home, at work, or out in the world.

Psychological type invites us to look at the way we see and act on experience. This model attends to the whole of human approaches to dealing with everyday problems. Psychological type affirms that:

- Sensory information stimulates us in complex ways
- Visceral reactions to stimulation are recorded and catalogued
- Patterns are observed, and they serve as ways to navigate daily challenges
- Anticipation of events and use of imagination alert us and generate possibilities
- Critical analysis enables us to find better solutions
- Reflection and critical consideration lead to clearer solutions
- Warm acknowledgment of engagement with others generates a sense of safety
- Personal valuation of events produces a passion for addressing perceived wrongs

If you know psychological type, you know that these eight statements identify a core benefit of how our use of Perceiving processes (Sensing and Intuiting) and Judging approaches (Thinking and Feeling) are manifest in Extraverted and Introverted ways. This alerts us to practical considerations to be found in each of the chapters, especially in the four new chapters added to the book. (Please note that the original titles and descriptions are maintained below but the chapters and titles were revised in the 3rd edition of this book.)

Chapter 6, "What Lies Underneath," explains the link between type and emotional intelligence. Our emotions are intertwined with personality in profound ways. Personality type gives us an understanding of those things that trigger various emotional reactions and offers a useful answer for how to create more positive emotional flow in our lives.

Chapter 7, "Getting There from Here," addresses the way that type influences our personal effectiveness during change, in our careers, while managing stress, and in enhancing health in modern life. Almost everyone feels that he or she is just above the waterline in responding to the demands of everyday life. Our lives are more complex and the pressures more consistent. No longer can we expect work to occur Monday through Friday, eight to five; it is now a 24/7 proposition. Our relationships are taking new forms as web-based networking extends how we think of community. Our lives are often run by the automatic pilot of our psychological type (and deep neuropath patterns), and the better we understand how to use our type effectively, the better we will become at using our natural talents to bring flow, well-being, and greater satisfaction to everything we do.

Chapter 10, "What's Up, Pops?" invites us to consider the interplay between generational issues and type. How does the influence of generational values affect type expressions? Are there differences in behavior between generations that vary by type? In other words, does an ESTJ at age twenty-two look more like an ESTJ at fifty, or do maturity and development blur the lines? Could a mature ESTJ begin looking like an ESFJ or INFP? Why does this matter? Depending on generation and type, there are different answers to these questions.

Chapter 11, "Continental Divide?" explores cultural variables and how they affect expressions of type. For example, Extraversion is about how stimulation from the external environment results in various behaviors. We know now what we only hypothesized in 1997—these expressions are colored by culture and are experientially evident in different ways. An Extravert in China is likely to express Extraversion differently than one in India, Canada, or the United States. In other words, the type process is the same but the expression of it varies by culture.

We have revised the other chapters in this book as well, adjusting the text when new research enriches understanding. Our lives have changed as our own children move into adulthood, and our experiences have brought fresh insights. We have worked with thousands of people since the initial publication of *I'm Not Crazy, I'm Just Not You,* and we are grateful for the insights they have brought to our use of type, which we now share with you in this revision.

New material has prompted a reorganization of the book. We have separated the material to make it easier for you in two ways: First, some of you are already conversant with the basics and are eager to move to new content. While we hear over and over that even experienced users find our approach helpful and refreshing, sometimes time is of the essence and you want the new stuff! It's here. Second, the new organization should allow you to use the book more easily as a handy reference.

The book is organized as follows.

Section 1: Foundations: Psychological Type from the Ground Up (Chapters 1 and 2)

This section provides a fresh look at what type really is. Far too many people associate psychological type with terms like Extraversion or Introversion or Thinking and Feeling and never really understand the underlying purpose and utility of these processes. It is important to know how Extraversion and Introversion affect our daily activities and how to use these energies for constructive management of personal stress. To do so, you need to get a firm grasp on the architecture of type. The focus of this section is to ground you thoroughly in the nature of type.

Section 2: Type Development: Psychological Type's Energy System at Work
(Chapters 3, 4, and 5)

Rather than a trait or descriptive model of personality, personality type is about the interactive flow of energy in how we perceive and manage our experiences. Type is a dynamic system of information and judgments about how to proceed, from the smallest choices to the largest decisions. Understanding the richness of this system opens the doors on potential that a set of "flat" descriptions can never provide. Think of type more as a gyroscope of moving parts in interaction with the world around it.

Section 3: *You*: Applying Personality Type to Enrich Individual Effectiveness
(Chapters 6 and 7)

At the end of the day, how you apply knowledge is what leads to effectiveness. This section looks at how personality type can be applied in very personal ways related to managing emotions and improving personal effectiveness. Chapters 6 and 7 are intended to enrich your way of using type.

Section 4: *Us:* Using Personality Type to Maximize Our Collective Strengths
(Chapters 8 to 11)

"Pathways of Communication" and "Valuing Differences" explore how type affects our efforts to communicate with and to value those with personality preferences different from our own. Communication has been referred to as a dangerous activity because the ways in which we can misunderstand one another are so numerous. Type provides a model to take control of our messages so that we deliver the meaning we intend. The human struggle to value differences is evident in homes and communities, as well as among nations. Type influences what we consider an expression of valuing and how we deliver such messages.

The chapters "Continental Divide?" and "What's up, Pops?" challenge us to consider how type plays out in the larger world of cultural and generational differences. We live within the context of our culture and of our relationships, which span generations. Our workplaces and our communities are more diverse than ever before. Though our friends in Europe and Asia have long experienced diversity in their large cities, we in North America are experiencing the most diverse migration into our cities in world history, as a look at recent demographics shows. Further, any astute observer of corporate life knows that we have multiple generations at work together in ways unlike previous generations. It is now commonplace to have a 31-year-old team leader supervising 55-year-old team members. Type offers us some insights on these phenomena.

Section 5: A Beginning: Psychological Type Opens Pathways (Chapter 12, 13, and 14)

Chapter 12: Follow the Evidence: A Quick Look at the Science

"Follow the Evidence: A Quick Look at the Science" addresses the question of the validity of Jung's theory of psychological types and the tools associated with measuring it. For the benefit of the general public, the professional practitioner, and the curious scientist, this chapter provides a look at the "science" of type assessment tools and how these tools and models fare through the application of rigorous standards. And while the science is robust, the ultimate test of value is if you and the user of type find the propositions of value in the management of your life.

The chapters "Beyond Patterns and Types" and "Knowledge Purchased" ask readers for mindful use of personality type at home and at work. Those values that lift us out of the muck of accusation, judgment, and repetition of bad patterns should free rather than imprison us. So often when individuals read the research describing "what is" in terms of behavior patterns, they interpret it fatalistically as "what will be," as if type preferences are absolute predictors of behavior. We state firmly that there is another choice. The choice is to know one's behavioral home base and to recognize the home bases of others. Understanding and insight can free us from mistrust and allow us to celebrate differences with confidence rather than disparage those differences in fear.

A book is only finished in the mind of the reader. Our hope is that this book takes on a "living" quality, prompting continued reflection, dialogue, and a reconsideration of how we behave in the world in relationship to one another and to the world at large. In the words of former National Geographic photographer Dewitt Jones, the question is, "Do you want to be the best in the world, or the best for the world?" Being the best for the world is only possible when you know the nature of your own mind. Psychological type provides a magnificent compass for that journey.

—Roger R. Pearman and Sarah C. Albritton
Winston-Salem, North Carolina, 2010

Prescript: Normal, Crazy, and In-Between: A Historical Glance at Type

What is "normal" human behavior? When we are troubled or amazed by what others do, we often remark, either with a furrowed brow or a gasp of delight, "It's just not normal to be able (or willing) to do that." We sometimes even hear the remark, "It's not normal to be so normal!" Some people just can't win the normalcy game. Even when we know intellectually that there are many ways to be normal, we still compare ourselves with friends, neighbors, colleagues, and celebrities, using them as a kind of personal checkpoint as if to say, "Compared with that person, I'm pretty normal." But just when we allow ourselves to feel comfortable, we may find ourselves in disagreements, experiencing disappointment, or mired in confusion because we misunderstood, or were misunderstood by, someone else. Our version of normality meets resistance from other normal people. Such moments cause many of us to pause and try to figure out what happened to make things go wrong. We may find ourselves muttering, "It seemed like a reasonable request to me; why did she look at me as if I were crazy?" or "I was just trying to be helpful and considerate! Why do I suddenly feel like I made a terrible mistake?" or "I worked hard to prepare a thorough presentation. Why did they keep asking questions that were irrelevant and outside the scope of what I was asked to do?" In essence, the situational question we perpetually ask is: What behavior in this setting will seem normal, reasonable, and acceptable? It troubles us how and why such differences of perspective occur and, if truth be known, we really want to know if one perspective is more right than the other.

Compounding, and too often confounding, the search for normalcy are the many so-called self-help and pop psychology books. These are often based solely on one person's experiences, but writ large to make those experiences seem normal and therefore applicable to you and me. Even self-help books that are not anecdotal are often based on research that has been conducted on a "clinical population." In other words, the people who were studied and on whom a book's assumptions are based are people who participated in a study because they were seeking professional help for an emotional or psychological problem. In fact, Jung's initial work was based on working with a clinical population and much of what he wrote is about exaggerations and difficult behavior.

The well-meaning psychologist or psychiatrist then writes a book for the general population based on the research about what treatment helped these people in the study, often neglecting to mention that if the reader isn't troubled by the same problem to the point of seeking professional help, the remedy in the book isn't likely to be a good fit. Further, these authors often make assumptions about "the rest of us" based on a small sample of people with admitted problems. Given the popularity of some of these books, it seems that true normality just doesn't sell to the reading public.

So, where is a description of regular folks with regular jobs trying the best they can to make the most of themselves, their families, and their lives? Where are some responses to life's everyday questions such as: Why do my spouse or kids and I consistently argue about this kind of thing? Why can't I get my ideas across to my boss, or to the other members of the volunteer group I work with? How can I learn to be a better listener and a better communicator in general? Why is this project so energizing while others are so draining?

In this book you will find some answers, or at least a clear road map to lead you to them. It is our attempt to identify and discuss the many layers and levels of ideas about normal human behavior found in the dynamic theory of individual differences called *psychological type.*

This theory of human behavior is based on sixty years of observation and research. Our work with psychological type began in 1978 and continues today. In our professional work as career counselors, therapists, managers, trainers, and later as corporate leadership specialists, we have used psychological type when appropriate to help individuals make career decisions, work through personal development issues, and become more effective managers and team members. Over nearly two decades we have trained or worked with thousands of individuals who, through an understanding of psychological type, have come to understand themselves and honor their own brand of "normal." We will present here knowledge that is substantiated by sound research (not based on anecdote or on purely personal experience) and helpful to the average person. A bit of history and background provides the context for this effort.

In 1921, Swiss psychologist, anthropologist, intellectual, and man of letters Carl Gustav Jung wrote *Psychological Types,* a book based on his study of many varied cultures, both ancient and modern. The majority of the book is a treatment of conceptions of difference and one-sidedness. He described all the major trends and insights about personality and offered his own modern-day explanation for two basic questions. First, how do normal human beings take in information—in brief, how do people know things? He called this dimension of personality *Perception*. Second, how do normal human beings make decisions or judgments about things? He called this dimension *Judgment*. Overlying these two core questions about mental functioning was a third dimension dealing with the question of where people get and expend their psychological energy. A great deal of his book looks at the nature of extraversion and introversion, and the special role these kinds of energy play in conscious and unconscious ways. A chief concern for Jung was how human beings find ways to compensate and accommodate to keep from being one-sided. In other words, if all you have is extraversion, you are one-sided and missing a great deal of life.

At about the same time, Katharine Briggs was asking the same kinds of questions. Katharine Briggs and later her daughter, Isabel Briggs Myers, were studying and writing about why different sorts of people succeed or fail at different jobs. When they read Jung's work, they found that it embodied all their ideas and more. They then began what became the lifelong task of bringing everyday application and understanding of Jung's insights to the general public—to "normal" people. Isabel Myers wrote to confidant Mary McCaulley, PhD, associate professor of psychology at the University of Florida, that while listening to radio reports on World War II, it occurred to her that a type indicator could help people find more suitable jobs in the war effort and thereby bring the war to a close more quickly.[1] She began to feel that if an instrument could be designed to help people identify their preferred Perceiving and Judging styles and the source of their energy, the insights gained would help them to value themselves and others more highly. Myers hoped that, with this knowledge, people could have more satisfying and successful educational and vocational experiences, as well as improved relationships. With these ideals to guide them, Myers and Briggs spent the next twenty years developing what is now known as the Myers-Briggs Type Indicator personality inventory, more commonly referred to as the MBTI. And with this increase in knowledge, new assessments have emerged; building on Myers's insights in some cases but changing some type assumptions in the way type is sorted or measured, these new tools are gaining ground and finding new applications around the world.

Inspired by fifty years of research with type and other measures of personal well-being and individual effectiveness, we focus now on deeper understanding of type effectiveness and development. To our knowledge, this development and work with Jung's model of psychological type is the only theory of human psychology that is based on normal populations and that emphasizes the *constructive use of differences,* rather than simply classifying and defining differences as matters of good–better–best or normal–abnormal outcomes. Measurement is not the focus; understanding patterns and how these patterns play out in everyday life is.

Jung's view is that the different cognitive styles of Perception, Judgment, and energy flow are just that—different. One is not inherently better or worse than another. Society may not take kindly to a model in which everybody wins, but it is our contention that this model is the key to successfully navigating the future. This deeply held belief is our motivation for writing. For if we—as individuals, families, communities, and societies—cannot learn to see value in the differing views and resources of others, we are surely lost. It is essential to understand that Jung and Myers are asking us to hold several complex assumptions at the same time:

1. Differences in cognitive styles affect behavior, and behavior patterns affect how we adapt and adjust to the demands of everyday life;
2. While the human propensity is to grow attached and hold on to various patterns of perception and judgment, our natural psychological system requires a balancing among various ways of perceiving and judging;
3. We are caught in an interplay between our conscious and unconscious processes, and the best compass we have is to understand our inner workings if we are to influence our outer choices;
4. Life experiences, chosen and imposed, affect all aspects of our being, even if some of the emotional and cognitive energy is stored away in the unconscious to provide future unsolicited tips and directions.

You might well ask at this point why you need to read this book. First, all around us we can see that human beings are struggling with the issue of valuing differences. This book, at its core, is about how we can identify, understand, and value human differences in constructive and productive ways. The better you understand your own natural tendencies and how they are expressed in your behavior, the easier it is to understand those things that you take for granted and/or assume are as true for others as they are for you—your interpersonal blind spots. This understanding enables you to attend to your own personal development needs, thus freeing you from the nagging fear, *What have I missed in this interaction?* With an understanding of type, you'll have a very educated guess about what is in your blind spot and can then take proactive steps to compensate. Just as important as what you learn about yourself is what you can learn about others. You may become aware of the dynamics and patterns natural to each individual; thus, you can learn to truly appreciate the richness of differences.

Second, we firmly believe you will find in these pages information that will aid you in every aspect of life—working, loving, parenting, and dealing with others. We have included many personal stories from our families, our work, and our volunteer experiences that we feel illustrate the important points. Yes, these are anecdotal, but take them in the spirit in which they are offered—not as glaring, bells-and-whistles events that only happen to special people, but as gentle teaching tales. You too can begin to notice similar incidents in your life if you keep your "type lenses" on. We will repeat over and over that type does not explain everything in human behavior and interaction. Far from it. But there is a pervasive quality about type that we and many others find intriguing, helpful, and often transformative. We hope our work can help you see that, too.

We offer a final piece of groundwork before diving into these important matters. As we have obviously taken issue with the generalities made from the research base in some other books, you should rightly be wondering about the nature of the research upon which we have based this work. Research into normal human behavior is a compelling enterprise. Researchers must make sure that those participating in the research represent regular, everyday people. As discussed earlier, for answers to questions about normal human behavior it is not helpful to study patients in mental health institutions or long-term therapy and then generalize the results to the rest of us. So, assuming the samples used are representative of people in general, researchers have to be sure that the way data are gathered and analyzed makes sense. Have other influences on behavior been reasonably accounted for? Was the research setting nonthreatening and nonbiased? We made sure that these and many other more technical questions were answered appropriately before we included the results of any piece of research in our work.

Research Base

The research that we have drawn on here comes from studies conducted all over the globe. We looked at research on everyday issues like stress, development, self-efficacy, career choices, management behaviors, and psychological type. Each research piece used an assessment of personality type and some other measure of behavior. When we found that at least three different studies suggested the same qualities about a type, we used the descriptors in our presentations to participants in our workshops. This material has been presented all over the United States, Canada, China, Europe, and Australia and we found that the descriptors were confirmed by folks of those types from all walks of life—home-keepers, office managers, ministers, line managers, counselors, and senior executives, to name a few.

We are confident in this material and have seen all the types respond well to the descriptors included here. We hope that understanding the source of the material and how it differs from many popular psychology books and other books on psychological type will help you become a more discerning consumer as well as give you the freedom to enjoy this work without having doubts about its validity. This work has produced material that allows for the exploration of the theory of psychological type, the dynamics of type, and how these can be used for personal and collective well-being.

The book's last section is written with practitioners in mind; we hope it will illuminate the science, best-practice approaches, and ethics involved in administering and interpreting the psychological type tools, with particular emphasis on the moral problems created when using psychological type. If you are currently administering or interpreting assessments and/or contracting for those services with an external vendor, this chapter will be critical to your handling of those endeavors. Psychological type has become the most written about and most criticized approach to understanding self and others that you will find in literature. Because of this criticism, a special section has been added on the science behind type and type measurement.

So, who is "normal"? In large measure, we all are. Our hope is that in these pages you will find insights into yourself and others that will provide you with the courage to celebrate, in all its many forms, the normalcy of us all.

Foundations: Personality Type from the Ground Up

"Seemingly chance variation in human behavior is not due to chance; it is in fact the logical result of a few basic, observable differences in mental functioning."[1]

—Isabel Briggs Myers, *Gifts Differing*

1 Habits of Mind
Jung and Psychological Type
looks at the basic preferences and their combinations that make up type.

2 A Messy Complexity
The Patterns That Create Expressions of Self
introduces how the preferences interact and relate to create a type pattern.

Habits of Mind

JUNG AND PSYCHOLOGICAL TYPE

t first waking in early dawn, we may be faintly aware of birds singing,
cars moving down the road, the feeling of an empty stomach. As we move
toward greater consciousness, the sensations slowly intensify toward a
complete and poignant awareness of being alive. Images from the previous
night's dreams may float through the mind; we may make some effort to give
meaning or bring order to the story. Slowly, recognition of the full day ahead
brings us to attention and makes us climb out of bed. For some, these early
moments of awareness are replete with wave after wave of physical sensation:
the sunlight on the curtains, the coolness of that certain spot on the sheets
that hasn't been occupied for a while. Others may be more aware of an inner
voice planning the day and reviewing the possibilities it holds. Some may
decide which things are most important to do today; a few will even announce,
whether or not anyone is around to hear it, "My to-dos today include…" By the
time we sit down for breakfast, our direction of awareness and attention has
already provided clues about our mental habits.

This direction of awareness, selectivity of attention, and focus of the
mind's eye from the earliest moments of morning to the final instant of consciousness before sleep at night make up an individual's psychological type.
Swiss psychologist Carl G. Jung's concept of a psychological type is, at its heart,
an examination of the way we attend to, bring order to, and make decisions
about our awareness.[1] Some psychologists have suggested that our perceptions are the realities about which we make judgments and take actions. If this
is true, understanding the mechanisms by which we formulate our perceptions becomes critical to understanding our habitual behavior. If personality
type theory is real, as we believe it is, habits of behavior are the expressions
of typical patterns of Perception and Judgment embedded in each person's
consciousness.

For example, a person who habitually focuses on the details of the world around her will likely exhibit behaviors concerned with precision, accuracy, and the order of details in the present moment. Likewise, if a person experiences life more like an impressionist painting, seeing few clear details but gaining a vivid image of the overall scene, we might hypothesize that his behaviors are likely to be concerned with patterns, possibilities, and nurturing an emerging vision to be fully expressed in the future. These are but two examples of the variety of interplay between habits of mind and observable behavior.

Psychological Type in Context of Individual Behavior Patterns

While hypotheses about behavior patterns can be based upon distinct and observable actions, using personality type to predict behavior is unwise; there are myriad other influences on behavior. Jung conceived of personality type as a habit of mind, not a fixed and unbreakable pattern, and his use of the word *type* was really shorthand for *typical*. American translations and current usage of *type* tend to imply *typecast* or *stereotype*, but this connotation was the farthest thing from the mind of Jung and from the minds of Katharine Briggs and Isabel Briggs Myers when they actualized Jung's theory in the Myers-Briggs Type Indicator inventory. The same can be said of the numerous relatively new publishers of personality type tools: they support an assessment of a dynamic system of psychological energy that taps into patterns of Perception and Judgment.[2] All of these tools are covered in detail in Appendix A (page 297). Fortunately, all psychological type assessments claim the same Jungian roots, which means that the insights outlined in this book apply, no matter what your source of type assessment may be. For example, in addition to the MBTI, you may have taken the Pearman Personality Integrator, which provides data on the use of all eight Jungian mental functions rather than a four-letter code.

We know, of course, that while we tend to be most comfortable with our habits, they do not always dictate or predict our behavior or responses. And so it is with our psychological type, or habit of mind. While the patterns of an individual's direction and process of attention are shared by others, each individual has a unique personal psychology and behaves in ways that may have other roots.

People's life experiences, the demands of their current situation, their developmental stage in life (the perspective of adulthood is a good deal richer than the one of childhood), and other inborn dispositions such as intelligence are all behavior-influencing factors in addition to psychological type. For example, if a naturally expressive person who gets energy from interacting with others is raised in an abusive home, he may learn that thinking out loud leads to pain. As an adult, he may revert to a silent thought process or a detached coping strategy when he feels threatened or stressed. A woman's biological clock or a man's midlife crisis may beget all kinds of behavior that are not expressions of natural type preferences. But their behavior and emotions are real nonetheless. This is precisely why we cannot make predictions of behavior or competencies based solely upon a person's type preferences. Much to the chagrin of many type enthusiasts, we must say loudly: type does not explain everything!

Yet to deny that we have habits is to ignore that we generally hold our forks the same way at every meal, put on our clothes in the same order, shave our legs or faces in the same pattern, react to questions with much the same facial expressions, and respond to certain stimuli in a consistent way. These habits of being pervade our thoughts and external behaviors. They do not, however, preclude or exclude other responses. When the situation calls for it, a healthy individual can adapt, breaking old habits and rising to the occasion. So the words *typical* and *habitual,* when applied to a person, do not mean that the person is rigid, fixed, or exclusive, but they do give some image, some sense of the person's patterns of seeing and responding to the world.

Amid the richness of experiences and situational demands, defined and discernible patterns of Perceiving and Judging information can still be reasonably discerned and understood. Lest anyone feel that applying personal traits to a pattern somehow compromises individuality, it's interesting to note that even fingerprints, the most renowned and overused metaphor of personal uniqueness, can be sorted into categories of recognizable patterns (the FBI, for example, sorts them into four classifications for faster identification—loops, arcs, whorls, and accidental lines). So too does psychological type provide a pattern or structure onto which our unique and individual experiences and mind-sets are grafted. With the understanding that it is but one of many influences on behavior, let us now turn our full attention to understanding psychological type.

An Overview of the Model

In his book *Psychological Types,* Jung suggested that we can sort typical mental habits among opposite poles of three personality dimensions.[3] The first, and perhaps most pervasive, dimension pertains to the primary source and direction of a person's mental energy. According to Jung's theory, the primary direction and source of psychological energy is focused toward either the outer world or the inner world. Jung used the terms *Extraversion* and *Introversion* to describe this distribution of energy. The second dimension, which he referred to as a mental or cognitive function, has to do with how we perceive information and what kind of information is initially attractive to us. The two poles of this dimension are *Sensing,* a preference for sensory data that we recognize via our five senses, and *Intuiting,* a preference for relational, abstract data that we recognize via what some might call our "sixth sense." Jung's third dimension, also referred to as a mental or cognitive function, pertains to our typical patterns for making decisions or judgments about the information we have perceived. One pattern, *Thinking*, involves decisions based on interest in and attention to an object with cause-and-effect analysis. The other pattern, *Feeling*, involves equally rational decisions based on personal values and relational impact of actions.

The American mother-daughter team of Katharine Briggs and Isabel Briggs Myers contributed to Jung's schema by adding a fourth polar dimension. This dimension has been adopted by nearly all assessments of personality type. It focuses on habits of external orientation either toward orderliness and decisiveness, called *Judgment*, or toward new information and "going with the flow," called *Perception*. They named these poles after the mental function to which they are related. As you will see, the Judgment orientation is associated with the Judging mental functions (Thinking and Feeling). Likewise, the Perceiving orientation is associated with the Perceiving mental functions (Sensing and Intuiting). This fourth dimension allows for quick identification of typical Extraverted expressions in all people;[4] it will be covered in detail later.

The four polar dimensions as presented by Jung, Myers, and Briggs are Extraversion (E) and Introversion (I), Sensing (S) and Intuiting (N), Thinking (T) and Feeling (F), and Judging (J) and Perceiving (P). Individuals have a preference for one side or the other of each of the four poles, thus creating 16 possible preference combinations that make up a psychological typology, a set of typical habits of mind.

Jung spent the majority of *Psychological Types* discussing his observations of a wide variety of perspectives on human differences. He pondered how human beings from incredibly different cultures could share basic qualities and yet be so different. From his studies he proposed that the psychological world is made up of polarities. His source for this theory is the presence of polarities in symbols found in all cultures. These range from the common—night and day, male and female, foreground and background, wet and dry—to the more philosophical, such as yin and yang, life and death, heaven and hell. Jung's point was that for a concept like heaven to have any substantial meaning, there has to be a contrasting concept of hell. He went on to propose that the psyche is also bounded by polarities and wrote about the polarities of consciousness and unconsciousness as well as, most notably, Extraversion and Introversion.

The psychological polarities Jung proposed are no different from the other polarities he observed and documented: just as we experience both night and day or wet and dry, we can and do utilize both poles of each dimension, but only in sequence, not simultaneously.[5] This is why the dimensions of this model are not set on a continuum of low to high. A continuum implies a simultaneous, measurable utilization of the opposites; Jung's model is based on the reality that one cannot focus perfectly on details and on generalities at the same instant. Individuals can, and most do, have access to and exhibit skills associated with each of the poles, depending on the situation. But we cannot access them concurrently. Therefore, the question in determining personality type preference is not "Which one do I do?" but rather "Which do I do first?" or "Which is most comfortable or reliable?" It is extremely important to realize that the presence of polarities and the reality of an individual's pull toward a pole does not imply an either/or situation. You are not entirely either an Extravert or an Introvert. Healthy, normal individuals have and use both poles, but they do have a preference for one over the other. Jung proposed that this is also true for both of the mental/cognitive functions included in his typology, and Myers argued similarly about orientations to the outer world when she added it as a fourth dimension in the MBTI.[6] As indicated earlier, nearly all other assessments of personality type include this dimension, as it addresses an aspect of Jung's theory related to a superior mental process that is aided by a secondary process, which is explained in more detail in the next three chapters.

The Model in Context: Ancient Traditions of Personality Observations

Jung, Myers, and others were not the first to observe personality types, nor was Jung the first to write about a typology of awareness. One of the oldest such typologies is part of the American Plains Indian tradition of the medicine wheel,[7] which assumes that each individual comes into the world with a way of perception that is but a beginning point in understanding others and the world. In this culture, one's task in life is to master not only one's own way of perception but to demonstrate understanding and good use of each of the others. To put it briefly, this model holds that each person is born into a particular way of seeing the world: the buffalo way, logical and analytical; the eagle way, seeing patterns and flying high above the details; the bear way, relational and connected to the environment; or the mouse way, grounded and close to the roots and details of life. The addition of assorted colors and directions to these basic descriptions (a person might be signified as a green bear looking inward, for example) honors the complexity and uniqueness of the individual while showing the patterns common to all people. Tribal elders identified the way of a child after much careful observation.

As tribe members demonstrated mastery in looking at and appreciating other people's ways, the elders granted stones to them for placement on symbolic medicine wheels. An individual's wheel was then carried in such a way on a man's shield or a woman's buckle that those approaching could see from the number and placement of stones how accomplished that person was in seeing other points of view. These Native Americans saw their life work as achieving movement around the medicine wheel to become expert at all views of life. This simple but elegant system was a model of the human psyche, and it informs us that type is a very old system with roots in ancient cultural understandings of processes. Myers and Jung provide continuity to this tradition with their contemporary revision of the theory. If you ever visit Monticello, the home of Thomas Jefferson, there is an exemplar of the medicine wheel with 16 positions around the circle that hangs in the foyer.

The Framework

Psychological type suggests that there is a pattern within each of us by which we engage with, perceive, and act on the world. This pattern can be determined by pondering the extent to which we are pulled toward one or the other pole of each of four dimensions:

(E)	Extraverting	**ENERGY**	Introverting	(I)
(S)	Sensing	**PERCEPTION**	Intuiting	(N)
(T)	Thinking	**JUDGMENT**	Feeling	(F)
(J)	Judging	**ORIENTATION**	Perceiving	(P)

We will review, in depth, each of the dimensions in the model, for it is vital to understand these polarities in order to cross the threshold leading to the heart of the type. Ultimately, personality type is less about preferences on a single dimension and far more about the dynamic interplay of the four preferences within a person's habits of mind that lead to typical behavioral expressions. The dynamic is understood in terms of how these dimensions relate to one another to create a sum that is truly greater than its individual parts.

The Model in Depth: Finding Your Own Home Bases

To find individual preferences, it helps to describe the two poles of each dimension and determine which has the stronger pull.

Sorting Among Extraversion and Introversion: The Mental Attitude

Your type preferences are on automatic pilot during every waking hour. They balance your external management of situations with internal pushes and pulls that motivate you. Though many people use the words *extraversion* and *introversion* in everyday conversation as a shorthand for "outgoing" or "shy," when Jung coined the terms they had a far more complex meaning. Extraversion and

Introversion in Jung's model have broader implications than mere differences of social acuity; they create an energy field.

Modern research suggests real differences in the brain activity of Introverts and Extraverts. Extraverts are stimulus hungry.[8] Extraverted minds seek external activity, change, and interaction to create the energy needed to guide the self through the day. Yet it is important to remember that we are not one-dimensional creatures. Within the person with an Extraverted preference, even while the Extraversion is active and the person is aware of this need for stimulation, Introversion is still at work outside of awareness. Within any person, it is never a situation of having access to the poles of the dimensions in an "either-or" fashion, but rather it should be considered in terms of "preference, and…" One's preference for Extraversion is always aided behind the scenes by Introverted energy processes. Though those processes are typically outside of ready awareness, they are very much in play, as we will see in later chapters.

This balancing process is also true for the person with a preference for Introversion, whose conscious awareness is likely to be focused on the inner world of thoughts and ideas. Nonetheless, their Extraverted processes are aiding and supporting them in the background while they navigate grocery aisles, highway systems, and boardrooms.

Jung referred to the Extraverted and Introverted processes as *attitudes,* and we will use his language to refer to them. For many people reading Jung's work today, attitude, used in reference to the processes of Extraversion and Introversion, causes a bit of confusion. We have come to use the word today to refer to a person's motivation level or stance toward life. But when Jung was translated to English in the 1920s, the word *attitude* had much more to do with physical positioning than with a state of mind. If you read murder mysteries written during the period, you will see the word used like so: "The attitude of the body was facedown with the left arm extended to the side." In talking about Extraversion and Introversion, Jung was concerned with the *physical direction of the mind's eye.* For a given individual, it is directed either mostly externally, seeking to exert and collect its energy from the world outside (Extraversion), or internally, focusing on and drawing sustenance from a vivid and rich inner world of thoughts and ideas (Introversion). Though assuming that we all use both energy sources, Jung theorized that any individual prefers one source over the other, much as one prefers left-handedness or right-handedness.

This balancing of energy is of practical significance. The person who prefers Extraversion is responding externally, seeking an event to be experienced. So strong is this impulse that the Extravert may talk out loud, even when alone, in order to experience an external event and make his thoughts real. All the while, his Introverted process is internalizing that experience, seeking to make sense of all that is happening externally. Without the functioning of

Introversion, the Extravert babbles like a shallow brook soon to be evaporated by the heat of living.

The individual who prefers Introversion is aware of the internal world of experiences and is generally less in tune with the Extraverted energy field. The Introvert uses Extraverted functioning as a practical way of getting from the sofa to the bathroom in an unfamiliar home, or finding the correct gate in a busy airport. But the trip provides no source of stimulation, and having arrived at the destination, the Introvert may wonder what route she took to get there. An Introvert without the functioning of Extraversion simulates a catatonic state of being.

Sometimes children give us the most natural and expressive examples of type in action. We, the authors, are inveterate observers of children, our own and others', and we will offer stories of them throughout to illustrate our points. And while we recognize that type is not the only force at work in these interactions, sometimes the type influence is so clear that we have to laugh out loud. A story from each of our households illustrates what can go on when Introverts and Extraverts get together.

Olivia and Luke Pearman are two years apart in age. Luke clearly prefers Extraversion and Olivia, the elder, prefers Introversion. Once, at the ages of about six and eight, they were in the car and Luke was giving a running commentary on all that he saw around him. "There's a red car…the radio is playing a good song…there's a McDonald's, I'm hungry…." After a few minutes, Olivia burst out, "Luke! It is what it is; be quiet!" Luke immediately responded, "I can't be quiet, Olivia. My brain keeps telling me things and I don't know how to turn it off!"

Tom, the father of Sarah's children, has a clear preference for Extraversion, while her son Wells seems to prefer Introversion. When Wells was a child it was not unusual for Tom to be talking to him about something at length and for Wells to finally ask, "Daddy, who are you talking to?" He'd tuned out all the "noise" many minutes before. One day on the way to kindergarten Tom was going on about something and Wells asked, "Daddy, WHAT are you talking about?" Tom, who knows a good deal about type, said, "Son, I was just thinking out loud. Sometimes I talk about things in order to understand them. Don't you ever do that?" Wells laughed as if he had caught Tom trying to pull a joke on him and replied, "No, Daddy, I don't. That's backwards."

In the business environment, Extraversion and Introversion can provide no end of misunderstanding. What to an Extraverted supervisor sounds clearly like a comfortable, lively brainstorming session can sound to an Introverted employee like a list of tasks for the upcoming quarter. We have heard many stories of team meetings in which Extraverts begin with one set of ideas about a solution to an issue and through lengthy, often animated discussion reach a conclusion entirely different from the starting point. This can confuse

Introverts, causing them to wonder which ideas to actually act upon—the initial plans or the later ones. Adding to the scene, some of the Introverts, with the benefit of time to reflect, may later make another series of suggestions that, when offered at that point, can be interpreted by the Extraverts as counterproductive—"Why didn't you just say so an hour ago? We already reached our conclusions. Now we have to get everybody together again to talk about it!" And so the circle dance can continue ad infinitum (or ad nauseam, depending on your viewpoint!).

This distinction between Extraversion and Introversion is profound but greatly misunderstood. People who have seriously reflected on their observations of life cannot reasonably question that the distinction exists, and no personality researcher in the last 60 years has had serious doubts about the presence of Extraversion and Introversion in humans. But the Americanized version of Jung's formulation has led to the false conclusion that Extraversion means outgoing and gregarious behavior, and that Introversion means shyness and withdrawn behavior.[9] The kernel of truth is that Extraversion seeks to initiate and Introversion is inclined to receive and reflect. Shyness, however, is a function of anxiety when in the presence of other people, and it occurs regardless of a preference for Introversion or Extraversion. It is more probably related to early childhood experiences. Likewise, gregariousness is also largely a function of expectation and training, and it occurs in Introverts and Extraverts alike.

In typology, in these habits of mind, Extraversion and Introversion are processes of charging our mental batteries. Some are aware of, and act upon, a need to initiate—to seek stimulus. Others are aware of a need for the energy that comes from reflection. Whichever process provides the main source of awareness, the opposite process fulfills needs that are beyond awareness.

The Extravert's relationship with the environment serves an important purpose. By definition, Extraversion means seeking energy from the world outside the self; thus Extraverts report feeling a real need to "think out loud." In other words, externalized thought takes on a richer, more complex meaning for the Extravert. Thoughts forced to stay inside without external expression may be experienced like the white noise of a radio tuned between channels where the frequency is sporadic. Sometimes the thought or idea only begins to make sense, the frequency only comes in clear and strong, after it has been brought outside the self. But the underlying goal of the initiation is to seek out and collect energy from outside the self.

The Introvert, on the other hand, is less likely to feel the need to externalize thoughts or ideas until the pressure to communicate with others requires it. Like a Japanese garden that offers new views as a person walks through it, the Introvert's new experiences or ideas are satisfying in and of themselves; energy comes through the peace and elegance of the internal garden rather than from outside stimuli. Extraversion initiates in the environment; Introversion is initiated within a person and spends its energy by painting an internal picture of what is real.

Extraversion and Introversion are as different to people as batteries and software are to a laptop computer; each is essential but they serve different purposes. The attitudes of Extraversion and Introversion, as psychological types, are the processes that create the energy field each person has with the world. This energy exchange can be represented in the following way:

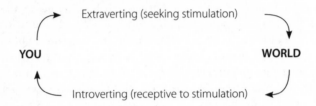

If you are new to personality type and want to discern your own preference on this dimension, take a moment to ask yourself, "Where do I get my batteries charged most frequently?" Do you get "mental juice" externally, by initiating, in which case your primary pull or preference may be for Extraversion? Or are you revitalized internally, by receiving and reflecting, in which case your preference may be for Introversion? Remember that you are doing both. But which is easiest and most energizing for you? Of which process are you most aware? Make a note in the margin of this page—*E* if you suspect you prefer Extraversion, *I* if you think you prefer Introversion.

Since this book was first published, the use of pagers, cell phones, email, conference calls, and various other connectivity technologies has grown exponentially, and global teams often require connections at all hours of the day and night. Everyone is plugged in! In workshops today, we hear even the most committed Extraverts tell us that they are exhausted from the unrelenting interaction and take the long route home from work with the phone turned off as well as other measures that, in days gone by, were the cherished solitary practices of those preferring Introversion. Anecdotally, the differences between the preferences now seem clearer in the "bounce back" time needed after a long, interactive week. The stories we hear suggest that, assuming a Friday evening start to private time, by lunchtime or afternoon on Saturday, those preferring Extraversion have recharged and are ready to meet the world again—community activities, family outings, and so on. Those with a preference for Introversion report wanting every minute of the weekend to restore their energy and get ready to go back out on Monday. This is not research; it is simply what we hear from people in our work and what we experience in our own lives.

Sorting Among Sensing and Intuiting: The Perceiving Functions

We have described Extraversion and Introversion as basic energy exchange processes. Now we turn to the mental functions. Taking in information and making decisions about information—Perception and Judgment—are core human mental functions. The perceptual dimension in type—that is, how we take in or perceive information—revolves around tendencies toward either specific and factual existence or theoretical and global existence.

Some of us are pulled toward concrete, matter-of-fact information that we experience directly and exactly. This pull to the pragmatic and realistic matters of life is referred to as Sensing Perception. Individuals with the Sensing preference are drawn to facts like metal to magnets; they feel an urge for clarity and prefer that the matters they deal with be of practical importance. These individuals often express their creativity by adapting familiar strategies to solve newly presented problems. This is the type of creativity displayed by Thomas Edison, who tried hundreds of possibilities before finding a workable light bulb filament: consistent adaptation of the known. People with a Sensing preference are thus often experienced by others as methodical, certain, adamant about details, and focused on the here and now.

Those who are pulled to the figurative, to ideas and various associations of possibilities, are said to have an Intuitive Perceiving preference. Rather than feeling the urge for clarity, people who prefer Intuiting have an urge to acquire knowledge and to seek complexity in information. The Intuitive Perception trusts ideas like the eyes trust light. The striving for the association of ideas is often so strong that, like two sticks rubbing together to create fire, Intuiting creates innovation. People with the Intuitive preference are thus often seen by others as imaginative, unconventional, intellectual, and having a mental focus on the future.

These qualitatively different perceptual pulls lead to profound differences of expression in communications. Often, those with a Sensing preference are drawn to the specificity, details, and action plan aspects of a project; those with an Intuitive preference are more likely to be drawn to the goals, models, and ideas framing the project. Without an awareness of these differing tendencies, the Sensing type might see the Intuitive type's reliance on models and theories as a person with his or her "head in the clouds," and the Intuitive type might see the Sensing type's interest in details and practicalities as being "a stick-in-the-mud." But a little reflection makes it clear that both types are needed to complete most complex projects, because the idea behind a project is as important as the details of the plan that implements it—one cannot exist without the other!

The same is true within an individual. A person whose primary pull is toward Sensing may often have hunches and a vision for the future but is more likely to spend energy talking about or exploring practical applications of an idea and may not act until the verifying data are in place. An individual pulled toward Intuitive processes is aware of details but is likely to put those details into a larger context in order to make meaning of them, perhaps talking about or exploring various abstract relationships between today's choices and choices that may crop up tomorrow.

These differences are profound and difficult to describe. Jung referred to the Perceiving function as "irrational,"[10] but *nonrational* probably works better in our current usage. Think about it. How do you come to know things? If we do base decisions on our perceptions of events, understanding where our perceptions originate is vital, yet the search is as for figures in the mist. Another teaching story from our children may illustrate both the dynamic tension between these modes of perception and the innate nature of the process.

Roger's son, Luke, and Sarah's son Wells have been best buddies from the start; they are very close in age. We suspect that Luke gets his information from external or Extraverted Perceiving, while Wells seems to be more tuned to Intuitive messages. One beautiful day when they were around four years old, they were outside swinging together, side by side. Luke was joyously exclaiming and reporting about all his sensory experiences: "The breeze is in my hair and feels cool! The sky is blue and so is that toy train and so are my pants! The grass is green and tickles my feet! The trees are green, too!" Wells, not to be outdone, shouted, "The trees are pushing the sky!" Luke's rejoinder, which reflected his Introverted Thinking desire for precision, was the sort many people preferring Intuiting feel they get from pragmatists. He said, "No, they're not."

No one told the children what to pay attention to or how they should experience that glorious afternoon. The verbal expressions they chose were absolutely natural. There they were, not ten inches from each other, both swinging, both facing the same direction, for all intents and purposes having the same physical experience, and yet their perceptions of it were so radically different. How do we know what we know? It is difficult to tease it apart, yet the pattern of difference between Sensing knowledge and Intuitive knowledge is undeniable.

For example, during an intense discussion by the members of a Research and Development Task Force for a financial company, those relying on Sensing kept pushing to use historical trends and specific data sources as benchmarks, but those with Intuitive preferences wondered aloud if the group was too buried in the past. Clearly both sides had important points to make. It is interesting, though, how during moments of stress we tend to exaggerate our typical responses and ignore other kinds of information. Professional observers of such situations often note these exaggerated states as people with opposing preferences play out their differences.

Here is another spot to stop and contemplate your own patterns of perception. Are you pulled more to the traditions, hard data, and sensory realities of life, or more to visions of the future that are guided by models and theories and ideas? Again, make a note in the margin of this page before going on, *S* for Sensing or *N* for Intuiting (as *I* denotes Introversion, *N* is used as shorthand for Intuiting).

Sorting Among Thinking and Feeling: The Judgment Function

Taking in information, as we all do through our Sensing and Intuitive functions, is but one part of the natural processing of information. Healthy individuals are also driven to decide on the merit or worth of information after it has been taken in. A plenitude of studies has shown the human tendency toward judgment. We are wired to make meaning out of information, to decide on its relative importance, its sensibility, and how it fits into our world views.[11] Jung suggested that we are pulled toward either an analytical, cause-and-effect type of Judgment (Thinking) or a value-oriented, idealistic, and accommodating type of Judgment (Feeling). Jung was quick to point out that both Thinking and Feeling are subjective and rational functions, but that the former places importance on the subjective experience of logic whereas the latter places importance on the subjective experience of personal values and how they affect outcomes. Jung wrote that Thinking types experience the world as an object, Feeling types as a subject.[12] In other words, those with the habit of initially stepping out of a situation and looking at the variables see the world as an object; those who look at the relations involved and step into a situation to attend to its effects on others see the world as a subject. The initial decision to step into or out of a new situation depends on what subjects hold the individual's interest and attention.

Individuals who are pulled toward Thinking Judgments are often seen as critical (thus less accepting), logical, and questioning. When assessing any situation, their likely first sequence of thought is *if A, then B*. The urge to verify information, to explore independent sources of information, and to insist on sequential reasoning is, for those with a Thinking preference, as natural as a river running downhill. The Thinking Judgment function is directed toward a particular outcome, moves with great momentum, and follows an orderly route to its destination.

Those with a preference for Feeling Judgments are often seen as accepting, trusting of emotions, fair-minded, and seeking of consensus. The urge is toward consistency with personal values rather than the apparent principles or logic of a situation. The first tendency is to examine how information and outcomes affect individuals. Feeling types may describe their acute awareness of the intricacies of a network as a delicate web that connects us all, such that movement anywhere on the web can be felt throughout the web, not just in the immediate area. Their thinking about a new situation is not likely to be *if A, then B,* but rather *if A, then B, D, N, and Q,* and that's just for starters. Feeling types respond first with acceptance of an individual and a desire to accommodate before bringing logic and analysis to a situation. Two examples illustrate how Thinking and Feeling often play out. One is from the business world, the other from a professional society.

During consultation with a manufacturing company, a vice president expressed great disappointment that the company was about to lose a very effective plant manager. The vice president had puzzled over the situation and was unable to see how to prevent the loss. By his account, this manager had gotten superior raises and other financial benefits, and was consistently given high marks on his annual review, which went into his personnel file. Asked to assess the situation and to intervene or at least clarify the reasons for the valued employee's departure, the consultant interviewed the manager. In that conversation the manager said things like, "I work hard for this company and get no appreciation. I can work anywhere for the money. I want to work where people really appreciate what I do—where I'll know that it matters that I come in to work, not just any plant manager with my expertise." Upon hearing this, the baffled vice president said again, "But we've given him raises! Stock! We point out all of his abilities during annual reviews! How can he not feel appreciated?" Simply put, the vice president had a Thinking preference and the manager had a Feeling preference. For the Feeling type, competency is basically assumed and regular expressions of appreciation are needed; for the Thinking type, appreciation is basically assumed and need only be confirmed by regular pay raises and/or increases in responsibility. Obviously the two have very different definitions of the word *appreciation.* This example came from one company, but we have heard virtually the same words from employees in many other manufacturing companies.

The other example comes from the board of a very small volunteer nonprofit organization. The board signed a contract with a speaker to present a workshop; it stated that after all the bills for the event had been paid, the speaker would receive a high percentage of the remainder. The speaker was a longtime friend to the organization and hoped the event would succeed so that the group would have some cash flow for future programs. The event was indeed a great success with lots of attendees. Six weeks later the treasurer of the organization reasoned that all the bills had been submitted, so he totaled up the figures and wrote the speaker a check for the appropriate percentage of the money left over. But three days after the check was sent out, another sizable and legitimate bill was submitted. *What should I do?* thought the treasurer. This bill significantly decreased the profits from the event, and therefore the speaker had been vastly overpaid within the context of the contract. To the treasurer, the proper action was clear: call the speaker and explain the circumstances. Especially since the speaker was a friend and wanted the program to enlarge the coffers of the organization, the payment would simply be renegotiated in light of the new information. No big deal.

But this board knew something about type. The treasurer knew he was the only person on the board with a preference for making Thinking Judgments and that all the others preferred Feeling. So, he thought, *It seems clear to me what to do, but I know others may have a different view. I'll ask the rest of the board what they want me to do.* That's when the real learning began. To the persons with a Feeling preference, the decision was equally clear—eat the loss. Their rational response was that this small organization depends on the good will of speakers in the area to virtually donate their time to present programs. Even with a successful program, the amount they paid the speaker was a pittance. To ask for a renegotiation of fees at this time would seriously damage the reputation of the organization and the network upon which it relied. From the board's perspective, it would be irresponsible to jeopardize the organization's ability to serve its members in the future because of a bookkeeping error. Thus, there were two radically different ways of approaching the same problem. The real gift of understanding type is the knowledge that there might be different but equally valid views about an issue, and that discussion about these views need not dissolve into an unpleasant personal argument.

Of all the psychological type dimensions, the distinction between Thinking and Feeling brings the most debate. Western culture generally values and teaches logical, linear, and analytical problem solving. It is often difficult at first for those whose true preference is for Feeling to separate it from such cultural conditioning. As consultants, we have seen over and over again in our work with major corporations the blind spot caused by over-reliance on Thinking attributes. We have often asked corporate workers to respond anonymously to the following query: "Visualize this organization five years from now, after it has developed self-directed teams (or whatever phrase the company uses for fully functioning teams). As you imagine your successful team, describe the characteristics that make it effective. What are you doing that helps you achieve the success you want?" Consistently the overwhelming responses are: "We listen thoroughly to each other." "Different views are tolerated and encouraged." "We care about each other." "We can take a risk without fear of reprisal."[13] This may explain why there has been exponential increase in titles such as *Emotional Intelligence, Care of the Soul, Servant Leadership,* and *Habits of Heart,* all of which tap into the need for balance in the workplace between these two equally rational ways of making judgments. When a Google manager noticed some of her teams were outperforming others, she wanted to know why. She was given an opportunity to study teams in Google, which resulted in Project Aristotle, which established that five key factors were critical, and the most important of which was psychological safety.

Interestingly but perhaps not surprisingly, this is the only type dimension in which we see gender differences in the general population. On a number of type assessments, a majority of women say they have a preference for Feeling, and a majority of men report themselves as having a preference for Thinking.[14] Much of the work that you see today on gender differences also describes quite accurately the differences between Thinking and Feeling Judgments, regardless of the gender of the person with the preference.

Some believe there is a kind of parallel development of these two processes. Our experience is that individuals have real, basic preferences that rely first on either personal logic or personal values.

Pause here again for reflection on your preferred method of making decisions. Mark *T* in the margin of this page if you have a preference for Thinking, or *F* if your preference is for Feeling.

Myers's Innovation: Sorting Among Perception and Judgment—Orientation to the Outer World

Myers agreed with Jung's notion that both the public self (Extraverted energy) and the private self (Introverted energy) combine with the mental functions of Perception and Judgment to create a complex system. She set out to simplify it by developing a way of examining typical Extraverted and Introverted mental functions through the use of a construct she called orientation to the outer world. Her suggestion was that the behavior and habits of the public (Extraverted) self give a strong clue about the dynamic of the individual's complete type orientation. She hypothesized that the poles of outward orientation could be recognized by decisive, orderly, and planned expression or by ad hoc, casual, and spontaneous expression. The former she referred to as *Judgment,* the latter as *Perception.*[15] By giving these the same names as the poles of the mental functions, she inferred that orientation preference, regardless of attitude preference, predicts whether a person's Judgment processes (Thinking or Feeling) or Perceiving processes (Sensing or Intuiting) are typically in the Extraverted mode. The alternate mental function, then, would typically operate in the Introverted attitude. In other words, if you Extravert Judgment, you Introvert Perception; if you Extravert Perception, you Introvert Judgment.

People with a preference for the Judging orientation are likely to express satisfaction with getting a job completed well before a deadline. They are driven to make decisions, to bring closure to things in the external world. While they are fully capable of handling last-minute changes and chaos, the voice in their head is likely to be saying, *If I had planned better, this wouldn't have happened. What can I learn from this to make sure it doesn't happen again?* These folks are likely to be very attached to their calendars and goal sheets and are often quite skilled at prioritizing the tasks necessary to meet a goal. Their to-do lists will almost certainly feature discernible orders of priority. The downside is a tendency to become attached to a particular outcome, rather than remaining open to new information that might lead to a more effective outcome. Still, the need for completion can work wonders when the going gets tough, and a proclivity for action can be crucial in today's fast-paced environment.

The person with a preference for the Perceiving orientation is pulled, in the external world, to remain open to new information, to go with the flow. Whereas people who prefer Judging might nag themselves to plan things better, the Perceiving type, though able to make and follow a detailed plan, may wonder, "If I plan or decide this now, will I be able to respond if something better comes along, or if I receive more information later?" Note, however, that research shows that actual procrastination seems to cut across both types.[16] In general, folks with a preference for Perceiving appear to the world to be fairly laid-back, unconcerned with the exact schedule of events because they are confident that the process will lead to the best outcome, whatever it may be. As a result, folks with a Perceiving preference are often very comfortable with ambiguity and last-minute changes. The downside of this pull is remaining open too long and missing opportunities for action. The benefit is that people with this preference are often more open to unexpected outcomes and may be able to find success where others would see failure.

Moments before Sarah and Tom were to be married, one of the bridesmaids rushed up to Sarah and said, "We are one bouquet short! I have no flowers!" Simultaneously, a groomsman approached and said, "We are one boutonniere short, too!" Rather than seeing this as a failure and feeling that all her hopes for a perfect wedding were dashed, Sarah assessed her resources and took the bouquet from the maid of honor and another from her sister, the matron of honor. She gave one of the bouquets to the empty-handed bridesmaid; the other she quickly disassembled and handed a single lily to the maid and another to the matron. From the remainder, she created a boutonniere for the groomsman. The wedding began on time, and because Sarah's mother grows prize-winning lilies, everyone in the church thought that the maid and matron of honor carrying a single perfect lily was a purposeful decision. For years after in that community, it was de rigueur for the maids of honor to carry a single-stem flower rather than a full bouquet. Remaining open to outcomes saved the day in this case. (Skeptics may rightly say that if Sarah had just counted the flowers earlier the whole crisis might have been avoided! Still, the unexpected outcome was a lovely new tradition that added something to their ceremony and to many others.)

You know what to do at this point. In which direction do you think you are pulled most in your dealings with the outer world? Do people around you see and hear you making decisions and judgments, reaching closure about the events in your life, or do they see you maintaining an air of flexibility and openness to whatever may come? Note a *J* in the margin if you think you

19

prefer a Judging orientation, or a *P* if you're more inclined to the Perceiving orientation.

Now thumb back through this chapter and find your margin notes; there should be four. Together they look something like ESTJ or INFP or ENTP or ISFJ. There are 16 possibilities (by convention, the four letters are listed in the following order: E or I; S or N; T or F; J or P). This is your personality profile, but for now consider it to be only a rough-cut hypothesis. Be open to changing your mind about it as you move through the rest of the book.

We will use the vocabulary from Table 1 regularly throughout the work, especially in the next chapter. It will be well worth your time to study this table carefully and familiarize yourself with the language of, for example, Extraverted Thinking and Introverted Sensing, and how that relates to the

TABLE 1
EXTRAVERTED AND INTROVERTED MENTAL FUNCTIONS

Self-Sort Profile					
Energy	*Perception*	*Judgment*	*Orientation*	**Extraverted Mental Function as Determined from Orientation Preference (J or P)**	**Introverted Mental Function**
I	S	T	J	Thinking (T)	Sensing (S)
I	N	T	J	Thinking (T)	Intuiting (N)
E	S	T	J	Thinking (T)	Sensing (S)
E	N	T	J	Thinking (T)	Intuiting (N)
I	S	F	J	Feeling (F)	Sensing (S)
I	N	F	J	Feeling (F)	Intuiting (N)
E	S	F	J	Feeling (F)	Sensing (S)
E	N	F	J	Feeling (F)	Intuiting (N)
I	S	T	P	Sensing (S)	Thinking (T)
I	S	F	P	Sensing (S)	Feeling (F)
E	S	T	P	Sensing (S)	Thinking (T)
E	S	F	P	Sensing (S)	Feeling (F)
I	N	T	P	Intuiting (N)	Thinking (T)
I	N	F	P	Intuiting (N)	Feeling (F)
E	N	T	P	Intuiting (N)	Thinking (T)
E	N	F	P	Intuiting (N)	Feeling (F)

Note: This table will be referred to many times, so study it and make a note of this page number for future reference. The self-sorting on most personality inventories produces a shorthand four-letter code that yields the system shown in Table 1.

Judging–Perceiving dimension. You may even want to dog-ear the table for quick reference later.

Research, both past and ongoing, shows that Jung and Myers were correct in their hypothesis that the 16 types are measurably distinct from one another.[17,18] In the following chapters you will read many descriptors of the different types as we, step by step, develop fully the picture that type can give us.

It is vitally important to remember here that for Jung these bipolar propositions assume that differences are valuable and constructive and are not to be overused at the risk of developing one-sidedness. Being different from others in one's perceptual or judgment pattern is neither good nor bad in and of itself. And it's also true that while all types are equally valuable, not all type expressions are equally valuable in all situations. This differentiation between a person's type and typical expressions of type is one we will return to over and over throughout this book. Keep in mind that our goal is to understand the typical patterns in the hope that understanding differences may begin a journey toward actually valuing human differences.

We must not leap to the conclusion that this understanding is equal to valuing the rich differences that arise from psychological types. Typology as a theory is straightforward, and it asserts that psychological type is a messy, sometimes chaotic dynamic that creates both clearly discernible patterns as well as tremendous variability in behavior. If personality type is used as a rigid, well-ordered system of defining, labeling, and predicting habits, it may be impossible to truly value differences. How can anyone value that which is stereotyped?

We hear more and more in recent years in casual discussion and in research literature that MBTI type "tells you what you are" or fails to, depending on what you're reading. We say over and over here, based on research and combined 70 years of experiences, psychological type is about pattern and preference, not absolute predictions and pigeonholing. We've added a full chapter (chapter 13) of current research and response to those wanting to dismiss the usefulness of psychological type based on interpretations from the wrong platform. An important facet of the usefulness of this model is born from its specific adherence to a unique model of bimodal preference, not continuous measurable trait. It cannot be compared to other tools using the same measurement metrics. It defies the whole concept of type to do so.

In this chapter we have covered definitions of the basic scales within the model of personality type. If we left you here, you might think that each of these dimensions is a stand-alone piece such that your profile would read ESTJ or INFP. But this model really comes alive in what are called *type dynamics*. Type dynamics help to answer questions such as, "What happens when your preferences on the individual scales start interacting with one another?" "Is Extraverted Intuiting different from Introverted Intuiting?" "Why can't my spouse and I understand each other even though three of our four letters are the same?"

The evidence we discuss in chapters 2 and 3 suggests that when Myers developed the J–P orientation scale she was on to more than just the orientations and their indications of Extraverted mental functions. She actualized Jung's model by showing two things: first, that the Extraverted and Introverted functions work in tandem with each other, and second, that one or the other function pulls more urgently on an individual, with the remaining one serving a supportive role. Chapter 2 will offer you detailed information on those dynamics. Further, when she explored orientations, Myers tapped into issues such as how our upbringing affects our development, how we are motivated to work, and the nature of tolerance.

Jung and Myers gave us a way to understand differences in Perception and Judgment. While these preferences have observable behaviors that are markers of mental processes, they are far from being static or two-dimensional. As our senses of smell, taste, and sight commingle to create an experience, our type preferences synthesize with experience to create the personality we exhibit. This mental synthesis is known as type dynamics. Dynamics are as different from individual preferences as a freestanding three-dimensional figure is from a flat two-dimensional picture. How these dynamics and basic preferences interact is the subject of our next chapter.

A Messy Complexity

THE PATTERNS THAT CREATE EXPRESSIONS OF SELF

I f you had a choice between seeing Michelangelo's *David* in person or looking at a picture of that remarkable sculpture, chances are excellent that you
would prefer to see the real thing. When showing our photo albums, we often
feel compelled to tell a story or describe the person in the photograph in order
to give a complete rendering of the picture. Should someone invite us to see a
story through a slideshow or the same story through a motion picture, we are
likely to choose the motion picture. We all are partial to three-dimensional
information. We want the motion, background, and simultaneous stimulation of sight, sound, and touch in order for the experience to feel real and be
fully appreciated. We think of ourselves as complex individuals who cannot be
adequately captured in just a snapshot—a videotape is likely to do a better job.
And in the age of videos on our phones, we've come to expect a small movie
production. In much the same way, learning about the eight dimensions of
psychological type provides just a flat snapshot of the mental processes. Type
dynamics, however, is the three-dimensional version; it is about the quality
of who we are and the dramatic integration of all our capabilities to provide
a response to the pressing needs of the moment. When, for example, within
two minutes we can have a logical debate with a colleague and then give heart-
felt sympathy to a friend who calls with sad news, we show our flexibility of
response and utilization of different mental processes.

Mental Markers

Our mental processes work so fast and are so immediate that in each moment
we process hundreds of thousands of pieces of information. Consequently, we
must acknowledge that any aspect of psychological functioning is complex. We
are left with looking at the behavioral markers that are the outcomes of these

23

mental processes. An illustration of this richness and complexity is captured in the word *synesthesia,* the term biologists use to describe the phenomenon of the exponential effect of various senses interacting to create a whole awareness that one sense alone could never accomplish.[1] Stimulating one sense promotes a reaction from another sense. For example, when trying to create a luxurious dining experience, it is vital to know that, from a biological perspective, the visual presentation and the aroma of the food are just as important as the taste because the interaction of those factors produces a level of stimulation that one of the factors alone could never achieve. Auditory stimulation (Mozart versus honking traffic noise) would also have an impact on the total experience.

Preferences at Interplay

Likewise, in psychological type, the dynamic *interplay* and *interaction* of the preferences add to the richness of type patterns. We must first understand, as Myers proposed, that the preferences are distinct processes that work together to make up the whole, in much the same way that our senses are distinct but interact to create depth of experience.[2] Because of this interplay and complexity, it is unreasonable to declare that any given behavior of a person is caused by a single internal factor; it is more accurate to say that a behavior is an expression of interacting factors such as the attitudes of Extraversion or Introversion with one of the mental functions. And it is more often true to say that a person's behavior at a given moment is an expression of what she is experiencing at that moment rather than to declare that she is behaving a particular way exclusively because of some trait or genetic quality.

As with our senses, each aspect of our psychological type serves an important function. Extraverted Sensing and Extraverted Intuiting serve to give us different types of external perceptions. Introverted Sensing and Introverted Intuiting provide a personal awareness of internal perceptions. Extraverted Thinking and Extraverted Feeling give us rational ways to respond to and interact with others in the world. Introverted Thinking and Introverted Feeling inform our reflective and introspective judgments about experience. And as nature would have it, we all have developed particular strengths with each of these mental operations. Though we each rely on all of them, they are not all equally expressive or apparent in our personalities. Understanding type dynamics gives us insight into the priority structure and nature of these mental processes in each of us.

Through the exploration of the dynamics of type to follow, you will gain an awareness of the three-dimensional nature of psychological type. We hope this awareness engenders a greater sensitivity to the complexity inherent in the mental processes suggested by type. Ultimately, learning about type dynamics provides a practical way to understand differences in perception, communication, and action. The dynamics of type enable us to see the adaptation of the individual to specific situations and better understand the resulting behavior.

Order of the Mental Functions: Drivers of the Mental System

Type theory says that because we cannot access all mental functions and attitudes at the same instant, we use (and are aware of) mental functions in a particular order. The mental operation used most often and of which we are most aware is called the dominant function and attitude. The dominant function is always used in the preferred attitude. For example, the dominant function for those who prefer Introversion operates in the Introverted attitude; for those who prefer Extraversion, the dominant function operates in the Extraverted attitude. The dominant function for all types is superior in awareness, utility, and reliability but not necessarily in the strength of its influence on our behaviors. A second mental operation, the auxiliary function, is frequently utilized and provides balance to the dominant but operates slightly outside our awareness. If the dominant process is Extraverted, then the auxiliary function will be Introverted, and vice versa. A third function, called the tertiary, explains a variety of responses we make, on occasion, which are quite different from either our dominant or auxiliary processes. A fourth function, called the inferior, is infrequently used and, though very powerful, is often quite outside our awareness.

To be true to the whole theory, we must add that the four remaining function/attitude pairs (if your dominant is Extraverted Intuiting, for example, Introverted Intuiting would be one of these four) operate far away from awareness, hidden deeply in the unconscious, and are usually inaccessible to us through any direct route. Some believe these to be the aspects of dynamics that make up the nature of our "other self." The other self is that part of us that is the opposite in gender attributes. For example, the male Extraverted Thinker who sometimes surprises even himself with tender, nurturing behavior may be expressing a Feeling function that resides deep in the feminine part of his psychology. Such matters are beyond the scope of this book. Suffice it to say that type theory suggests that deep within us we use all eight mental function/attitude pairs to serve conscious and unconscious purposes. Our goal here is to get a grasp on the use of the four primary mental functions, as these make up so much of our conscious awareness and drive our choices.

Dominant and Auxiliary Functions

Jung hypothesized that among a person's preferences is a dominant, or leading, mental process (Sensing, Intuiting, Thinking, or Feeling) that is used in the preferred attitude (Extraversion or Introversion). He further theorized that there is an auxiliary or supporting mental process (again either Sensing, Intuiting, Thinking, or Feeling) that is used in the non-preferred attitude.[3] In Table 1 at the end of chapter 1, each type is listed with its Extraverted and Introverted mental functions. If you refer to that table, you will see that both ISTJ and ESTJ use Extraverted Thinking. For ESTJ, Extraverted Thinking is the dominant function, but for ISTJ Extraverted Thinking is the auxiliary function, while Introverted Sensing is the dominant function. Table 2 lists the full dynamic order of awareness for each type. If you choose to use Table 1, just remember that because the dominant function is always in the preferred attitude, for Introverted types the dominant function can be found in the Introverted mental function column, while for Extraverted types it can be found in the Extraverted mental function column.

An important point: just as we cannot consciously Extravert and Introvert at the same time nor perceive with our Sensing and our Intuiting at the same time, we cannot both attend to information and decide on it at the same time. Out of habit, one of the two will lead the way for the other.

The dominant process is the leader, the "captain of the ship," psychologically speaking.[4] It is the mental process of which we are most aware and on which we rely most heavily. In healthy individuals it is the most well-developed process, and nearly all type experts would agree it is the process that develops

TABLE 2
TRADITIONAL HIERARCHY OF TYPE DYNAMICS

	EXTRAVERTED TYPES							
	ESTJ	ENTJ	ESFJ	ENFJ	ESTP	ENTP	ESFP	ENFP
Lead	Te	Te	Fe	Fe	Se	Ne	Se	Ne
Auxiliary	Si	Ni	Si	Ni	Ti	Ti	Fi	Fi
Tertiary	Ni	Si	Ni	Si	Fi	Fi	Ti	Ti
Least-used	Fi	Fi	Ti	Ti	Ni	Si	Ni	Si

	INTROVERTED TYPES							
	ISTJ	INTJ	ISFJ	INFJ	ISTP	INTP	ISFP	INFP
Lead	Si	Ni	Si	Ni	Ti	Ti	Fi	Fi
Auxiliary	Te	Te	Fe	Fe	Se	Ne	Se	Ne
Tertiary	Fe	Fe	Te	Te	Ne	Se	Ne	Se
Least-used	Ne	Se	Ne	Se	Fe	Fe	Te	Te

first in children. (It is especially difficult to determine the sequence and timing of type development with Introverted children, as they keep their dominant process to themselves!) For the majority of people, using the dominant process is very comfortable, efficient, and usually fairly effective.

The auxiliary process operates in support of the dominant process and, to our own awareness, usually behind the scenes. If, for example, a person's dominant function is a Judging function (Thinking or Feeling), the auxiliary Perceiving process (Sensing or Intuiting) is busily feeding the Judging process either ideas or data about which to make decisions. Conversely, if a person's dominant process is a perceiving process, the auxiliary Judging process is in the background determining which of the many data or ideas are reasonable or valuable to pursue. We often are less aware of our auxiliary function at work, yet it is always there. Sometimes this lesser awareness can lead us into misunderstandings. And as we said, this brings complexity to understanding and, ultimately, richness to seeing differences among individuals.

Using the Secondary

When we interact with others using our auxiliary function, we may appear a bit blustery or evasive. Introverted Perceiving types (led by Introverted Sensing or Introverted Intuiting) may be quite unaware of how critical or final their Extraverted judgments (Extraverted Thinking or Extraverted Feeling) seem to others. Extraverted Judging types may be equally unaware when their Introverted Perceptions come across to others as noncommittal and confusing.

Let's look at a person whose preferences are for Extraversion with Sensing attention to details and who prefers to analyze those details in a Thinking way. In this case, Extraversion would combine with either Sensing or Thinking to become the dominant mental process, and the non-preferred but still active Introversion would combine with the other function to serve as the auxiliary process. You can see now why Myers's addition of the J–P scale, indicating which function is used in the Extraverted mode, was so critical to a full understanding and identification of type dynamics. In this example, without knowing the person's preference for J or P, it would take many discussions to begin to identify which mental function serves as the dominant function. Myers's contribution was enormous.

Using the Four Functions

Remember, type theory holds that all four mental functions (Sensing, Intuiting, Thinking, and Feeling) are always present within a person but are used by different individuals with relative degrees of awareness and reliability. In other words, to get at the complete dynamic within each type, we must identify a lead attitude and function, auxiliary attitude and function, tertiary attitude and function, and least-used (inferior) attitude and function. This ordering is an outcome of each person's habits of mind and generates the expressions of self about which we can make sense of, if we are patient.

Consequently, we are more likely to be aware and make deliberate use of our lead attitude and function, while our least-used attitude and function may be rarely utilized consciously. The least used is often referred to as inferior; as the lead function is superior in consciousness, the least used is inferior to consciousness. The order of conscious access, according to type theory, is as shown in Table 2.

Taken together as listed above, this structure of functions provides a shorthand model for understanding selectivity in habits of perception and judgment. This enables the type-knowledgeable person to read a four-letter abbreviation of preferences as sorted by personality type instruments not just as Introversion, Sensing, Thinking, and Judging (ISTJ), for example, but rather as a *dynamic* preference for a dominant process of Introverted Sensing supported by an auxiliary process of Extraverted Thinking. Later in the chapter is a description of the dominant and auxiliary functions for each of the types, but even as we proceed toward it, we remind you again: people are not types. We have a multiplicity of potential responses that show our complexity and capacity to adjust.

We are individuals with unique experiences, competencies, and a one-time special combination of genetic material. Like the Taoist philosophy asserting that there are patterns among changes, fixity among chaos, and movement within stability, psychological type proposes that it is the nature of humankind to live in a complex, handmade lacework of social and interpersonal relationships.[5] Habits of mind—psychological type—act in combination with other innate dispositions to influence how we perceive and judge these relationships. Perceptions and judgments, in turn, promote typical expressions in behavior that tend to be consistent and enduring. The structure that supports these habits and typical behaviors is psychological type.

Remember Polarities and Compensation

Two reminders: first, types exist due to different poles of energy (Extraversion, Introversion), Perception (Sensing, Intuiting), and Judgment (Thinking, Feeling); second, each of the functions provides avenues for dealing with life's challenges. There is a kind of mental compensation that occurs to allow us to utilize those "understudy functions," which often don't get much time on center stage but nonetheless stand at the ready for the moment when the lead becomes tired or ineffectual.

Basic Dynamic Purpose

The poles of psychological type create energy fields that serve particular psychological purposes in the same way a magnet must have both a positive and negative pole to create its energy field. Thus, polarity is the underlying structure of type. Keep in mind that an important structural aspect of this model is that the polarities create an energy exchange system such that energy spent in one area is compensated for in another. Consider an example of the Extraverted Intuitive type (ENFP or ENTP) who spends enormous energy at work creating and processing ideas and models throughout the day but who, at the end of the day, takes the long way home to provide quiet, reflective time to make decisions and bring order to the day's events. This enables her to be calm and attentive with her family. Without necessarily thinking, "I need to balance my type," but rather following her own impulses, she is attending to a primitive urge to take care of herself. See Table 1 in chapter 1 to remind yourself of the frontline components of balance for each type in the balancing energy exchange system. Dire stories about those who ignore this basic internal urge for balance are all around us. Consider the constant distress of those who feel compelled to react to every situation or to run from the difficult situations they encounter daily. This kind of distress has consequences to health and long-term well-being.

Think also of the executive with preferences for Extraverted Thinking (ESTJ or ENTJ) who spends all day Extraverting his Thinking judgments around a group of close associates, but who fails to allow himself time for reflection and for internal evaluation of priorities. His failure to listen to his internal voice will almost certainly lead to burnout as he depletes his natural energy without providing time for renewal by balancing his Introverted and Extraverted needs. It is easy for such individuals to feel shallow, to become rigidly judgmental, or to simply see all things as untrustworthy. It makes sense that if he distrusts his own instincts to the extent of hurting himself, how or why should he trust anyone else? This lack of balance is likely to be experienced acutely by those around him who endure the behavior born of such rigidity and narrow focus. If only he were aware of the effects of his behavior on others and the systems within which he operates, he might feel compelled to pay more attention to the internal voice calling for balance in his life. If this situation continues long enough, his internal exchange system will essentially force him to use a least-preferred cognitive function, the one most unlike his dominant function, to direct his focus of attention and making of judgments. This usurping of power by the least-used mental function will make his life, and the lives of those around him, utterly unsettled and miserable until he takes the time to attend to his need for balance. The full nature of this process is discussed in chapter 4.

Dynamic Compensation

In later chapters, similar analysis is provided to illustrate the rules of compensation for each type's dynamics. For Jung, compensation is largely an unconscious process by which individuals simply take care of themselves without much ado.[6] Nonetheless, understanding the process of compensation is essential because it provides balancing of the mental processes, adaptation to situational demands, and an understanding of the complexity of behavioral expressions that emerge for each individual.

A Messy Complexity

We could say in general that an individual with preferences for INFP is an Introverted Feeling type who Extraverts Intuiting, and that the two attitudes work with each other to create a balance between perceiving and judging information. But in real life, due to the situation of the moment or to individual life history, the rule of compensation may work very differently and lead to very different behaviors for one INFP when compared with another. Typically calm, reserved, and gentle individuals, INFPs may nevertheless be very aggressive, energetic, and analytical when presenting their ideals.

Tension Among the Dimensions

To adapt to the world and adjust to the variety of demands facing us, we call on the dimension of ourselves that seems most appropriate at the time. In addition, an internal dynamic dance plays among the dimensions that make up personality type. Simply sorting oneself along the type dimensions, say as an ESTJ, is a shorthand way to describe the dynamic tension going on between Extraverted Thinking and Introverted Sensing. It's important to note that this dynamic between Judgment and Perception and between Introversion and Extraversion directly influences our typical expressions in everyday life.

As mentioned, many significant influences on a person's behavior are outside the realm of personality type. While type can be a profound force in how we experience life, people are not types. Discussing his own descriptors of the different personality types, Jung said, "Every individual is an exception to the rule. Hence one can never give a description of a type, no matter how complete, that would apply to more than one individual, despite the fact that in some ways it aptly characterizes thousands of others. Conformity is one side of man, uniqueness is the other."[7] Understand, then, that the personality is a complex energy exchange system, which is balancing and compensating in perpetuity.

Habits of Mind Leading to Expressions

It might be satisfying if the formula for predicting behavior and for under-standing others was a simple set of letters. But basic formulas serve only lim-ited ends. Individuals are so complex that we should truly be delighted to have even a glimpse of the basic energy, perceptual, and decision-making patterns inherent in each person. Given that type expressions provide a set of clues—not a complete psychological story—they provide an opportunity to begin exploring ways to further understand and value different perspectives within a rational framework.

When first learning about type, many people want a detailed and thor-ough description of this dynamic for each type. This is often motivated by the desire for something that will explain it all without gaps or overlaps, but by now you know this is not a constructive or even accurate use of type. Observing typical expressions of type is far more representative of the adapting, respond-ing, and developing adult. Any detailed description would tend to ignore many other influences on each individual and imply a more fixed system of psychol-ogy than really exists. Consequently, we will examine typical expressions of type dynamics using adjectives and phrases rather than entire paragraphs or other long prose descriptors. These descriptors give a very clear image of the patterns without precluding the host of other qualities that are also likely to be present.

The descriptors in Table 3 are of typical expressions of attitudes and functions such as Extraverted Thinking, Introverted Sensing, and so on. As described in the prescript, our research began by examining all of the stud-ies we could find on psychological type.[8] Each study was examined to make sure that the people in the study were typical (no clinical groups, for example) and that the behaviors under study were typical—reading habits or manage-ment practices, perhaps, but not depression or eating disorders. We sought to identify research that used adequately large samples and sufficiently controlled conditions, and included assessments of behavior via both a self-report for-mat and observation reports from others. Once all of the studies were selected, we began looking for overlaps in the results. When the same descriptor for a type showed up in three different studies, it met our criteria for inclusion here. One reason we do not use full-paragraph type descriptions is that too often (in our experience about 35 percent of the time) the detailed descrip-tions simply do not work for individuals, though they may in fact verify that the MBTI inventory sorted their preferences correctly.[9] In the years fol-lowing this analysis, additional studies with multiple instruments and rater observations have been completed, and these studies inform our revised edition.[10]

Our goal is to present you with kernels of truth about the typical expressions of the preferences, both in terms of their natural expression and of their expression by people experiencing stress. Thus, for each type you will find descriptors of the normal, well-rested expressions of preferences, as well as descriptors of those preferences when an individual feels pushed, stressed, or particularly worn out. Keep in mind that the descriptors generally capture the dominant use of each pattern (Introverted Intuiting or Extraverted Sensing); about half to two-thirds of the patterns will still apply when the preference pattern is identified as the auxiliary or supporting attitude and function. We will look first at the descriptors of the attitudes and functions and then at how the combinations of these expressions make up the dominant and auxiliary dynamic.

Preference Does Not Equal Competence

Instead of seeing a person with Introverted Intuitive preferences as Mr. or Ms. Abstract, or someone with Extraverted Feeling preferences as Mr. or Ms. Sweetness, recall that a typical expression merely reflects the way one generally responds. Type neither predicts competence in a given role nor reveals the richness of life experience brought to the task at hand. Type preferences are more than a formula! When you too quickly dismiss a person because of perceived type expressions, you may needlessly eliminate opportunities for talented individuals to contribute to your life and work. For example, there are plenty of individuals with a preference for Thinking who aren't good at analysis, as well as those with a preference for Feeling who need relationship skill training. By definition, psychological type is a messy complexity that provides a mere first step toward understanding oneself and others.

It is important to note that types are attracted to interests and work activities that "feed" the type energy. For example, the accounting field has a large number of Sensing-Thinking-Judging (STJ) individuals as the precision and concreteness of numbers and the logic of accounting fit a psychological need. No surprise that a large number of counselors report preferences for Intuiting-Feeling-Perceiving (NFP). In this case, the attraction to personal stories and personal meaning satisfy a need so these patterns are pulled to this career. This is not to say that the other type patterns are absent from these careers—only significantly infrequent, and when the other types are in these careers, it is for very different reasons. For example, the ENFP accountant says that her career helps solve individual personal problems while the ISTJ counselor says observing others systematically work toward wellness is satisfying. This is covered in detail in chapter 7 and Table 18.

Fragments of All Preferences

You can and should see some of yourself in all of the lists of type preference descriptors. As discussed earlier, healthy adult development suggests that an individual can call upon any function in either attitude as required by a given situation. This story illustrates the difference between type preference and a situational type expression.

Roger and a friend who knows type were walking together in an unfamiliar city, trying rather unsuccessfully to follow directions to a restaurant. Seeing their confused expressions, a passerby said with a smile, "You two look a bit lost. May I help you find your way somewhere?" After getting them back on course, she cheerfully went on her way. As she did so, Roger's friend said, "Thank heaven for Extraverted Feeling types!" Roger's response: "No. Thank heaven for Extraverted Feeling, regardless of who is doing it!"

The point is, neither Roger nor his friend knew that stranger's personality type preferences, and it didn't matter. What did matter was that in a moment of seeing two lost people, she chose to use an Extraverted Feeling expression to respond to the situation.

We began this deliberation with the premise that type is about how we adapt and respond to the world given our patterns of Perception and Judgment. As the patterns become clearer, it seems more obvious that knowing your own dynamic aids in understanding your interpersonal style, and that studying the gifts of other types uncovers your interpersonal blind spots. This self-knowledge can lead to insight regarding your relationships, leadership style, learning methods, and areas that need development.

The complexity and richness of type begins to reveal itself when you combine the expression of the preferred perception and decision-making processes. Using Table 3, you can create an impressionistic portrait of a psychological type by combining the descriptors of its dominant and auxiliary functions.

An even more complete impression of type dynamics can be gained by connecting each set of descriptors for the relevant lead and auxiliary role of each type. From this you begin to see how important it is to consider type valuable as an expression of heart—the patterns of psychological comfort. We've done this for you in Table 4.

As we pull the preferences together to find an expression of the whole type, remember that only portions of the auxiliary descriptors will hold true for each type. For Introverts in general, the Extraverted auxiliary is toned down somewhat in the amount of energy exhibited, though the term may be accurate. For example, an INTP who has Extraverted Intuiting as auxiliary may not be seen as generally jolly, uninhibited, or friendly; however, in a comfortable environment among friends, those terms may be quite applicable. This is the pattern for all of the Extravert descriptions when applied as the auxiliary expressions of Introverts.

TABLE 3
EXPRESSIONS OF THE ATTITUDES AND FUNCTIONS

INTROVERTED SENSING

(Dominant for ISFJ, ISTJ; Auxiliary for ESFJ, ESTJ)
thoughtful realists
unhurried
test ideas with facts
careful, calm, and steady
consistent and reliable
fastidious
loyal
unassuming

Under stress may become
stingy, unemotional, overly conventional

Introverted Sensing is a function drawn to the concrete and specific details of any information presented. This leads to carefully moderated responses to questions or tasks. People with this preference believe in economy of effort, that performing a task consistently and persistently now will conserve the energy that otherwise would have to be spent later to correct mistakes. Because they are pulled to immediate concrete information, they often seem very realistic.

EXTRAVERTED SENSING

(Dominant for ESTP, ESFP; Auxiliary for ISTP, ISFP)
action-oriented realists
practical
reliable
forceful
thorough
excitable
good-natured
know who, what, when, where
good at easing tensions

Under stress may become
unscrupulous, unkind, opportunistic, rigid

Extraverted Sensing is expressed in quick-paced reporting in factual, pragmatic terms. Often pulled toward action-oriented responses, individuals with this preference seem efficiently forceful about getting the job done. After giving thorough attention to the specifics of any given situation, such people often have a good-natured response that suggests that whatever the problem, it can be solved.

TABLE 3
EXPRESSIONS OF THE ATTITUDES AND FUNCTIONS *(Continued)*

INTROVERTED INTUITING

(Dominant for INFJ, INTJ; Auxiliary for ENFJ, ENTJ)
value knowledge for its own sake
introspective
scholarly
like ideas and theory
evaluate motives
see to the heart of important problems
appreciative
formal
value intellectual matters

Under stress may become
withdrawn, retiring, dreamy, hardheaded, reserved

Introverted Intuiting is pulled toward the future and toward possibilities. This function is like an inner eye focused on what could be, rather than what is. As a consequence, individuals with this preference often seem scholarly or studious, as if looking toward the center of a problem. This tendency may show up as, for example, a knack for summarizing a long conversation in one sentence. Interpersonally, individuals who prefer Introverted Intuiting are seen by others as calm and capable of concentrated attention.

EXTRAVERTED INTUITING

(Dominant for ENTP, ENFP; Auxiliary for INTP, INFP)
action-oriented innovators
adaptable
verbally fluent
resourceful
active, enthusiastic
friendly, jolly
uninhibited
like rapid tempo

Under stress may become
distracted, impulsive, unrealistic in expectations, hasty, noisy

---

Extraverted Intuiting has an enormous appetite for external possibilities. This leads to quick pursuit of ideas in conversations, a fast-paced search for information, and an interpersonal style that seems to adapt at will. Because individuals with this preference are drawn to many different experiences, they often have a resource bank of ideas to call on to aid them in discussions. This function exerts a fun-loving attitude—an interpersonal style of active engagement in whatever is going on.

TABLE 3
EXPRESSIONS OF THE ATTITUDES AND FUNCTIONS *(Continued)*

INTROVERTED THINKING

(Dominant for INTP, ISTP; Auxiliary for ENTP, ESTP)
reflective reasoners
quiet, detachedly curious
analyze vs. run their world
organize ideas
value intellectual matters
seen as independent and autonomous
often critical and skeptical
original and imaginative
often unconventional

Under stress may become
rebellious and nonconforming, restless, self-centered, and defensive

---

Introverted Thinking is a pattern often experienced by others as a detached curiosity. This curiosity leads those who prefer it toward active but quiet analysis of nearly everything. Reveling in the complexity required to deal with the world, they are frequently seen as independent minded (their model of how things work may be very different from mainstream thought, but INTPs have their reasons). Interpersonally, they may express skeptical acceptance of the world around them.

EXTRAVERTED THINKING

(Dominant for ESTJ, ENTJ; Auxiliary for INTJ, ISTJ)
action-oriented thinkers
critical, resourceful
proactive and systematic
have a basic formula about the world
energetic, prefer a rapid pace
reasonable and analytical
expressive, fluent
mentally versatile
have high aspirations

Under stress may become
arrogant and condescending, reckless and aggressive, opportunistic

---

Extraverted Thinking is a mental pattern of actively analyzing experience and information and expressing this analysis in an energetic fashion. Individuals with this preference are often seen as having a plan or model to help adapt to and manage the world around them. Resourceful with ideas and suggestions, Extraverted Thinkers are often fluent critics and have ideas on how to improve just about anything put before them.

TABLE 3
EXPRESSIONS OF THE ATTITUDES AND FUNCTIONS *(Continued)*

INTROVERTED FEELING

(Dominant for ISFP, INFP; Auxiliary for ENFP, ESFP)

reflective harmonizers
quiet, deferent
care about values and people
artistic (aesthetic)
introspective
unusual or unconventional thinkers
arouse liking and acceptance in people
sensitive

Under stress may become
irritable, touchy, suspicious, undependable

Introverted Feeling is often exhibited in quiet, deferent attitudes. Individuals expressing these preferences seem sensitive to the environment around them. Because the first response of Introverted Feeling is to accept the other person, a great deal of energy is spent helping the other to be comfortable. Given the inclination to focus on values as a basis for reacting to events, individuals with this preference seem unconventional to those with a focus on logical answers.

EXTRAVERTED FEELING

(Dominant for ESFJ, ENFJ; Auxiliary for INFJ, ISFJ)

action-oriented cooperators
sympathetic
sociable and friendly
empathetic
affiliative, warm
want inclusion
outgoing, gregarious
idealistic
facially expressive
energetic

Under stress may become
impulsive, hasty, sentimental, fussy, self-dramatizing

Extraverted Feeling is expressed in an energetic, cooperative fashion with attention to social interaction in sympathetic and friendly behaviors. Often given to expressive engagement with others, when Extraverted Feeling is being used it appears to be drawn to others seeking inclusion in social affairs. While given to a cooperative spirit, individuals with this preference act quickly to address issues they see, believing they can achieve an idealistic goal that could help improve the human condition.

Conversely, those who have an Introverted auxiliary may be initially inclined to deny that descriptions of Introversion apply to them. Yet when they think about the times they allow themselves to be reflective, quiet, and calm, they may find that Introversion does indeed describe them in such episodes. Whatever your type, keep in mind that you are less likely to be aware of the typical expressions of your auxiliary. A developed, mature, appropriate expression of the auxiliary is probably clear on certain occasions. As you read the descriptors, consider both the rewarding and the problematic interactions you've had with various individuals. You may never know the type preferences of those involved, and there is actually no need to; it is enough to know that the expressions you listen to daily are at least partially the result of orderly differences in Perception and Judgment.

Sometimes it helps just to know that there is a valid reason you may be on the same wavelength with some folks but not with others. Likewise, these type descriptors give us a lens for understanding that interpersonal problem areas are not necessarily the result of diabolical plots spawned in the dark of night to irritate you and to stymie all your good work! This framework of type, while it doesn't explain everything, invites us to take a step back during difficult situations and ask whether part of the misunderstanding has to do with differences in type expressions.

Pondering type differences may lead you to see that the various ways people express themselves have a lot to say about their habits of mind, and that how such variations are interpreted by a given observer has a lot to say about the habits of mind of that observer. For example, people who are expressive and warm about personal experiences may merely be exhibiting a natural expression of Extraverted Feeling. Yet some observers may suggest that such behavior is designed to manipulate or control those around them. Who is right? These communication questions are rich, and we discuss them in depth in chapter 8, but to gain the most from that discussion you need to understand the patterns of expression laid out in Table 4. Knowing that there are tangible, legitimate differences in Perception and Judgment opens the doors of communication and provides the foundation for valuing differences.

As we have explored, type is an elegant model of habits of mind—the ways we seek energy, attend to information, and make decisions. It features a system of ordering habits that is useful and pragmatic and demonstrates that people seem to have primary and secondary styles that are most evident in their typical expressions and ways of doing things.

Thanks to the complexity and sufficiency of the model of psychological type, we have the opportunity to make better judgments about our interactions, make more choices in what to say and do to be influential, and develop a better understanding of our personal histories. But as is true of any model, no matter how constructive and incisive, it can be distorted and misused.

TABLE 4
DESCRIPTORS FOR THE 16 TYPES

Extraverted Sensing Types

TYPE	
DOMINANT/LEAD FUNCTION DESCRIPTORS	**AUXILIARY/SUPPORTER FUNCTION DESCRIPTORS**
Most aware of…	*Fully functioning but less aware of…*

ESTP	
Extraverted Sensing	**Introverted Thinking**
realistic, action-oriented	reflective reasoners
practical	quiet, detachedly curious
reliable, thorough	analyze vs. run their world
forceful	seen as independent and autonomous
excitable	good-natured
know who, what, when, where	often critical and skeptical
good at easing tensions	often unconventional
	original and imaginative

Under stress may become

unkind, unscrupulous,	*rebellious, nonconforming,*
opportunistic, rigid	*restless, defensive*

ESFP	
Extraverted Sensing	**Introverted Feeling**
realistic, action-oriented	reflective harmonizers
practical	quiet, deferent
reliable, thorough	care for values and people
forceful	artistic
excitable	introspective
know who, what, when, where	unusual or unconventional thinking
good at easing tensions	good at easing tensions
	arouse liking and acceptance in people
	sensitive

Under stress may become

unkind, unscrupulous,	*irritable, touchy,*
opportunistic, rigid	*suspicious, undependable*

TABLE 4
DESCRIPTORS FOR THE 16 TYPES *(Continued)*

Extraverted Intuitive Types

TYPE	
DOMINANT/LEAD FUNCTION DESCRIPTORS	**AUXILIARY/SUPPORTER FUNCTION DESCRIPTORS**
Most aware of…	*Fully functioning but less aware of…*

ENFP

Extraverted Intuiting	**Introverted Feeling**
action-oriented innovators	reflective harmonizers
adaptable	quiet, deferent
verbally fluent	care for values and people
resourceful	artistic
active	introspective
like rapid tempo	unusual or unconventional thinking
enthusiastic	arouse liking and acceptance in people
friendly, jolly	sensitive
uninhibited	

Under stress may become

distracted, impulsive, unrealistic in expectations, hasty, noisy	*irritable, touchy, suspicious, undependable*

ENTP

Extraverted Intuiting	**Introverted Thinking**
action-oriented innovators	reflective reasoners
adaptable	quiet, detachedly curious
verbally fluent	analyze vs. run their world
resourceful	seen as independent and autonomous
active	often critical and skeptical
like rapid tempo	often unconventional
enthusiastic	original and imaginative
friendly, jolly	
uninhibited	

Under stress may become

distracted, impulsive, unrealistic in expectations, hasty, noisy	*rebellious, nonconforming, restless, defensive*

TABLE 4
DESCRIPTORS FOR THE 16 TYPES *(Continued)*

Extraverted Thinking Types

TYPE	
DOMINANT/LEAD FUNCTION DESCRIPTORS	**AUXILIARY/SUPPORTER FUNCTION DESCRIPTORS**
Most aware of…	*Fully functioning but less aware of…*

ESTJ

Extraverted Thinking	**Introverted Sensing**
action-oriented thinkers	thoughtful realists
resourceful, critical	unhurried, careful
proactive and systematic	test ideas with facts
have a basic formula about the world	calm
energetic, like a rapid pace	steady
reasonable and analytical	consistent and reliable
expressive, fluent	loyal
mentally versatile	fastidious
have high aspirations	unassuming

Under stress may become

arrogant and condescending, reckless and aggressive, opportunistic	*stingy, unemotional, overly conventional*

ENTJ

Extraverted Thinking	**Introverted Intuiting**
action-oriented thinkers	value knowledge for its own sake
resourceful, critical	introspective, scholarly
proactive and systematic	like ideas and theories
have a basic formula about the world	evaluate motives
energetic, like a rapid pace	see to the heart of important problems
reasonable and analytical	appreciative, formal
expressive, fluent	value intellectual matters
mentally versatile	
have high aspirations	

Under stress may become

arrogant and condescending, reckless and aggressive, opportunistic	*retiring, dreamy, hardheaded, reserved*

TABLE 4
DESCRIPTORS FOR THE 16 TYPES *(Continued)*

Extraverted Feeling Types

TYPE	
DOMINANT/LEAD FUNCTION DESCRIPTORS	**AUXILIARY/SUPPORTER FUNCTION DESCRIPTORS**
Most aware of…	*Fully functioning but less aware of…*

ESFJ

Extraverted Feeling	**Introverted Sensing**
action-oriented	thoughtful realists
prefer cooperation	unhurried
sympathetic	test ideas with facts
sociable and friendly	careful
affiliative	calm
warm	steady
want inclusion	consistent and reliable
outgoing	loyal
gregarious	fastidious
idealistic	unassuming

Under stress may become

impulsive, hasty,	*stingy, unemotional,*
sentimental, fussy, self-dramatizing	*overly conventional*

ENFJ

Extraverted Feeling	**Introverted Intuiting**
action-oriented	value knowledge for its own sake
prefer cooperation	introspective, scholarly
sympathetic	like ideas and theories
sociable and friendly	evaluate motives
affiliative	see to the heart of important problems
warm	appreciative, formal
want inclusion	value intellectual matters
outgoing	
gregarious	
idealistic	

Under stress may become

impulsive, hasty,	*retiring, dreamy,*
sentimental, fussy, self-dramatizing	*hardheaded, reserved*

TABLE 4
DESCRIPTORS FOR THE 16 TYPES *(Continued)*

Introverted Sensing Types

TYPE	
DOMINANT/LEAD FUNCTION DESCRIPTORS	**AUXILIARY/SUPPORTER FUNCTION DESCRIPTORS**
Most aware of…	*Fully functioning but less aware of…*

ISTJ

Introverted Sensing	**Extraverted Thinking**
thoughtful realists	action-oriented thinkers
unhurried	resourceful
test ideas with facts	proactive and systematic
careful	critical
calm	have a basic formula about the world
steady	energetic, like a rapid pace
consistent and reliable	reasonable and analytical
loyal	expressive, fluent
fastidious	mentally versatile
unassuming	have high aspirations

Under stress may become

stingy, unemotional,	*arrogant and condescending,*
overly conventional	*reckless and aggressive, opportunistic*

ISFJ

Introverted Sensing	**Extraverted Feeling**
thoughtful realists	action-oriented
unhurried	prefer cooperation
test ideas with facts	sympathetic
careful	sociable and friendly
calm	affiliative, warm
steady	want inclusion
consistent and reliable	outgoing, gregarious
loyal	idealistic
fastidious	
unassuming	

Under stress may become

stingy, unemotional,	*impulsive, hasty, sentimental,*
overly conventional	*fussy, self-dramatizing*

TABLE 4
DESCRIPTORS FOR THE 16 TYPES *(Continued)*

Introverted Intuitive Types

TYPE	
DOMINANT/LEAD FUNCTION DESCRIPTORS	**AUXILIARY/SUPPORTER FUNCTION DESCRIPTORS**
Most aware of…	*Fully functioning but less aware of…*

INTJ

Introverted Intuiting	**Extraverted Thinking**
value knowledge for its own sake	action-oriented thinkers
introspective	resourceful
scholarly	proactive and systematic
like ideas and theories	critical
evaluate motives	have a basic formula about the world
see to the heart of important problems	energetic, like a rapid pace
appreciative, formal	reasonable and analytical
value intellectual matters	expressive, fluent
	mentally versatile
	have high aspirations

Under stress may become

retiring, dreamy,	*arrogant and condescending,*
hardheaded, reserved	*reckless and aggressive, opportunistic*

INFJ

Introverted Intuiting	**Extraverted Feeling**
value knowledge for its own sake	action-oriented
introspective	prefer cooperation
scholarly	sympathetic
like ideas and theories	sociable and friendly
evaluate motives	affiliative, warm
see to the heart of important problems	want inclusion
appreciative, formal	outgoing, gregarious
value intellectual matters	idealistic

Under stress may become

retiring, dreamy,	*impulsive, hasty, sentimental,*
hardheaded, reserved	*fussy, self-dramatizing*

TABLE 4
DESCRIPTORS FOR THE 16 TYPES *(Continued)*

Introverted Thinking Types

TYPE	
DOMINANT/LEAD FUNCTION DESCRIPTORS	**AUXILIARY/SUPPORTER FUNCTION DESCRIPTORS**
Most aware of…	*Fully functioning but less aware of…*

ISTP

Introverted Thinking	**Extraverted Sensing**
reflective reasoners	realistic, action-oriented
quiet, detachedly curious	practical
analyze vs. run their world	reliable, thorough
seen as independent and autonomous	forceful
often critical and skeptical	excitable
often unconventional	good-natured
original and imaginative	know who, what, when, where
	good at easing tensions

Under stress may become

rebellious, nonconforming, restless, defensive	*unkind, unscrupulous, opportunistic, rigid*

INTP

Introverted Thinking	**Extraverted Intuiting**
reflective reasoners	action-oriented innovators
quiet, detachedly curious	adaptable
analyze vs. run their world	verbally fluent
seen as independent and autonomous	resourceful
often critical and skeptical	active
often unconventional	like rapid tempo
original and imaginative	enthusiastic
	friendly, jolly
	uninhibited

Under stress may become

rebellious, nonconforming, restless, defensive	*distracted, impulsive, hasty, noisy, unrealistic in expectations*

45

TABLE 4
DESCRIPTORS FOR THE 16 TYPES *(Continued)*

Introverted Feeling Types

TYPE	
DOMINANT/LEAD FUNCTION DESCRIPTORS	**AUXILIARY/SUPPORTER FUNCTION DESCRIPTORS**
Most aware of…	*Fully functioning but less aware of…*

ISFP

Introverted Feeling	**Extraverted Sensing**
reflective harmonizers	realistic, action-oriented
quiet, deferent	practical
care for values and people	reliable, thorough
artistic	forceful
introspective	excitable
unusual or unconventional thinking	good-natured
arouse liking and acceptance in people	know who, what, when, where
sensitive	good at easing tensions

Under stress may become

irritable, touchy,	*unkind, unscrupulous,*
suspicious, undependable	*opportunistic, rigid*

INFP

Introverted Feeling	**Extraverted Intuiting**
reflective harmonizers	action-oriented innovators
quiet, deferent	adaptable
care for values and people	verbally fluent
artistic	resourceful
introspective	active
unusual or unconventional thinking	like rapid tempo
arouse liking and acceptance in people	enthusiastic
sensitive	friendly, jolly
	uninhibited

Under stress may become

irritable, touchy,	*distracted, impulsive, hasty,*
suspicious, undependable	*noisy, unrealistic in expectations*

Those seeking shortcuts in understanding and in making sense of situations will no doubt use this model as a sword to direct and control others. In the chapters ahead we will continue to explore the natural expressions of the preferences, the importance of the inferior or least-used functions, the moral issues with using psychological type, and how these types fit into communication and valuing.

As you read each page you should keep in the forefront of your mind that the goal is to extend human understanding and development. Any other use works against the intent of the theory. The simple fact is that millions who have taken the Myers-Briggs Type Indicator inventory or other psychological type tools have merely scratched the surface of what type can provide in their lives. With studious attention to the ideas in this and the next several chapters, you can move closer to the realization of those for whom type means so very much: pathways of valuing and development that raise the quality of our lives.

Type Development: Psychological Type's Energy System at Work

"The years teach much which the days never knew."[1]

—Ralph Waldo Emerson

This section provides a deeper exploration into the dynamics and development needs of the types. The goal in type development is to make our perceptions clearer and our judgments more sound.

3 **Elements of Balance**
Processes That Keep Us Mindful
reviews how all of the levels of type play out in our lives.

4 **The Teacher Within**
Lessons We Cannot Ignore
gives a deep look at the role of the inferior function and its relationship to dealing with stress.

5 **Using the Ruby Slippers**
The Role of Type Development
looks at the key processes in individual development from the perspectives of the types.

Elements of Balance

PROCESSES THAT KEEP OUR MINDS FULL

Psychological type is about a series of balancing acts. Within the context of human mental health, balancing is a process, not a state of being. If we accept Jung's definition of type, it is clear that the balancing of a person's Extraverted and Introverted energy through the Perceiving and Judging functions is essential to healthy adaptation and responsiveness. Balancing is an ongoing requirement for a person's continued development and growth. For example, the individual who gets stuck in Judgment becomes judgmental and rigid. Without attention to perception, this individual is out of balance and will become stale, one-sided, and uncomfortable. Likewise, the person stuck in Perception becomes incapable of making decisions, which leads to an equally stale and uncomfortable personality. The cost of one-sidedness in life is very big.

Imagine the psyche as a heavy-duty kitchen sponge, with ideas and data perceptions providing the liquid necessary for it to work and decision-making criteria providing its fiber. For the sponge to work best, liquid and fiber must balance properly. If the sponge is too dry, lacking all liquid, it becomes brittle and will crumble in your hands if you use it for serious work. In the same manner, if the sponge is supersaturated with water—like the psyche overindulged in perception—it merely flops over the edges of your hand and is too soft and porous to be used for serious work. When we think of psychological balance in this way, we can see that type gives us a different way to understand our psychological discomforts—they may be a sign that our adaptation to experience has slowed and we are out of balance. The message from the psyche is, "Attend to your own processes."

As discussed earlier, type dynamics are expressed and identified as the combination of attitudes (Extraversion and Introversion) with the mental functions of Sensing, Intuiting, Thinking, and Feeling. We can identify the Extraverted–Introverted function dynamic for each type by sorting the preferences for the Judgment and Perception orientations as shown in Table 1 (page 20). The power and richness of the dynamic processes driving our Extraverted and Introverted mental functions were fully explored in the last chapter, but a brief summary is appropriate here before moving to the next level.

Type Dynamics Review

Type theory suggests that all mental functions are used in varying degrees and that the complete dynamic within each type consists of a lead (dominant) attitude and function, a secondary (auxiliary) attitude and function, a third (tertiary) attitude and function, and a least-used (inferior) attitude and function. The order of these preferences in an individual is an outcome of the habits of mind enjoyed by that person. Consequently, we are more likely to be aware of, and make deliberate use of, our dominant function, while our least-used attitude and function may be rarely utilized consciously. This is why the least-used function is referred to as inferior; the lead function is called superior because we are more conscious of it; and the least-used is called inferior not because it is less worthy or less important but because we are least conscious of it. For a full table of the hierarchy of functions for each type and discussions about type dynamics, you may refer to chapter 2. Chapter 4 will look at the richness and lessons of the inferior function in great detail. We have taken time to review the concept of type dynamics here because it is central to understanding the nature of each typology. As noted, these attitudes and functions perform a variety of balancing acts that enable each of us to experience life fully and respond to life with purpose. But there is more.

New Depth to Preference Interactions

In addition to evidence for traditional type dynamics, there are data to support expressions of various interactions of the type preferences. For example, an ENTP has the well-known dynamic of Extraverted Intuiting with Introverted Thinking. Little discussed until now is that this type also has distinct behavioral expressions that result from interactions between Extraversion and Perception (EP), which we will refer to as the *outer image*; between the Perceiving function and Perceiving orientation (NP), which we call the *motivator*; between the Judgment function and Perceiving orientation (TP), which we call *inner tension*; and between the Perceiving and Judging functions (NT), which we call the *cognitive core*. Each of these interactions has a unique set of expressions demonstrated in the research that truly show the beauty and complexity of each type.

In our research, we sought evidence for the interactions in the same way we identified evidence for the various expressions of preferences. To meet our criteria for inclusion, evidence had to come from at least three differen sound research sources and had to be verified by our database. The terms *image, motivator, inner tension,* and *cognitive core* are based on the central psychological issue in each kind of interaction.

For each of the types, the interactions among the preferences are as shown in Table 5.

Symbolic Elements of Balance

After analysis of all the psychological type-related research, we searched for patterns in the data. If, as Jung suggested, psychological type is a kind of compass that guides a person's behavior, then it follows that the individual is the center point of type. If, as he further speculated, we carry within us the history of patterns of human thought in the form of archetypes, type itself is a later development of an archetypal system in the evolution of human consciousness.[1] With these possibilities before us, exploring the interactions and their symbols is a worthy pursuit indeed.

Outer Image

How you are perceived by another person during a first meeting might surprise you, but the type interaction we call outer image is like a mirror that shows the

TABLE 5
ELEMENTS OF BALANCE FOR EACH TYPE

	EXTRAVERTED TYPES							
	ESTJ	**ENTJ**	**ESFJ**	**ENFJ**	**ESTP**	**ENTP**	**ESFP**	**ENFP**
Outer Image	EJ	EJ	EJ	EJ	EP	EP	EP	EP
Motivator	TJ	TJ	FJ	FJ	SP	NP	SP	NP
Inner tension	SJ	NJ	SJ	NJ	TP	TP	FP	FP
Cognitive Core	ST	NT	SF	NF	ST	NT	SF	NF

	INTROVERTED TYPES							
	ISTJ	**INTJ**	**ISFJ**	**INFJ**	**ISTP**	**INTP**	**ISFP**	**INFP**
Outer Image	IJ	IJ	IJ	IJ	IP	IP	IP	IP
Motivator	TJ	TJ	FJ	FJ	SP	NP	SP	NP
Inner tension	SJ	NJ	SJ	NJ	TP	TP	FP	FP
Cognitive Core	ST	NT	SF	NF	ST	NT	SF	NF

often distorted impressions others receive. Since abundant evidence suggests that judgments are made about you within the first fifteen seconds of an interaction, the importance of gaining this self-awareness cannot be overstated. It helps us understand how so many quick misjudgments are made and how we might ask more appropriate questions of each other in order to get past the outer image.

Understanding outer image provides the motivation to pause before we jump to conclusions about people when we first meet them—perhaps we'll better understand why they may behave so differently during an introductory conversation than in more in-depth interactions. It also shows how we ourselves can be so easily misread by others upon first meeting. For example, an energetic and spontaneous EP may completely misread a reserved and restless IP as being disinterested. At a minimum, we are invited to consider how we present ourselves and to suspend judgment on interactional styles different from our own.

With the question, "If someone took an interpersonal snapshot of you during the early moments of conversation, how might they describe you in the interaction?" we get a match between the answer to the question and the descriptors of the interactions of the attitudes and orientations (EJ, EP, IJ, IP). Those descriptors and answers map to the descriptors shown in Table 6.

Consider these snapshots of outer image the next time you meet an acquaintance or someone new to you. What are you responding to in them, and what may they be responding to in you? We have seen this information have transformative effects in interview skills training and executive coaching. As the saying goes, you never get a second chance to make a first impression. Understanding these interactions and making considered choices in your future behavior helps you make the most of new opportunities.

Motivators

Unfortunately, many talented and capable individuals miss opportunities because they are unaware of how their outer images are perceived by others. Likewise, many people feel unmotivated and are not sure how to infuse life into tasks or work. This results in unhappy experiences and poor evaluations.

Viewing this issue through the lens of type, an important insight leaps out. Regardless of preference for Introversion or Extraversion, a special motivation for engaging with the world is set in motion when the external orientation (J or P) interacts with its matching Extraverted function. All energy is directed externally and with the same purpose. When the Perceiving orientation interacts with either Sensing or Intuiting (whichever is the preferred Perceiving mode), or when the Judging orientation interacts with either Thinking or Feeling (whichever is the preferred judgment mode), there is an inspired cooperation between the two, as if each is egging the other on to heights unattainable by either one alone. Therefore, the motivating interactions are SP, NP, TJ, and FJ.

TABLE 6
OUTER IMAGE

ADAPTABLE LOOKING

EP

Extraversion and Perception
active and energetic
seek novel experiences
informal and spontaneous
often uninhibited, like rapid tempo

IP

Introversion and Perception
adventurous but reserved
changeable, nonconforming
restless and individualistic
tend to delay action

DECISIVE LOOKING

EJ

Extraversion and Judgment
fast moving and energetic
confident-looking and charming
often conform
talkative, sometimes blustery
conscientious

IJ

Introversion and Judgment
introspective and persevering
often quiet and modest
deferent but hard to convince
may overcontrol impulses

TABLE 7
MOTIVATORS

SP

Sensing with Perception
adaptable realists
focused on the present
seek new, present experiences
adapt to immediate situation
efficient with personal energy
keen awareness of the present
believers in economy of effort

If natural motivators are denied may become
distracted, inattentive, unstable, lazy

NP

Intuiting with Perception
adaptable innovators
independent
seek out new challenges
unconventional
challenging
fluent and expressive
nonconforming
imaginative
original

If natural motivators are denied may become
fickle, pleasure seeking, distractible, unable to delay gratification, restless

FJ

Feeling with Judgment
benevolent administrators
responsive
observant of people and their needs
informal
expressive and energized in relationships

If natural motivators are denied may become
overly evaluative of others' motivations, preoccupied

TABLE 7
MOTIVATORS *(Continued)*

TJ
Thinking with Judgment
logical decision makers
tough-minded
analytical
executive
critical, often skeptical
precise
deliberate
steady
ambitious
If natural motivators are denied may become
tense, stern, hardheaded, dominant, conceited

For SP and NP motivation or exhilaration may be experienced as a sense of limitlessness, flow, and lack of boundaries, like a fully rigged ship on a smooth, wide ocean under a clear sky with perfect winds at your back. For FJ and TJ exhilaration may be experienced as a keen sense of steady accomplishment with clearly defined needs, parameters, and priorities. Their ship has navigated the ocean, has land in sight, and is using the wind to execute the perfect docking.

When people were given the instructions, "List the adjectives that describe what your experiences are when the moment is 'just right'; what are you typically engaged in doing, or not doing, when this feeling is triggered?" the descriptors shown in Table 7 match those of the interactions of orientations and their associated functions (SP, NP, TJ, FJ). In addition, when asked to consider what might become of this motivated spirit if it is denied, there is a list of "may becomes." When these natural motivators are kept at bay for any great length of time, those undesirable behaviors may emerge with a message that says, "It's time to get back in balance!"

Learning about our natural motivators provides us with a way to understand and affirm our experiences. It also provides a road map for exploring more opportunities that allow full use of this interaction as well as what comes from living and working in a situation that continually denies these very natural urges and needs. The suggestion is not that we must have working environments that always allow these preferences to be expressed, but that we plan activities that encourage their regular expression. For example, if present-focused seekers of new experiences like those with SP preferences live all day in the critical, analytical, tough-minded environment preferred by TJs without providing themselves with outlets for their fluid adaptability, then two outcomes are probable. First, they are likely to become distracted or lazy and consequently reduce their contributions at work. Second, the TJs are likely to believe the SPs are resistant and difficult.

If you supervise or manage others at work or at home, do you have a sufficient understanding of the various motivators that provide the basic personal satisfaction needed for them to do a good job? Are you in an environment yourself that provides opportunities for your natural motivators to express themselves? As you plan activities and experiences for family members, you might keep this in mind when assessing whether the program in question will affirm the natural motivators at work in their types. What may seem to an NP parent like an idyllic camp or school environment could actually bring out the worst in the FJ youngster who is forced to attend. Type should never be the only data point used in making these determinations, but taking it into consideration can contribute greatly to illuminating our blind spots.

Inner Tension

Just as we need time for our natural motivating force to express itself outwardly, we need space to allow our private, internal world an opportunity to flourish. Beyond our Introverted mental function, we need to recognize and honor the internal push and pull we experience occasionally as part of our typology. This process, like that of our outer presentation and our natural motivators, is essential to a healthy recognition that our orientation to the world calls on one aspect of us while our inner operations call on another aspect of our experience. We each have a built-in mechanism that serves as an action inhibitor, for it calls on us to look inward.

Regardless of a preference for Introversion or Extraversion, this mechanism operates as the interaction between our preferred orientation (J or P) and our Introverted mental function. These interactions (SJ, NJ, TP, and FP) are experienced as a tension between outer orientation and inner mental work. For example, in the SJ interaction the orientation for Judging pulls toward decision-making and closure even as the Introverted Sensing function wants to gather more data. In the TP interaction, the orientation for Perceiving creates a strong pull to remain open and to gather more information even as Introverted Thinking urges making a competent, analytical decision.

Asked to think back on a poor decision and to answer the questions, "What are you like when you realize you have either decided too quickly or waited too long for a decision? How might the people in your life experience you while you are in the midst of that process?" the descriptors intersect with those of the type interactions noted in Table 8. Asked how they might be viewed by others if they stay in this psychological state too long, a further list of verified "may becomes" was generated.

Note that this does not describe those times of agitation when everything is wrong and everyone around you knows it. Rather, this interaction looks fairly calm externally but feels uncomfortable inside. We can think of it as the internal frustration that often precedes a breakthrough of some kind. This interaction is perhaps the most difficult to understand precisely because we are so internally focused that we are unaware of how we appear to the rest of the world. All types feel internal unease; their concurrent external behavior often is an adaptive, socially acceptable response to the condition. Table 8 delineates how others see us behaving while that is going on.

These interactions present us with information about those times when we merely go through the motions in outer life because we are actually focused on processing information in our inner life. As noted, this is at odds with the external pulls indicated by our typological orientation. When we begin to feel an internal fire, a rush to get on with it or the laboring sense that we would get on with it if we had enough information, then our system of dealing with the world is bordering on imbalance.

Two quick examples illustrate the significance of this interaction. After exclaiming that SJs "don't make bad decisions," a number of ESTJ and ESFJ women in separate workshops reported to us that they knew their first marriages were ill-fated before they ever walked down the aisle. But the invitations had been sent, gifts had been received, their parents were committed to the marriage, and all of the guests were planned for. The external world confirmed the decision to get married while data in the internal world profoundly argued against it. According to their reports, all of the energy invested in the ceremony outweighed the internal energy that was trying to alert them to problems elsewhere. Many of the SJs argued that they don't make bad decisions but acknowledged that some of their decisions are made based on poor information. After confiding their bad marital experiences, these same women said they had never revealed this information before out of fear that others would see them as crazy.

In another example, an INFP we know was visiting a large city 1,200 miles from home and decided to visit a special store to purchase gifts for his two children. The store sold only stuffed animals—thousands of them. Every day for four days he went to the store on lunch breaks and after dinner and reviewed all of the choices. A friend who accompanied him observed that he was methodical, calm, and focused on making the decision, and spent an enormous amount of time looking for the right animals, the ones that felt right for his kids. Inside, however, he was anything but calm, methodical, and focused—more like confused, distracted, and irritated at himself. He simply could not decide. The reason was that his Perceptive mode took in all the information and the Judgment function evaluated all the options, which leads to indecision. Like the ESTJ and ESFJ women, the INFP felt crazy—they were simple children's gifts, after all!

It is a relief to realize that a rational model can explain the spots we get into. This mechanism is an alarm that encourages us to stop and ask, "What do I really need in order to respond to the situation before me?" Knowing enough to ask and answer this simple question can lead to new arenas of personal growth.

TABLE 8
INNER TENSIONS

NJ
Intuiting with Judgment
visionary decision makers
persistent
strive toward inner vision
driving
determined
sensitive about demands
often seen as thorough and industrious
If stuck in this "psychological place" may become
hardheaded, fussy, blustery

SJ
Sensing with Judgment
realistic decision makers
steady
reliable
seek order in the environment
dislike ambiguity
stable
conforming
fastidious
often moralistic
favor conservative values
do the "correct thing"
If stuck in this "psychological place" may become
overcontrolled, opportunistic, intolerant, unable to recognize their own anxiety

TABLE 8
INNER TENSIONS *(Continued)*

TP
Thinking with Perception
analytical and skeptical
associate ideas in unusual ways
tolerant
often seen as clever
enjoy orderly frameworks
enjoy the environment
observant and curious

If stuck in this "psychological place" may become
hasty, evasive, self-indulgent

FP
Feeling with Perception
affiliative and adaptable
tolerant
relatively uncontrolled expression
responsive and softhearted
enjoy humor

If stuck in this "psychological place" may become
impulsive, distractible, hasty

Cognitive Core

Human growth depends on our ability to stretch our ways of processing and responding to information. If we fail to acknowledge tension, multiple research studies tell us we are likely to pay a price by way of difficult relationships and episodes of ill health.[2] Type gives us a way to access some of the potential stretch areas by recognizing the dynamics and interactions of our preferred functions.

At the core of this typology is the basic interaction of the preferred Perceiving and Judging functions (ST, SF, NT, NF). When all of the other expressions of the preferences fade, the habits of mind that result from the interactions of the mental functions provide a bedrock on which you can build an understanding of each type's world view. This knowledge is sufficient to analyze television commercials, speeches, characters in movies, and how individuals approach learning. For example, car television commercials that accentuate efficiency (ST), safety (SF), personal expression (NF), or performance (NT) are pulling on the innate core of type patterns. Listen carefully to the words (concrete or abstract) and the focus (self or system), and you will hear coverage of a type's core.

To the questions "When you plan or anticipate your day, what are people likely to see or hear from you?" and "What are you using to help you decide

TABLE 9
COGNITIVE CORE

ST

Sensing with Thinking
efficient
tough-minded
reasonable
matter-of-fact
practical
verify facts—weighs, measures
orderly
self-controlled
power-oriented
self-satisfied
internally consistent

If often kept from the preferred plan may become
overcontrolled, rigid, intolerant, overly conventional, unresponsive to personal needs

NT

Intuiting with Thinking
system
competence
psychologically minded
ingenious
analytical
focus on theoretical relationships
like autonomy
often clever
have defined interests
pride of objectivity
methodically attentive to theory, model

If often kept from the preferred plan may become
argumentative, overconfident, indifferent or wary, condescending

TABLE 9
COGNITIVE CORE *(Continued)*

SF

Sensing with Feeling
factually oriented
gentle and modest
seek to meet needs
safety
comfort
express personal warmth
seen as compassionate
responsible
conscientious
patient with detail
focus on things concretely affecting others

If often kept from the preferred plan may become
overly conventional, formal, despondent, or very disinterested

NF

Intuiting with Feeling
meaning
personal expression
tender-minded
enthusiastic
insightful
seek new projects, complexity
flexible
identify symbolic and theoretical relationships
aesthetic
inventive, nonconforming
unconventional thought processes

If often kept from the preferred plan may become
snobbish, self-pitying, withdrawn, fearful, anxious, dreamy, distractible

---

on the activities of the day?" the answers overlap with the descriptors of the interactions of the cognitive functions found in Table 9. These are the basic descriptors that capture the most typical qualities of the types. If you were asked to identify descriptors of how you might be seen if your plans for living out each day get frequently interrupted, a variety of "may becomes" like those found in Table 9 may emerge.

Clearly, there is value in recognizing one's core processes—those that feed and nourish us throughout the day. We encourage you to make sure there is time in your day to allow for your preferred way of making choices and acting. Though it is not always possible to engage in our most natural behavior, we can recognize the need to do so and be more deliberate about creating such psychological spaces.

Each aspect of the typology of individuals provides information about basic needs, drives, and requirements for balance in everyday life. Keeping an awareness of one's own processes is hard work that demands the fullest attention and recognition of one's type. The evidence suggests that type is a fact. The only question is whether we will ignore it or use it to enrich our possibilities. Type provides a place to begin understanding oneself and others in the context of normal human development. It takes extraordinary courage to own one's habits of mind and to recognize their limitations. It takes tremendous energy to seek to stretch beyond these habits and tendencies in order to fulfill your potential. Such courage and energy are the stuff of moral character, available to all but accessed by few.

The Teacher Within

LESSONS WE IGNORE AT OUR PERIL

Teachers attempt to show us how to pay attention to information, to direct our focus on priorities. They also may reveal our ignorance. Some of our earliest learning experiences are with schoolteachers and with our parents, teachers of another kind. As we grow older and become more judicious about how we spend our time, we make our own decisions about what is worth knowing and who we trust to be our guide. We become more aware of the inner voices of experience that guide us. As we grow in maturity and understanding, we realize that the greatest teacher is the one within.

Psychological type provides a letter of introduction to one such teacher within us. Many people familiar with type refer to this teacher as the inferior function, or the least-used function.[1] As the name suggests, this function is seldom called upon and used in daily life, at least not consciously. Yet it is not weak, unimportant, or even lacking in activity. Jung noted that he meant "inferior" to consciousness, not in psychological strength. We propose that it is best to think of the inferior function as emerging in three roles: conscious use, adaptive use, and compensatory use. Check Table 2 in chapter 2 (page 26) or Table 10 (page 66) in this chapter for a refresher on identifying the inferior function for each type.

Conscious Use

Conscious use of the inferior function means you intentionally call upon it to enable you to manage a situation that is somewhat out of the ordinary. Type theory suggests that someone with preferences for INFP may prefer to plan a presentation by listing as many ideas as are relevant to the topic with a focus on value-laden content. When, for any number of reasons, that person intentionally plans a logical, orderly, systematic presentation, he or she is calling upon Extraverted Thinking to help. When used this way, The Teacher who lives within each of us is giving two lessons: first, we can accomplish many things when we put our minds to it, and second, we have developmental needs that are good to address in a conscious way—sort of a "try it, you might like it" lesson.

Adaptive Use

Adaptive use of the inferior function is best explained by remembering times when you dealt with a situation productively and were also aware that you behaved very differently than usual. You might have thought, *Gosh, I didn't know I had it in me.* The lesson here is that you do. You have the resources necessary to manage challenges as they emerge. It's a matter of adapting to the situation by using your least-developed function. In this role, The Teacher is quietly ensuring our success and preparing us for lessons as we reflect on our accomplishments.

Compensatory Use

Compensatory use of the inferior function occurs when we are tired, highly stressed, and have depleted the natural resources found in our dominant and auxiliary functions. Some people working with psychological type refer to this as being "in the grip of your inferior function." Essentially, in lieu of a strong dominant function, the inferior seems to rise up from the unconscious and rule our behavior—sometimes for an hour, sometimes for months. The inferior function attempts to compensate for the loss of balance within the psychological makeup of the person. Of all the taskmasters we must

TABLE 10
IDENTIFYING THE INFERIOR FUNCTION

	INFERIOR FOR EXTRAVERTED TYPES			
	ESTJ/ENTJ	ESFJ/ENFJ	ESTP/ESFP	ENTP/ENFP
Teacher	Fi	Ti	Ni	Si

	INFERIOR FOR INTROVERTED TYPES			
	ISTJ/ISFJ	INTJ/INFJ	ISTP/INTP	ISFP/INFP
Teacher	Ne	Se	Fe	Te

face, this is perhaps the sternest. It demands that we recognize the unhealthy imbalances in our life. Table 10 shows each type and its teacher or inferior function.

Lessons Too Good to Ignore

There is very little published empirical data about the Teacher. We have many case examples, as do others, but it is inappropriate to generalize too far from such reports. Yet the power of the Teacher within us gives a compelling call to attend to many questions.

Often the conscious and adaptive use of the inferior function happens so quickly that we hardly notice it. The conscious choice of using one's inferior function may happen as a strategy for managing a particular human interaction. The adaptive use of the inferior function may simply emerge as a result of the situational pressures at work on an individual. Table 11 summarizes the characteristic expressions of the Teacher in conscious and adaptive ways. Compensatory expressions are wholly different and are discussed separately later in the chapter.

TABLE 11
CONSCIOUS AND ADAPTIVE USES OF THE INFERIOR

Type	Teacher	Conscious Use	Adaptive Use
ESTJ, ENTJ	F i	Choosing to be warm, friendly	Internal awareness of personal values
ESFJ, ENFJ	T i	Planning a logical presentation	Solving a human puzzle through principles
ESTP, ESFP	N i	Internal focus on future	Following a hunch
ENTP, ENFP	S i	Concentration on task details	Managing by sequencing information
ISTJ, ISFJ	N e	Expressing ideas about the future and about meaning	Changing course midstream
INTJ, INFJ	S e	Explaining current awareness	Spontaneously focusing on Sensing information
INTP, ISTP	F e	Active expressions of appreciation	Responding empathetically
ISFP, INFP	T e	Fluent verbal critique	Expressing logical connections, systems

In the compensatory use of the Teacher, we have surrendered typical control to this function.[2] Because its emergence during this depleted state often presents a raw and even distressing picture, it may have more of a psychological punch to it. In the vernacular, it is heavy artillery. The inferior function is an exacting taskmaster, but learning to use it is necessary to balancing the psyche.

Our experience indicates that if one should ignore the lessons of the inferior at any point in life, the Teacher's lessons will come back stronger, more demanding, and more difficult to manage. Using the inferior function simply means that a challenging teacher has arrived and is knocking at the door. The compensatory teacher is one over whom we have little conscious control.

The Inferior Lags Only in Development, Not in Strength

Of the inferior function, Jung wrote, "it lags behind in the process of differentiation…its true significance remains unrecognized."[3] Jung points out that the inferior is "merely backward" when compared to the favored function. Keep in mind, however, that it still serves an important role in Jung's "self-balancing psyche." For example, if you become overly dependent on the expressions of your dominant function, the compensatory inferior will erupt from the unconscious to impose balance.

Identifying Expressions of the Compensatory Inferior

Knowing the characteristics of the inferior of a type is not sufficient for understanding the role of the inferior in development. You must identify the expression of the inferior in your life, both the effort to consciously use it and the times when it expresses itself outside of your control. Once you feel you have identified the way this teacher operates within you, seek out information from others who have seen your inferior function in action and have them identify its effects on you and others. It is important to recognize the unique influence of the inferior, separate from the other functions.

While you are getting a handle on the nature of the inferior function in your own life and behaviors, it is important to realize that simply identifying it is not enough. The next step is to develop a method of transforming the energy and insights you gain into useful conscious material. This transformation of energy from recognition to constructive use requires hard work. Journals are very useful; having an effective personal guide works, too. Keep in mind, however, that you may not be able to directly access your fourth mental function; in some of us it is far from awareness and simply cannot be easily activated.

Reincorporating the compensatory inferior function—integrating it— means acknowledging that it has a legitimate voice in your life and can be a valuable guide when needed. Many of the lessons of the inferior function lie beyond recognition and thus transformation of its presence and nature are veiled. After much conscious work, you may not realize a lesson has been learned until well after the fact. It is helpful to know that your inferior function may encourage certain behaviors; understanding their connection to yourself and others begins the reincorporation of your newfound strength.

Be attuned to the simple rule that the inferior function of your type produces specific expressions. In other words, while your inferior function shares some general characteristics with others of your type, many of the particular expressions of it in your life will be unique to you and driven by your history.

Division of the Types

Jung differentiated among the types by identifying the combined attitude and dominant cognitive function (for example, Extraverted Sensing and Intro-verted Thinking). Because the dominant cognitive function directs the overall type, his first division was between the Judging (Thinking and Feeling) and the Perceiving (Sensing and Intuiting) functions. Using this schema, the various types are separated first by the Judging function and then by the Perceiving function. This difference is profound because it permeates the type and alerts you to the probable inferior—the very cognitive function in the same category that is opposite the dominant (such as Extraverted Thinking that has an inferior Introverted Feeling).

On each of the following pages of this chapter, you will find a summary of the hallmark qualities of each type, followed by a statement concerning the typical compensatory expression of the inferior. These are followed by a brief listing of activities and ideas concerning type development for the inferior.

Keep in mind that the inferior is the least-used function. As such, it is the one we are least likely to be aware of when it is expressed. Even those who know type very well find it easier to identify the inferior function of others than to identify expressions of the inferior function in themselves!

The compensatory inferior function may be expressed for a few hours one day, or it may take over for months. If ignored, it grows in strength. Acknowl-edged and explored, it becomes a new guide.

Please note that we view type behavior as expressions of the habits of mind. We feel using language such as "INFPs act this particular way…" to describe a type is a less fluid and more rigid dynamic than experience indicates is reasonable. Therefore, you will at times note that the language used here is different from the usual descriptors of type.

The following descriptions provide a basic outline for the purposes of stimulating study and conversation. Your personal experience will no doubt alter how you might write a description. These descriptors have the following structure:

    I. Hallmark qualities of type
    II. General descriptors of the compensatory inferior
    III. Activities for inferior function awareness

Compensatory Inferior Descriptions

In the descriptions that follow, we need to remember that the inferior function is simply least consciously active for us. The function is quite active in the unconscious realm, quietly gaining energy and collecting experiences relevant to the function that is involved. As pointed out earlier, there are times we access the least-used function to help us address a current situation. But we do not have the active conscious use of this function as we do our most preferred mental habit of Sensing, Intuiting, Thinking, or Feeling. Consequently, our inferior function possesses a considerable amount of independent will, as it is least under conscious control.

    Ironically, it is when we have lost conscious control because we are very tired, extensively stressed, or have overconsumed alcohol or other drugs that the inferior function will emerge and drive our behavior. It is compensating in two ways. The inferior function is taking its moment in the spotlight to compensate for all its time in the dark world of unawareness. More important, however, it is informing you of an imbalance, of a need to compensate for the overextension of your natural strengths and the depletion of your energy. In the vacuum created by this overextension and depletion, the inferior function gets to express itself with considerable magnitude, as seen in the following descriptions.

The Judging Types

EXTRAVERTED THINKING (ESTJ, ENTJ)

Inferior Function: Introverted Feeling

Typical Extraverted Thinking

Individuals whose typical patterns are Extraverted Thinking are likely to appear analytical and focused on cause-and-effect logic in their outer world.

Often methodical and thorough in behavior, those who prefer Extraverted Thinking direct their energy to solving complex problems. Attention is naturally drawn to models and overall goals, with concurrent emphasis on issues of competence and logic.

Typical Compensatory Introverted Feeling

When the inferior function of Extraverted Thinking emerges, it is generally a negative and excessive pattern of overly personal sensitivity. Introverted Feeling in its positive form is characteristically warm and open to concepts and ideas that bring meaning to life. Meaning is found in relationships and loyalties in typical Introverted Feeling ways; however, in its compensatory form, Introverted Feeling is a barbaric and mournful voice demanding to know "What do I live for?"

Feelings of worthlessness are exacerbated by a lack of ability to fully communicate one's feelings. This lack of expression only seems to reinforce a faulty conclusion of incompetence. There is a withdrawal from others as these feelings seem inexplicable. It is as if the self is demanding that you look inward and acknowledge the power of relational values and symbols.

Possible Activities for Type Development

Creative activities that have to do with art, such as drawing symbols or designs that represent feelings or the colors of one's moods, allow the natural Extraverted attitude to access information about the experience. Unlocking the Introverted Feeling energy and giving it life serves both the inferior and the dominant function.

INTROVERTED THINKING (INTP, ISTP)

Inferior Function: Extraverted Feeling

Typical Introverted Thinking

Individuals with a pattern of Introverted Thinking are generally focused on principles and megamodels that explain data, theories, and experience. It seems that the more complex the problem, the more energized these processes become. Criteria, rules of evidence, and verifiable data are major concerns of Introverted Thinking.

Typical Compensatory Extraverted Feeling

In a mode of positive expression, Extraverted Feeling seeks friendship and mutual appreciation. Usually sensitive to rejection or hostility, Extraverted Feeling becomes excited by cooperation and mutuality. In a compensatory mode, Extraverted Feeling is driven so hard by the feeling of being disliked that it overwhelms all in the wave of its expression. This negative emotion has a needy quality that is so strong that individuals who see it coming get out of the way.

This moving away by others inadvertently verifies the sense of being unappreciated. The emotions are well out of control for those who prefer Introverted Thinking. This causes anxiety and perhaps even some bitterness at the power of these emotions. By its own nature, compensatory Extraverted Feeling may establish superficial relationships to dispel energy from the inferior function. It is as if the self is demanding recognition of the importance of your passions and how they support your thinking life! You are not just independent but must be interdependent with others, if you hope to achieve life's goals.

Possible Activities for Type Development

Make an effort to write poetry or some other written expression of the overflow of feelings. Even listing words that express aspects of one's feelings will give life to and momentarily capture the experience. Ask a close friend or significant other to look at the poetry or word list, and invite him or her to note which expressions capture positive qualities of your relationship. This will ensure that the basic needs for both analysis and affirmation are met. Labeling the feelings is a basic start; specific experiences need to be associated with each label.

EXTRAVERTED FEELING (ESFJ, ENFJ)

Inferior Function: Introverted Thinking

Typical Extraverted Feeling

If ever there were a natural at creating relationships, the individual with Extraverted Feeling expressions is it; the hallmarks for Extraverted Feeling are cooperation and personal invitation. Seeking mutuality, Extraverted Feeling shares openly and connects easily with others. Generally, in the face of conflict, a chief strategy of the Extraverted Feeling pattern is to identify the positive qualities or ideas in each person's view.

Typical Compensatory Introverted Thinking

If the typical positive and mature expression of Introverted Thinking is confidence in one's ability to make sense and meaning out of experience, the compensatory expression of this tendency is a compulsion to find the answer by seeking an expert. This compulsion exists because the compensatory Thinking judgments have been turned on the self, creating considerable self-doubt. This doubt can seemingly only be managed by seeking the sage who will bring an end to the quest for meaning. So critical and negative can the Introverted Thinking voice become that even everyday experience can become twisted.

Social gaffes such as expressing a condolence at a wedding or congratulations at a funeral horrify the Extraverted Feeling. This type of experience reinforces the Introverted Thinking's message that one really is not so competent and capable after all, even in social affairs. It is as if the self is demanding recognition that your thoughts and plans are important; give them more attention and your personal relationships will be enriched!

Possible Activities for Type Development

Identifying accomplishments in one's social life can be a benefit to Extraverted Feeling. Often, because it is so natural, active involvement in social activities is not recognized for its contributions to oneself and to others. Creating a report of the week's activities will highlight the distribution of your energy and, if thorough enough, will give you a reminder of the needs of your inner world. A concrete look at how you spend your time will show you whether directing some energy toward new and stimulating situations would be feasible. Introverted Thinking wants a plan and wants to know how energy is being used to achieve your life goals.

INTROVERTED FEELING (INFP, ISFP)

Inferior Function: Extraverted Thinking

Typical Introverted Feeling

The general behavioral expression of Introverted Feeling is a passionate conviction to values and commitments. Often quiet and reserved, one typical hallmark of Introverted Feeling is a marvelous adaptability. Generally, there is little flash, but a great deal of energy is put into those activities that are connected to the most deeply held values.

Typical Compensatory Extraverted Thinking

While Extraverted Thinkers are known for their abilities to see many sides of a problem and to rapidly analyze the pros and cons of options, in its negative state Extraverted Thinking becomes a dictator, unyielding and maladaptive. So compulsively reductive and hairsplitting is the compensatory Extraverted Thinking inferior pattern that it can lead to the conclusion that you and those around you are incompetent.

The obsession with rightness and specificity eventually turns in on the self, unleashing a critical voice that tries to prove how incapable the Introverted Feeling is at taking discernible action. It is as if the self is demanding you to look at the inner map for direction but always stay attuned to the weather outside. Ignore the ability to analyze situations at your own peril; seek clear understanding of alternatives, but evaluate them using your own criteria.

Possible Activities for Type Development

With pencil and paper in hand to record information, discuss with a significant other recent choices you have made. What were the options and the various factors associated with each choice? Explore the values involved; which ones seem to emerge at the top of the list? By giving life to those values in written form, you energize your thinking so that the Extraverted function can see the criteria used in the inner world. Extraverted Thinking is less likely to unleash its critical voice when it understands the role that critical values play in feeding the psyche.

The Perceiving Types

EXTRAVERTED SENSING (ESTP, ESFP)

Inferior Function: Introverted Intuiting

Typical Extraverted Sensing

The hallmark expression of Extraverted Sensing is a firm, concrete, realistic attention to experience. The reliance on sensory experience has rarely failed the Extraverted Sensor; consequently, the Extraverted Sensor is comfortable dealing with immediate problems. Energetic and careful in its mature state, the typical Extraverted Sensing function is expressed in skillfully addressing situations, whether they involve people or machines.

Typical Compensatory Introverted Intuiting

Rather than experiencing a rich world of interconnections and possibilities, which is common to Introverted Intuitive processes, in the compensatory state this function is filled with dark fantasies and eerie expectations of the future.

The internal awareness is of seeing all the dire possibilities without being able to adequately express feelings or possibilities about them. This difficulty causes some withdrawal from others, for their presence only encourages the inferior function and reinforces the dark feeling of incompetence in social relationships. It is as if the self is demanding that you pay attention to the connection between the concrete reality of life and the more symbolic value that reality may present.

Possible Activities for Type Development

Do something completely different from yesterday's routine. Afterward, intentionally look at how you did it and compare it to yesterday's experience. What are the differences, outcomes, and similarities? Explore the value of the routine and the virtue of a new strategy. What is gained and what is lost? Study the relationship between previous goals and actual accomplishments. The lesson is that a long-range view is useful; today's consequences follow from yesterday's actions. So envisioning several futures provides the possibility that you can begin to consciously decide which future you would prefer, using hunches to get you there.

EXTRAVERTED INTUITING (ENFP, ENTP)

Inferior Function: Introverted Sensing

Typical Extraverted Intuiting

Extraverted Intuiting expresses itself with a focus on possibilities and innovation. These types are inclined to make connections between experiences and facts. New connections provide new stimulation, which maintains and incites the making of more connections. Connections sometimes add insight and depths to projects already underway. In relationships with either people or ideas, individuals with this pattern look for new ways to enrich their experiences.

Typical Compensatory Introverted Sensing

Mature Introverted Sensing is aware of and enriched by details, but, in its compensatory form, details are laden with emotional overtones, perhaps leading to the sensation that a fact or specific awareness establishes and proves a premonition. This can become a compulsion in which the importance of a piece of external evidence or a bodily sensation becomes exaggerated beyond all reasonable concern. Such an excessive focus on a work project or on foods, hygiene, or bodily functions reinforces the unspoken and underlying fear that life is about to take a major turn for the worse. It is as if the self is demanding that you look at the richness around you before leaping to a new precipice. Spend some time developing inside images before seeking new ones.

Possible Activities for Type Development

Use a relaxation exercise and imagine a journey you would like to take. The journey can include images from previous vacations or other actual experiences. Be sure to begin your journey in a dark room and focus on the difficulty of discerning the details of a lightless place; perhaps a room from a childhood experience will create the proper sense of darkness and aloneness. Follow the journey wherever it leads, but be sure you end up in a lighted place, maybe a room you remember as special because of the warm, pleasant memories it evokes. Focus on the details of the experience and enjoy it for your sake.

INTROVERTED INTUITING (INFJ, INTJ)

Inferior Function: Extraverted Sensing

Typical Introverted Intuiting

Hallmark expressions of Introverted Intuiting are the independent, often individualistic, pursuit of innovation in ideas and activities. Introverted Intuiting expresses itself through an inspired understanding of experience. These preferences are often those of individuals who are very interested in theories and models of meaning but also willing to splice and remold old theories to accommodate new ideas. Such people are often quite goal-directed and will pursue their ends even if unpopular or unconventional; to them, a difficult challenge means a greater opportunity.

Typical Compensatory Extraverted Sensing

Extraverted Sensing has the natural strength of collecting evidence from the environment—people, things, places. The fluid experience of information enables those using Extraverted Sensing to describe their experiences well. But in its compensatory form, Extraverted Sensing leads to incorrect deductions from a single fact; at times a simple smell can lead to the catastrophic conclusion that a relationship is over. There is no step-by-step logic leading to the conclusion; it is as if the conclusion already existed and merely required the observation of a random fact to allow it to be arrived at.

The consequences of the resulting behavior can make a fool of the Introverted Intuitive. Concerned with competence and possibility, the Introverted Intuitive person is horrified to discover that errors in logic or offenses to others seem to be the order of the day. Further, no explanation for the behavior can be made that is reasonable to others because it was based on a single fact from which an unreasonable conclusion was drawn.

Possible Activities for Type Development

Travel to the nearest art gallery or museum, giving yourself the day to absorb the details of artistic expression. Ask yourself which details stand out in a given piece. See if there is a pattern to the details you select. Go back, view the art again, and purposefully focus on another aspect of the art. See if the piece changes in your perception or if the meaning of the work alters. In this way you can experience in a constructive way the role of detail induction and how focus alters meaning. Also, get involved with crafts and cooking.

INTROVERTED SENSING (ISTJ, ISFJ)

Inferior Function: Extraverted Intuiting

Typical Introverted Sensing

The Introverted Sensing pattern of attention produces an accurate and thorough picture of reality, but it may remain unshared. These preferences incline an individual to seek practical rather than new solutions or procedures to problems. Painstaking with details, individuals with the Introverted Sensing pattern care about getting things done on time and according to precise specifications. When carrying out tasks, they will not stop until satisfied that all that could be done has been done. They are consistent and persistent doers.

Typical Compensatory Extraverted Intuiting

When the mature functions of Introverted Sensing, which have the natural strengths of clarity and specificity, give way to the inferior, a sinister and pessimistic mood settles on the individual. Events in the impersonal world seem directed as if part of a general plot to destroy one's happiness. A simple phone call from a friend relating some benign recent event may be interpreted as if it were a warning of and precursor to the end of a relationship or some other ghastly state of affairs that is coming soon. People in this state of mind make deductions unsupported by facts.

The nagging awareness that this is so creates a self-defeating cycle of saying, "Well, look at my bad judgment. I don't have all the facts, but looking at the facts I do have and the kinds of judgments I am making, something bad is bound to happen." Under the circumstances, some minor difficulty proves that the inferior was right and that you are right to feel terrible about your life. It is as if the self is demanding that you look to connections between today and yesterday, and that you plan for possibilities tomorrow.

Possible Activities for Type Development

Work on a hobby or other activity that you haven't worked on for a long time. Visit someone in the hospital, go collect seashells, check in with a friend from a long time ago—just do it. It will remind you of your strength and show you that possibilities abound that are neither dire nor foreboding. Some folks report that renting the most sinister movie they can find helps them realize just how much the inferior is playing with their minds.

A Final Word

The inferior function is a natural teacher that reminds you when your energies are depleted, shows you new avenues for development, and can be called upon when the situation demands its gifts. And as a teacher, it demands your utmost attention and greatest respect.

It is difficult to respect something that seems foreign to us or at least somewhat at odds with our typical way of responding to those around us. Yet one may learn to respect something that seems unlikable if for no other reason than it has a great deal of influence. Take as an example the fact that electric power running through our homes can be helpful *and* destructive. Its capacity merits our respect and proper treatment. In a similar fashion, we need to understand that the inferior function can play a positive part in our psychological development. It is present and has a great deal of energy. There are times we can use it as we need it, and it allows us to adjust to a situation.

But as we have seen, there are times the inferior function emerges out of control. Our capacity to recognize this when it happens and to understand the message that we are in need of adjustment in our daily lives is essential for the inferior function to be productive in our lives. If it does nothing more than turn on a mental light bulb that tells us we are working too hard and are ignoring those most important to us, it is a teacher worth having around.

Using the Ruby Slippers

THE POWER OF TYPE DEVELOPMENT

C onsider for a moment *The Wizard of Oz* as a contemporary tale of type development. The story is about a girl, Dorothy, stranded in a strange land on the other side of the rainbow. Because she inadvertently squashes a bad witch upon her arrival, the local good witch grants her a pair of ruby slippers.[1]

Viewing the story as a matter of type development (bear with us!), Dorothy is ripped from her frame of reference and sent on a path of discovery (a Sensing process). She meets a scarecrow wanting a brain (Thinking function), a tin man wanting a heart (Feeling function), and a lion wanting courage to face the future (Intuitive function). The unique resources of all the characters are required to get Dorothy to Oz, where an all-knowing presence—the Wizard—is supposed to be able to return her home and grant her assistants their requests as well. But the Wizard won't help them until they face their fears and struggle against the dark forces that threaten to undo them. When they succeed in doing so, it turns out that the Wizard has no magic; still, he is wise and caring, which enables him to fulfill the desires of Dorothy's companions. Dorothy's own wish, though, is bigger—she wants to go home, and that requires leaving her friends behind to sail in a balloon back over the rainbow, a simple plan foiled by an accident. In the end, she gets home only by submitting to the power of the ruby slippers she had from the beginning of the journey. The moral of the story? There really is no place like home, and the power to get there is with you all the time.

Our Yellow-Brick Road

Dorothy's story offers an excellent analogy to our own lives. Her path—the yellow-brick road—is like ours: often broken, rarely straight, and featuring no end of characters en route to the desired destination. The story is poignant to us because it is a metaphor for the need to befriend our mental functions one by one and gather them up to successfully complete our life journeys and achieve our goals. These functions, like the new friends Dorothy meets, can contribute to one another and lead to greater wisdom than any could achieve alone. Together, they ultimately overcome formerly insurmountable obstacles. While psychological type is about understanding our habits of perception and judgment, it is also a developmental model. Development implies growth, movement, and evolution. As such, type suggests that there are internal forces that move us toward greater maturity and increased ability to deal with life's challenges. Ultimately, all development is about adjusting and adapting to change while trusting our natural and reliable talents.

Normal individuals move each day toward activities that ensure survival. Whether or not we are conscious of our individual psychology, how it enables us to adapt and adjust is important; being alive necessitates responding to the stresses and choices that come our way. If we do not adjust, we may suffer serious physical or psychological consequences. Development implies a continually improving capacity to adjust and adapt to environmental demands. The questions psychologists ask often have to do with how, and how consistently within people, such development occurs. You could live a perfectly happy life without knowing anything about psychological models, including psychological type; you could go through life developing your abilities without knowing that's what you were doing. Some phases of life simply feel better, easier than others. You recognize lessons in life that help you move forward more smoothly. The mechanisms of personal adjustment, change, and adaptation do not require names in order to function; they still play out.

Patterns Leading to Insights

The beauty of learning human patterns is that we can accelerate insight into our way of seeing things and responding to life's ups and downs. Because we have the capacity to explore and learn, we can understand our personal and collective psychological development. Perhaps such understanding enables us to live richer, fuller lives. Knowing how our minds work does not necessarily relieve us from particular stresses, but it may make them more bearable and manageable and allow us to capture lessons that help steer us past future episodes.

Learning about psychological type as a framework for habits of mind provides us with choices we would not ordinarily have, which means more freedom—any increase in choice is an increase in opportunity. We can come to understand, for example, that even though we may be at our best in situations calling for critique and analysis, we can still learn to be empathetic and accommodating. If we do, we have made a personal advance. As we move down our personal yellow-brick roads, we are more likely to enjoy the journey as our range of choices increases. We may not get to Oz any more quickly, but the ability to make conscious choices will ensure that we are more mature and less naive when we get there—and that we will have more fun along the way.

Other Developmental Factors

In the same way that a model of the mind's workings, such as psychological type, is useful, understanding developmental forces within us can be equally practical. For example, if you learn that you are likely to become less physically able with age, you might decide to move into a house with fewer rooms to clean, no lawn to mow, and no stairs to climb. The same is true of psychological changes: if we know they are going to happen, we can be prepared for them. One way of preparing is to understand the three assumptions of development in psychological type: first, type is part of our mental self-regulation; second, we specialize, then integrate, mental functions; and third, development begins within as part of our adaptation to the world outside.

Type as Self-Regulating

One developmental aspect of type is that our minds maintain self-regulating processes that enable us to adapt and respond as our environment changes. Self-regulation means that without effort or even being aware of it, our psychological makeup finds a balance between being active and reflective, between having a narrow internal focus and a broad external focus, and so on. In type terms, our minds Extravert and Introvert, Perceive and Judge as needed to maintain our general style and sense of well-being.

Self-regulating has to do with keeping internal balances between perception and decision-making, and maintaining the energy distribution between Extraversion and Introversion. For regulation to occur, there must be sources of energy and mental functions that need direction and utilization. As children grow, they begin to test drive their various mental functions, and their preferences emerge very early. For example, some researchers believe that the preference for Extraversion or Introversion appears within the first six months of life.[2] But children, like the rest of us, must internally regulate their preferences, which is not necessarily a conscious process. Otherwise, for example, a person preferring Extraversion would carry out no Introversion functions, and, thus, would relentlessly seek experiences without ever giving any thought to what was being experienced. Fortunately, we are equipped for a natural exchange between the two processes. This regulation is true for all of perception and decision-making. Like Dorothy, whose capacities increase as she gains supporting characters, so it is in psychological type, where the proper utilization of mental functions increases our ability to adjust.

In concrete terms, this simply means that as we go from experience to experience, say English 101 to Math 110, or from the boardroom to the family room, we use different perceptions and decision-making strategies to deal with whatever is presented. English may require us to call on the metaphorical, intuitive side of our imagination, while math may need more specific sensing attention and analytical thinking processes. The boardroom may be the place for decisive, directive action, while the family room may call on a more spontaneous, fluid, go-with-the-flow type of interaction. We change without deliberation if we have already learned what will most likely produce a desirable outcome. In other words, we self-regulate our actions, responses, and perceptions.

Type Moves from Specialization to Integration

A second developmental aspect of type is that we develop specialized mental functions before we integrate other mental capacities. Whatever our type, we must be clear and consistent in expressing it before we can gain clarity about other aspects of our personality. The clearer we are about our preference for Extraversion, for example, the more likely we are to be clear when we also use Introversion. An INFP—with Introverted Feeling as his primary process, assisted by Extraverted Intuiting—is more likely to know when he is exercising Extraverted Thinking if he is clear about his own type. If we know what habits we have, it is very clear what habits we don't have. This is a critical aspect of type development: we know our type, we are clear about our type, and then we understand the other dimensions of type we can use. But before we can really learn to use these functions in a conscious way, we need to become fully aware of the nature of our own type dynamics—that is, to learn to wear and use our psychological ruby slippers.

The ruby slippers have the power to transform frame of reference and quality of life once they are recognized for their natural worth. From the perspective of psychological type, we are more likely to transform our lives when we accept our preferences and get on with the business of learning about the appropriate use of the less preferred mental functions. For example, if you are clear about preferring to use Extraverted Sensing to manage your daily challenges, you can use it to seek ways to explore other aspects of your abilities—perhaps your Extraverted Sensing will lead you to a workshop that teaches people to get in touch with their Intuiting. Such a workshop fits a need, addresses a natural strength, and provides a door for future development.

We spend a good portion of early life developing our natural preferences; during the second part of life we spend time identifying and using other preferences that do not come so easily to our awareness. Some books on midlife change and transition point out that after we spend twenty years or so learning, developing, and adjusting to our work and life partners, we begin to become more aware that time is running out, and so we seek out new challenges.[3] We insist on new experiences because we do not want to look back later and regret not exploring or changing when we had the chance. Type assumes that the same processes are at work on the use of mental functions. If we spend the first part of life developing Extraverted Feeling, we may pursue Introverted Thinking activities in the second part—rather like eating fish for twenty years and then developing a hankering for pork.

Type, Adapting to Challenges, and Parenting

As noted above, type theory says we must specialize in a specific pattern of using Perception and Judgment before we can successfully explore other aspects of mental processes. In a sense, the power of our psychological ruby slippers lies in our type, our home base, our personal framework. Understanding your own type offers help on the developmental journey, the destination being to learn when and how to appropriately use those aspects of yourself that you have kept on a mental shelf. Whether or not people know about their psychological types, those who cannot develop clear, appropriate use of their types—who have never experienced being valued or appreciated for the perspective they bring—cannot fully understand or realize their potentials. The two most obvious places a person can be prevented from developing natural expressions are in the family and in school. While conducting career counseling with a young woman, for example, a friend of ours helped her interpret her MBTI inventory. As our friend described the process of Intuiting to the client and she confirmed that this was her preferred way of perception, she began to cry. Later the woman said, "You know, this is the first time in my life I have ever felt that anyone understood me. All these years my family and teachers told me I was crazy, and I was about to believe it myself. I have tried and tried to see things their way, but they never once thought it would be worthwhile to try to see things my way. Now I know I am not crazy. It is such a relief." Type gives us a stability of direction to manage the waters of change and to pursue other abilities that might otherwise be ignored. The purpose of this development is to enable us to more wisely address the daily demands of life. What a tragedy when our oars and rudder are taken away just when we start the long journey. This is to say that type development starts early and lessons learned in childhood have lifelong implications.

Parenting and adult/child relationship applications for using type are the topic of many questions that have come to us over the years. Whether you are a parent (by birth or adoption), favorite relative, or childcare provider, wondering how best to connect, correct, and motivate the children around us is a constant quest. There are good data pointing to the existence of innate facets of our personality that are with us from the womb. Anecdotally, Roger's wife, Angela, and Sarah can tell you the children they carried were different from the very start of the process, and certainly became different and unique personalities from birth to now, grown adults living in the world. Thus begins the "nature" side of the nature versus nurture paradox.

Immediately, we, as parents and other well-meaning adults and teachers, enter the scene. Nurturing begins an immediate and profound influence on us. There are many, many books written about all this, some better than others, and all try to capture what ultimately can't be captured—a complete explanation of why we are who we are. Why we love what and who we love. Why we struggle or glide; why we succeed or fail. Most parents want nothing more than for their children to live happy and productive lives, and, if we're honest, to reflect well on our efforts to do the right things over the first 18 years. "It's the toughest job you'll ever love" is more than a cute saying in a new parent's greeting card. How can type help?

Throughout this book and in the following chapters in particular, we have parsed out every conceivable combination and permutation of type preferences and our best thinking on what the research says about the motivations and meanings of how different types show up in different ways. Our purpose is always to promote curiosity, understanding, and, spirit willing, valuing of those differences. But here's the thing about kids: they're not completely fixed in their personalities and behaviors, nor should we strive for them to be, especially in their younger years. We invite our readers throughout this book to think of preferences, not traits—to appreciate the power of a type expression when it serves a situation well, rather than get hung up on predicting or assuming a person's four-letter type.

This is especially true when it comes to interacting with children. Children need one thing above all else in order to thrive—a secure knowledge of their true belonging, no matter what. Within that context they can try on many different ways of being to discern for themselves what feels right to them throughout their natural stages of development, specializing, generalizing, and experimenting as they go. Understanding type and type preferences gives us, as adults, every reason to understand that each kid is different and, with observation and experimentation, to find ways to support a child's safe zones and stretch zones, freedoms and boundaries.

When Sarah's oldest child, Wells, was a toddler in a Montessori school, she had already noticed patterns that suggested he preferred introversion and intuition. While alert and curious in a group of children, his pattern was to watch from the edges for a while before deciding how he wanted to engage with the bustle. He wasn't shy or anxious, he was fully enjoying himself while watching. She and his father learned not to push or coax him too much—he always found his way, making friends, and often by the end of the afternoon he'd be the one in charge of the games and imaginary stories all the others would play their part in. As two extraverted parents, it was always a challenge for them to not over-support or to keep themselves from pushing him into things before he was ready. They weren't always successful!

The Montessori school prized its open floorplan classroom with no dividers for private space. It wasn't long before Sarah was getting calls from the teacher that Wells was taking a "work tray" from its shelf and going into the small, more private adjacent cloakroom to do the tasks. They weren't happy about it. She asked if they'd ever had any other students do that. The answer? "Well, yes, a small handful every year, now that you mention it." Sarah did a tutorial on personality type for a few of the teachers, with a special focus on introversion and extraversion. She suggested that rather than having all the shelves with the work trays lining the walls leaving one big open space, that a few of them be placed perpendicular to create smaller enclosed spaces in the room for those children who needed a reprieve from the "big room" all day. They were kind enough to indulge her suggestion and were thrilled with how much calmer and more engaged all the children were. Regardless of whether or not Wells grew up to claim a preference for introversion, at that time of life he was express-ing his desire for smaller, more enclosed, and intimate spaces. As an observant parent with a knowledge that all of us have "gifts differing," Sarah was able to advocate on his behalf, not by pigeonholing him with a label but by generating a hypothesis, staying curious, and encouraging other adults to not make him or other children "wrong" for doing things differently than the norm.

As you read through the following pages and chapters, we invite you to consider how you might apply these lessons to the young people in your life. How might you experiment with different ways to show that you value your children's expressions of personality? As they move into youth and young adulthood, what are you noticing about their communication patterns, and yours? Armed with all the possibilities we have written about here, are you willing to ask questions and try some small experiments in order to better understand what's going on, rather than leaping to the conclusion that your own natural biases and history write for you? All of the applications of psy-chological type in this book are especially critical when thinking about our relationships with children.

Shame versus Guilt as Parental Control Tools

Dr. Brené Brown has researched, written, and spoken compellingly about the profound difference between shame and guilt. Put simply, guilt is the sense that we *did* something wrong. Shame is the sense that we *are* something wrong. To quote Dr. Brown, "I define shame as the intensely painful feeling or experience of believing that we are flawed and therefore unworthy of love and belonging—something we've experienced, done, or failed to do makes us unworthy of connection."[4] We all know the feeling of shame. It's a human condition. And as parents we have the opportunity to help minimize the negative impact of shame and to give our kids some coping tools for when it, inevitably, comes calling.

As parents, especially with small children, it is crucial that we get our language straight about this. Why is it so important? Here's what Dr. Brown's research showed: Shame self-talk (e.g., "I am bad"), is highly correlated with addiction, depression, grief, anxiety, eating disorders, and violence. It is isolating and leaves us feeling powerless to respond. If I "am" something, how can that ever change?[5]

Guilt is the discomfort we feel when we realize our *behavior* hasn't been in integrity with our values. We recognize the discomfort and feel motivated and empowered to change our behavior to bring ourselves back into alignment. "I made a bad choice; I will choose differently next time" versus "I am bad; what use is there to even try to be anything different?" Shame paralyzes. Guilt galvanizes.

For example, when a child tells you, with chocolate all over their hands and face, that they didn't eat the candy bar, your words matter. Telling that child that it's clear they are not speaking the truth, that they have told a lie, and that we have family rules/values about that behavior is a constructive use of guilt. Boundaries are in place; there is room for correcting the mistake or making amends, learning lessons, and moving on. The child can internalize "Uh-oh, I did a bad thing. I don't want to do that bad thing again. I don't like time out…" (or whatever consequence might follow).

If, on the other hand, they are told, "You are a liar. How dare you lie. I can't trust you because you are a liar. Go to your room. I don't want to see you right now." The internalized message is very different. Now there is an "I AM" statement embedded that, over time, is shaming. What kind of person is a liar? A bad one. I don't belong. I am unlovable and disconnected.

Take the casual, everyday use of "Be a good boy/girl!" as if they are ever anything other than that. Or "You're a bad boy/girl for…" Those are shame messages designed to control a child's behavior. Another example is "Don't be lazy" versus "Please pick up your dishes after using them." Those shame-based messages can become crippling over time (you *are*) versus guilt-based messages (you *did*). The same is true at school and work, by the way. Bullying, shaming language is incredibly toxic, and while it might result in an immediate fix, the long-term impact is harmful and unproductive.

At a scenic overlook in the mountains, Sarah watched as a family's youngish child—seven or eight—was looking out over the vista. The little girl spotted a river far below and began extraverting her imagination of what it would be like to walk beside that far-off ribbon of water. "Look down there. I bet it's shady and cool, with tall grass and animals drinking. Do you think there are fish down there? It looks so green...." Whereupon one of the adults with her wheeled around telling her to shut up. "We just got up here and you're already wanting to go off somewhere else? For once can you just be quiet and appreciate where you are? You always want something you don't have and I'm sick of it. We're NOT going down there!" The child's eyes filled up and her lip trembled (as did Sarah's when their eyes met briefly). That was at least 25 years ago, but the memory is still vivid. The child's natural expression of extraverted intuition was deeply misunderstood and shamed into silence. "It was like watching a beautiful full balloon deflate in front of my eyes," Sarah said later when recounting the story.

Think of all the commands with a type bias that children hear all day, every day:

Speak up! [Rejection of the young Introvert]
Be quiet! [Rejection of the young Extravert]
Get some common sense! [Rejection of the young Intuitive]
Have a little imagination! [Rejection of the young Sensor]
Stop contradicting me! [Rejection of the young Thinker]
Stop taking things so personally! [Rejection of the young Feeler]
Be flexible! [Rejection of the young Judging preference child]
Get it done! [Rejection of the young Perceiving preference child

When we consider all the many ways that our type differences can create misunderstandings, it is deeply important that parents and anyone with responsibility for caring for children find constructive language to discuss the behaviors in question without questioning the bonds of lovability and connection within which children thrive. Modeling this language for other children is important, too. Sibling and peer language can be equally damaging when it threatens a child's sense of worth and belonging.

Owning Your Baggage

One of the best things we can do as grownups with children in our lives is to take responsibility for our own behavior, good and bad. Many parents feel the need to hide their mistakes, struggles, and foibles from their children. This may range from putting on a good face about a hard thing confronting an adult to refusing to apologize to a child for a mistake. But how else will children learn that mistakes and failures/hardships are an important part of life, and that making them, fixing them, dusting off, and getting back up is natural and acceptable in a family? Role modeling that is important. Celebrating a job well done is just as important, too. We aren't suggesting pulling out the family budget spreadsheet to explain to your five-year-old why you're worried about losing a complex piece of business at work. We *are* suggesting sharing with a child, in age-appropriate language, that you are feeling disappointed that something you worked hard on didn't go as planned. Role modeling that resiliency is powerful. When the moment comes that the child has a setback, they will feel less alone and more confident that you truly understand what it feels like and that it's okay to talk about it and feel whatever the feelings may be.

Years ago, Sarah was picking up her youngest, Emmy, from high school. Emmy bounded into the car and as they pulled away Emmy said, "We got our report cards today!" "Great!" Sarah replied. "How'd you do?" "Five As and a B-plus!" (You know where this is going, don't you? Of course you do!) Sarah's unfiltered NT view of the world kicked in, always looking for the ways to improve on things, and these terrible words flew out of her mouth, "Cool! Wow. Huh. What's up with that B-plus? Why'd you miss that last A?" To Emmy's credit, her NF preference teared up and she mustered a power- ful claiming of her worthiness and self-respect "MOM! Why can't you focus on the five As rather than the B-plus?" We can neither confirm nor deny that there was an expletive or two in there! Sarah was horrified at her blunder and ashamed for ruining what should have been a pure moment of well-deserved pride. Rather than bouncing the hurt back to Emmy by getting mad with her emotional response or rationalizing her own behavior with "I was just asking! Jeez!" Sarah sought to redeem herself by pulling over at the next opportunity, looking Emmy in the eyes, and apologizing sincerely while also congratulat- ing her heartily. While she can't claim a complete cure by any means, Sarah considers that moment a lightning-bolt lesson to be aware of how naturally a critique can fly out of her mouth and what it can sound like to others, no mat- ter how well intended. There's a lot more than type to that story, but type gives us a place to discuss the biases and worldviews from a platform of difference, not right or wrong. And from a family perspective, Sarah was so proud of how Emmy held her accountable rather than swallow her emotions about it. That transparency is a place we can heal from. Secrecy, shame, and defensiveness offer no such redemption or resolution.

Being a parent doesn't mean you stop being a fallible person. You enter those new family dynamics with all the same baggage you had the moment before your little human came into your world. If anything, children will mag- nify the chinks in your persona and offer you opportunities for growth more reliably than anyone else in your life. (That's a nice way of saying, they show us where we've got crooked logic and false beliefs in need of an upgrade! It can be painful.) Sarah likes to call kids our "Zen masters." The wonderful cave scene from *The Empire Strikes Back* between Luke Skywalker and Yoda explains it well. They're standing outside the cave Luke fears the most, and he asks Yoda, "What's in there?" Yoda replies, "Only what you take with you." Our children, however, they come into our lives, hold our highest hopes and our darkest fears. And when we choose to be a parent, into the cave we must go. No exceptions. Jung's model of psychological type helps us to understand that of all the things in that cave we might fear, we need not fear the natural differences among us. There is a balance created from cooperation among the perspectives that can make us all stronger and more resilient if we humble ourselves to the lessons.

Big Spirits, Little Bodies or "You Don't Treat Me like a Dumbass"

Sarah was flying home through Dulles airport one Friday afternoon. It was overcrowded, hot, and everyone was tired and mildly on edge, jockeying for position to be first in line when their flights were called. At the front of her line, talking to the gate agent, were two women, probably a grown daughter with her mother, dressed in attire from another country, clearly not speaking or understanding English well. Others were beginning to get annoyed, worried they were being blocked from their planes (though they were not). Sarah became aware that the energy of the crowd was that these women were dumb or a problem somehow—that they were going to get in the way. There was an air of aggravation and impatience.

It dawned on Sarah in that moment that for all we knew, these women were highly acclaimed scientists or authors or doctors in their country. But for the barrier of language, we might all be in awe of them, rather than annoyed or mistrustful of them. And further, if the shoes were reversed and we were in their country, we'd be the ones hanging on the sleeve of the gate agent trying to be sure we were in the right spot and all the locals would find *us* ignorant and annoying.

It is an easy leap to recognize that children are the same way. As many before have observed, we are not humans having a spiritual experience, we are spirits having a human experience. If that's true, then children are big spirits in little bodies. When they're born, they don't speak the language here, they don't know how their bodies work, they don't know the customs, and all kinds of things that foreigners in a new land need to learn. In the spirit realm, there's no telling how powerful and revered they were! As parents/elders/community members our job is to be their tour guide, not their prison guard. We speak the language, we know how some things work, but to treat children as "less than" because of that is to do them and ourselves a disservice. We miss big opportunities to learn when we disrespect the humanity and inherent worth of each child in our orbit or when we try to mold them to our own image. From a type perspective, type is a powerful way through which their spirit is expressed.

When Eliza, Sarah's middle child, was a toddler, she quickly became the organizing force for timeliness and order in that Perceiving household. Sarah realized one day while playing with Eliza in her playhouse, teaching her the concept of "open" and "closed" with a door to the little house, that her vocal quality was much more pleasing and welcoming on the word *open* and much more clipped and harsh on the word *closed*. Hello NP type bias! Sarah caught herself and worked hard to present both options as equally appealing whenever they played that game. In the somewhat chaotic three-kid, two-cat, and one-dog household, the silverware drawers and cupboard doors were often ajar, and Eliza's very first word came when she closed a drawer with a definitive push and said "THERE" with pride in the closure she brought to that drawer and that moment. Sarah laughed *and* got a chill. Sarah thought, *She's not like me—oh no! And oh yes!* Therein lies the beauty and the pain of loving and raising children.

One last story. When Wells was 15 or so he was telling Sarah one Friday afternoon about several different close friends who were grounded for the upcoming weekend, leaving him at loose ends for plans. As he recounted their transgressions and the various parental responses, Sarah was both perplexed and nervous. She rather felt like the other parents' punishments exceeded the crimes but, being a single mom at this point in life, she also began to second-guess her own parenting. Was she too lax? Was she doing this wrong? So Sarah said to Wells, in all seriousness, "Should we be fighting more? Do I let you get away with too much?" He just laughed and said, "No, I think we're good. We don't need to fight about things." But she wasn't satisfied and pressed him further, "But WHY? Why do all your friends keep getting in trouble and WHY don't we fight more?" He thought a moment, looked over at her, and said, "There's not much to fight about because you don't treat me like a dumbass." Oh. Just that simple. Just that hard.

So, parents, own your psychological baggage, and show your kids some respect. It's not about being permissive; it's about being real. Let the type information here support and guide your efforts in understanding, loving, and valuing yourself and *all* the humans you interact with, with an extra dose of tenderness for the younger ones.

Psychological Type Is a Dynamic Force in Development

Psychological type would be of little value if it did not provide for our need to adjust to changes and challenges in life. Good students learn from previous experiences and use those lessons to address similar situations. Type reminds us of the attention we pay to situations and the conclusions on which we can act. Type suggests that the things that frighten us at age twenty may be used to our advantage at age 40. For example, if you were afraid of making logical, orderly—Extraverted Thinking—presentations in the early part of your career, chances are that in order to advance, you learned to do it anyway. Healthy individuals learn to use those aspects that increase their likelihood of achieving success. Type development requires that our mental processes are distinct from one another, that we can appropriately identify and deploy them as the situation requires, and that we have a "well-oiled" home base of primary and supporting processes that alternately focus our perceiving and judging situations.

Jung proposed that as we grow older, our internal psychological mechanisms demand challenge and opportunity. Like a tulip bulb that knows when to grow and unfold, our internal psychological processes stimulate change of their own accord and timing. Those who prefer Intuiting may find themselves passionate about a Sensing-related hobby in their thirties, for example, because it allows for the expression of the non-preferred perception without threatening the more basic preference.

Other Developmental Models

To understand the significance of type as a developmental model, we need to recognize that type is different from other developmental perspectives. Other models assume that human development occurs in a relatively sequential manner, moving from simple to complex behaviors. Further, development at a later stage requires competence at an earlier stage. For example, you can learn to walk only after you have learned to crawl.

By contrast, type does not assume sequential development. Type is like the inner veins of a tree, influential and essential to growth but allowing it to occur in any direction in response to the environment. Further, though type does not assume the sequential, hierarchical development of preferences, it does presume that human behavior is quite complex and serves many purposes. For perceptions to get "clearer" an individual needs to seek to develop Extraverted Sensing and Intuiting, Introverted Sensing and Intuiting—these are four windows on reality of experience. To make judgments more "sound" an individual needs to develop Extraverted Thinking and Feeling, and Introverted Thinking and Feeling so that all available considerations lead to wise discernment. And developing these eight functions are possible and more conscious choice on what to use when is desirable *without* the loss of the main pattern that serves as our compass in life. In other words, an ENFJ will depend and enrich this pattern by learning about and accessing the other functions when needed to adapt and respond in life.

What We Have Learned

In somewhat practical terms, type development is about what we have learned to do and what we have avoided learning to do. For example, those who have a natural preference for Extraverted Thinking and have learned this way of making decisions quite well are less likely to have used or developed Extraverted Feeling. Being comfortable as verbal, analytical, systematic problem solvers, they act that way more often than not and gain reinforcement for it more often than when they express themselves in other ways. Thus, they may tend to simply ignore Extraverted Feeling throughout life.

But type development is the process of activating those previously unacknowledged functions, learning their capabilities, and using them in appropriate ways. If you spent the first half of life enhancing your natural patterns of Perception and Judgment, you will develop more completely when you work on the less-used patterns. Learning when to appropriately use your non-preferred mental functions and to use them well is the goal. It is the same as the medicine wheels of the Plains Indians mentioned in chapter 1. Life's journey is one of growing awareness of, appreciation for, and skill in using expressions outside your natural view. When you gain this ability, you earn the privilege of placing a new stone in your wheel. Those who meet you and observe your understanding of many perspectives will know that you are truly wise.

Much of the literature on adult development focuses on the important tasks of growing up, selecting a career and a mate, being creative in one's work, and making choices about contributions to be made later in life. Additional adult development material is focused on physical and mental changes. There is very little on the personal, inner psychological work we must do to move successfully through life. In many regards, psychological type theory gives the largest scope of mental development of any current model. Jung's injunction is clear: learn to do your inner work and everything will be okay. Learning techniques like active imagination, meditation, mindfulness, and inner dialogue are steps in the direction of inner work needed by all.

Learning from Experiences

Some of the most interesting work on adult development is emerging around research on the lessons people learn from their various life experiences.[6] The assumptions guiding this work are that we are attracted to those things we do well and avoid those things that we believe we do not do well. Throughout our early adult life we select experiences and challenges that we feel reasonably able to accomplish. As we get older, it becomes increasingly clear that the experiences we avoided at an earlier time would have taught us valuable lessons that could be very useful now. Thus, we strive to excel at our strengths, but we avoid confronting our weaknesses until it is absolutely necessary to do so in order to continue to achieve greater levels of satisfaction.

For example, if you graduate from college with a degree in industrial engineering, chances are you will pursue a job with a firm that needs an entry-level industrial engineer. Let's assume you are generally able and ambitious, you receive promotions, and you excel at the work the company needs you to perform. One day, however, you are promoted to supervisor. Within a few months, you wish you had taken the human relations courses you pooh-poohed in college and the professional development workshops you avoided early in your career, because now you need insights regarding motivational and leadership skills. Having assiduously avoided such "soft topics" to pursue expertise in engineering, you are now woefully unprepared to tackle supervisory tasks. More alarming is that further success may depend on learning things now that you could have easily learned earlier. But you quickly set about learning these skills and vow that you will not get caught like this again. Assuming that you do learn the skills necessary to supervise, and you perform very well, you are now promoted to a position as unit manager. While the lessons of leading and supervising those with less experience or expertise were difficult enough, you now need the ability to persuade peers and make public presentations to upper management and clients. If you have not prepared for such a day, you may once again wish you had learned the skills needed for this new challenge earlier.

In Appendices B and C (pages 299 and 303) we have provided charts linking various personal or work experiences and the mental functions. Simply find the intersection of type functions and activities to see the kinds of things that can enrich or further activate that function for you. Enriching these mental functions increases capability for future effective responses and deepens our type pattern—not at the cost of the pattern.

Echoes of Type Development

This model of lessons learned and lessons avoided has a very strong parallel in type development. Type theory says that type preference is part of the reason we are attracted to specific interests and activities, and that these are reinforced by a sense of accomplishment. Later, we have to learn things about ourselves that we have ignored in order to maintain a healthy view of the world.

We suspect that, as more researchers explore the processes of adult development and move beyond looking solely at the tasks of development, these basic principles of type will be supported. After more than four decades of asking questions about type development of thousands of program participants, we have enough evidence to suggest that type development is a very real and powerful force in adult growth. It is clear that, properly understood, type can aid adults throughout their lives in making more conscious choices and in avoiding the blind spots that can plague them.

In adult life we constantly strive for effectiveness—for the ability to produce results, which is explored in chapter 7. We want to be effective as partners, parents, associates, managers, and in any other role we can imagine. We want our needs to be understood and satisfied through our engagement in relationships, work, parenting, and all the other roles we choose. If we decide to be parents, we generally want our kids to grow up to be happy, healthy, and successful individuals. If these things happen, we think of ourselves as effective. When we prepare a presentation for work, we do our best to design it to be effective. Electricians want to install wiring, switches, and outlets in such a way that power is safely distributed in a structure, and if they do so they think of themselves as effective.

Developing Efficacy

Often we are effective because we have sought experiences that give us the abilities to do the job, or we model our efforts after someone who has done the job well (parents, for example, usually do not go to parenting school but rely on their observations of other parents, especially their own). What we really want is more than effectiveness; we want efficacy. *Efficacy* means making more conscious choices and actions based on the use of all of our capacities rather than merely acting out of routine. Efficacy is the awareness and use of our skills, our knowledge, and the limits of our capabilities. It is the belief that no matter what comes our way, we can adapt, adjust, and develop a strategy to respond. The ultimate end of type development, like Dorothy's use of the ruby slippers, is efficacy: consciously using our powers to get us where we want to go.

To explore the development of the 16 types, Table 12 provides two descriptions for each type. The first is a description of qualities of those people who are clear about their types and who have been observed as being effective in using the behaviors that result from their types. The second is a description of the qualities needed to obtain greater efficacy. To increase your own efficacy, you might ask others who know you well what kinds of things you could do to learn new behaviors, to respond differently, and to immerse yourself in new ways of getting things done. The intent behind listing some activities and ideas to consider is merely to give you hints and trends; these are by no means prescriptive or comprehensive.

TABLE 12
TYPE PATTERNS IN ADULT DEVELOPMENT

ISTJ

Introverted Sensing with Extraverted Thinking

When developed	Pragmatic, detail-oriented, consistent, rely on past experiences, concise, focused, serious, orderly, methodological, practical, decisive, reserved, predictable, organized, realistic, it takes time to get to know them, trust facts, want and make structure, conscientious, calm, make time to be alone, hard to dissuade once mind is made up, responsible, energized by data
For efficacy	Learn to trust the inner voice and the Intuiting of others, create opportunities for complete freedom from closure, learn multiple decision-making models, engage two or three more people in problem-solving than they normally would

ISFJ

Introverted Sensing with Extraverted Feeling

When developed	Organized, succinct communicators, want thorough understanding of facts before acting, service-oriented, enjoy helping others, careful, reliable, realistic, concise
For efficacy	Seek opportunities to let go; immerse themselves in activities such as art classes or philosophy debates at a local university, get involved with psychologically minded programs, join a book club

INTJ

Introverted Intuiting with Extraverted Thinking

When developed	Play out conversations in their heads, like planned changes, like new challenges, reflective, independent, see the big picture, oriented to the future, determined, purposeful, resourceful, ask why, hard-driving, relentless about precision, use principles for decision-making
For efficacy	Commit regularly to a social help volunteer organization, seek out others who share many of their qualities but have achieved success in very different ways from them, engage in group training programs with a physical component, such as rafting, to drive focus on the moment

TABLE 12
TYPE PATTERNS IN ADULT DEVELOPMENT *(Continued)*

INFJ

Introverted Intuiting with Extraverted Feeling

When developed	Quiet problem solvers, have global perspective, avoid conflict, like many points of view, enjoy generating options, work with complex people problems, establish enduring friendships, decisive, attentive to other people
For efficacy	Identify physical and social activities that challenge their worldview and require them to live explicitly in the moment, attend training programs on giving and receiving feedback and promptly implement the training, develop a regular time for selected activities

---

ISTP

Introverted Thinking with Extraverted Sensing

When developed	Logical, factual, focus on what is relevant to here and now, constantly analyzing, often seen as detached, thorough, practical-minded problem solvers, highly value independence
For efficacy	Seek opportunities that require brainstorming and long-term project management with others, regularly engage in personal planning about goals for the next ten years, attend seminars about trends for the future, pursue marriage- or relationship-enrichment seminars, groups, or similar short-term experiences

---

INTP

Introverted Thinking with Extraverted Intuiting

When developed	Love problem-solving, complexity, and new ideas; analytical, build mental models, like to synthesize ideas, strive for objectivity, like problem-solving as exploration, avoid small talk, want specific and direct feedback, are constant gatherers of information, impersonal, tolerant, seen as critical
For efficacy	Attend seminars on relationship development such as marriage- or relationship-enrichment workshops, develop frequent opportunities for feedback from the folks they work with, get involved in community or social projects, complete a group survival program in a wilderness area

TABLE 12

TYPE PATTERNS IN ADULT DEVELOPMENT *(Continued)*

ISFP

Introverted Feeling with Extraverted Sensing

When developed	Take pride in self-control, seek affiliation, use orderly ways to nurture others, careful about facts, reflective about current situations, seen as quiet and introspective, express commitment and appreciation in specific terms
For efficacy	Volunteer to lead a social help group, develop contacts in professions very different from their own, seek feedback on problem-solving style, attend project management and problem-solving seminars, look for non-work-related activities

---

INFP

Introverted Feeling with Extraverted Intuiting

When developed	Reserved, intense, passionate about values, like to facilitate discussion, seek harmony, dislike being caught off guard, enjoy autonomy, genuine about values, go with the flow, stealth risk-takers, often the social conscience in a group, inner directed, perfectionistic, oriented toward causes, relentless searchers for what is meaningful, intrigued by complexity, prefer win/win situations
For efficacy	Seek seminars in forecasting and trend analysis, take lessons in public speaking and debate, try out for community theater roles, attend local business forums, annually develop a five-year plan, learn several conflict management techniques

---

ESTP

Extraverted Sensing with Introverted Thinking

When developed	Energetic seekers of experiences, get caught in the moment, keep communication brief, decide by talking, outgoing, meet deadlines just in time, seen as forceful and excitable
For efficacy	Take time for regular periods of quiet and reflection in which they purposefully avoid describing in detail what happened in various situations but make general lists of their possible meanings, take leadership of a six- to eight-month project, pursue retreat opportunities in varied physical environments

TABLE 12
TYPE PATTERNS IN ADULT DEVELOPMENT *(Continued)*

ESFP

Extraverted Sensing with Introverted Feeling

When developed Enjoy amusement and physical play, active, resourceful when dealing with people, focus on the immediate, find the easy way to do hard things, have low need for closure, like to solve conflict as a go-between, curious about social interactions, like nature, usually can give the facts of a situation

For efficacy Take courses or seminars in conflict management, seek opportunities to work with people more technically trained than themselves on selected projects, write in a journal about personal reactions to people and situations, develop contacts with people in hobbies and activities that are very different from their natural interests

ENFP

Extraverted Intuiting with Introverted Feeling

When developed Involved with many different tasks, work in short intense spurts of energy, have insatiable curiosity, love creating ideas, trust others at face value, diplomatic, have difficulty deciding, trust hunches, exuberant, spontaneous, accommodating, challenge systems and rules, take pride in adapting to situations, insightful about people and their needs, easygoing, warm, work well under pressure, optimistic, good at reading between the lines

For efficacy Seek several short-term projects that require attention to financial, operational, and service tasks; seek individual performance hobbies that are completed with a group (such as watercolor painting classes), find opportunities to focus on specific experiences such as group problem-solving on a local historic district issue

ENTP

Extraverted Intuiting with Introverted Thinking

When developed Value change, like to learn, avoid routines, take risks, future-oriented, slow to trust, verbally critical, think while talking, eclectic, make changes often, quick-thinking, love ideas and intellectual challenge, ingenious, adventurous, questioning, defiant, delegate the details, like a quick pace

For efficacy Engage in physical routines with a conscious focus on what, why, when, how, where, and who; make a yearlong commitment to a social service volunteer agency, take courses in project management with an engineering bent to the topics, develop networks in service-oriented businesses for comparisons

TABLE 12

TYPE PATTERNS IN ADULT DEVELOPMENT *(Continued)*

ESTJ

Extraverted Thinking with Introverted Sensing

When developed	Competitive, want completed jobs to be done right, organized, direct, frank, have a sense of urgency, high energy, seek and make decisions, reliable, outspoken, matter-of-fact orientation, develop pragmatic skills, results-oriented, expressive of critical analysis
For efficacy	Attend collaboration training, find opportunities to develop creative writing skills (stressing, for example, motivation, vision, global systems), ask for a project that requires careful and moderately slow analytical processes, pursue community involvement in agencies and programs that require individual rather than group problem-solving

---

ENTJ

Extraverted Thinking with Introverted Intuiting

When developed	Reasoned, logical, curious, fair with high expectations, like to control, focused on the future, organized, logical action takers, seek variety, energetic about many topics and interests, like immediate planning, persistent, pursue closure, want to have fairness in relationships, motivated by challenges
For efficacy	Put themselves on task forces that deal with issues only tangentially related to their main work, develop relationships with those who appear to feel best about addressing individual needs rather than working on systems problems, identify as many relationship and people outcomes as financial or achievement outcomes from working on projects, tasks, or selected jobs

---

ENFJ

Extraverted Feeling with Introverted Intuiting

When developed	Warm, friendly, empathetic, lively, approachable and initiating, doers, flexible, want to be trusted, like humor, sensitive to criticism, enjoy innovating and acting on new ideas, want others to be comfortable, bridge builders among people, try to make others feel important
For efficacy	Volunteer to help organize and deliver services in a health-related social service, attend seminars on critical thinking and scientific problem-solving methods, develop hobbies that rely on spontaneous responses, seek regular discussions with individuals who successfully manage conflict to review the strategies they use

TABLE 12

TYPE PATTERNS IN ADULT DEVELOPMENT *(Continued)*

	ESFJ
	Extraverted Feeling with Introverted Sensing
When developed	Committed and dedicated to others, respectful, nurturing, active listeners, enjoy a variety of people, organized, give attention to details related to people, talkative, sympathetic, tactful, realistic, radiate sympathy, motivated by appreciation, orderly in small matters, often seen as gregarious
For efficacy	Attend abstract, intellectually loaded seminars on financial topics, participate in local debate clubs, identify and network with individuals involved with theoretical topics or imaginative endeavors (such as art, music, or theater), find three or four opportunities each week to meditate

Developed Types

The descriptions above give you our best handle on the home base—the natural psychological ruby slippers. They are followed by the qualities that type needs to develop in order to achieve efficacy in later life. Keep in mind that these are the actual words used by individuals to describe their own types and their observations of other types.

As we move through our daily chores, we choose to behave in ways that reinforce who we are and that support things about which we feel positive. We have a system for noting benchmarks in life—entering college, graduating, taking a first job, getting married, and so on—but we rarely make note of the changes that occur quietly in our minds. Adjustments we make, lessons we learn, actions we take today that we would not have taken earlier are signs of significant internal events. In much the same way, each individual's psychological type undergoes change and transition.

Type unfolds and develops of its own accord; in supportive conditions it grows and blossoms, contributing to self-esteem and to the lifelong paths each of us make. Like Dorothy in Oz, we move down the road of life, and if we are attentive to the lessons of experience, then we activate energies and talents that enable us to face difficult challenges and respond appropriately to them. In normal circumstances, we come equipped to manage life and adjust to its daily demands. But we are rarely comfortable settling just for clarity about our capabilities in the moment; we want to become more and exceed current expectations. The urge to move on, to seek new challenges, to squeeze more from life comes from within. Type theory tells us that the journey down the road of life can be made intelligently and with awareness of who we are and what we can become. And in learning new lessons and developing new capabilities, we never leave behind our natural strengths; in fact, we may enhance them through our acceptance of new opportunities.

In a sense, type development is the process of moving up a spiral of ever-increasing awareness of, and capacity to use, our mental processes of Perception and Judgment. We circle around our most central part as we move up the spiral, and if we are in tune with our growth, it deepens our perceptions and judgments which serve us throughout life.

You: Applying Personality Type to Enrich Individual Effectiveness

"An idea not coupled with action will never get any bigger than the brain cell it occupied."[1]

—Arnold H. Glasow

This section explores the powerful application of psychological type in our emotional intelligence, career choices, approaches to stress management, and general personal effectiveness.

6 What Lies Underneath
Using Type to Enhance Emotional Health
invites an exploration of the interplay in our emotions and type patterns.

7 Getting There from Here
Increasing Personal Effectiveness at Work and at Home
links our strategies for becoming more effective in both our professional and home lives.

What Lies Underneath?

USING TYPE TO ENHANCE EMOTIONAL HEALTH

S tefan noticed the shift on Erica's face from a slight smile to a slight plaintive look. Without checking his perceptions of her reaction, he concluded that what he had just said irritated her. When he did not acknowledge a shift in her reaction, Erica decided that Stefan really didn't care about what was important to her regarding the matter at hand. She felt disappointed and saddened by the emotional disconnect. As she withdrew from the conversation, Erica suggested that the topic needed broader consideration. Stefan decided that if Erica was unhappy about something, she should speak up.

Stefan's personality type, ESTP, plays out in the following way: his Extraverted Sensing process naturally observes subtle changes in the faces of those around him as well as details in his general environment. His Thinking process is Introverted, often leading him to keep his thoughts to himself unless asked about his perspective. Erica's INFP type tends to lead with Introverted Feeling, which prompts her to quickly evaluate whether a situation is off course or not aligned with her expectations. This is an internal process, and she isn't likely to quickly articulate what is on her mind; rather, she may tend to use her Extraverted Intuitive process to look at the context and push for the "big picture." Both are feeling that the interaction doesn't have a pleasant ending and neither is quite sure what to do about it.

Stefan and Erica's interaction is laden with emotions and this interaction will serve as an example throughout this chapter. Emotions are intertwined in every aspect of human experience. While scholars argue about the nature, source, and utility of emotions, what is not in question is the power of emotions to affect judgment. In fact, there is sufficient evidence from research on individuals with damage to the emotional centers of the brain to show that without emotions, we are unable to make effective decisions. Emotions are underneath the surface of conscious thought. Just as our personality type is an automatic pilot influencing what we see and how we decide, the color and heat of our perceptions and judgments is provided by our emotions.

In recent years, studies of the importance of emotions have led to models that posit emotions as based in a kind of intelligence that is essential to a healthy and fulfilled life. Any model of intelligence implies that some kind of information (in this case, emotion) is perceived and managed to make effective choices. This implies that the weaker our abilities to perceive or manage emotions, the less effective we will be; conversely, the stronger our abilities, the more effective we will be. We can think about these abilities in the following way:[1]

Abilities for Perceiving Emotions

A: Recognizing your emotions
B: Identifying context of your emotions
C: Recognizing others' emotions
D: Anticipating others' emotions

Abilities to Manage Emotions

E: Identifying emotional responses
F: Matching emotions with situations
G: Evaluating the emotional needs of others
H: Demonstrating appropriate responses

At the end of this chapter, complete a personal survey of behaviors related to these abilities in order to familiarize yourself with these ideas. The letter associated with each ability is reflected in the personal survey and is provided for your reference.

Becoming aware of these abilities to perceive and manage emotions can encourage us to become more mindful of the complexity of emotions and its links to our behavior. We can think of these abilities as "bedrock" aspects of emotional intelligence, but these are by no means the most immediate areas of concern. We may not be able to adjust bedrock abilities, such as how quickly we recognize emotions on another person's face; however, we can recognize and change behaviors that affect the quality of our relationships. Becoming skilled in creating a dialogue for mutual understanding is the key. In the case of Stefan and Erica, each of them was able to see that the other had a slight change of facial expression and each was able to track it to a change in emotion. As we will see, each of their personality types plays into their triggers and expressions, or lack thereof, of emotions. An important point must be kept in mind: *all types can be emotionally intelligent or emotionally problematic.*

Emotional intelligence presents some hard truths about emotions you need to consider regardless of your personality type:[2]

- **We generate our emotions.** No one "causes" us to experience a given emotion. Another individual's behavior may prompt various thoughts and reactions, but the emotions are generated by *our* mind and body system. Our emotions are ours, and two of the most important questions you can ask are, "Why does this situation/behavior/circumstance prompt a particular emotion from me?" and "Does this get me what I want?" As outlined below, type is a key player influencing our triggers and our reactions.

- **Our emotions are greatly affected by our "mind maps" of our experience.** A mind map is simply a way of thinking about life situations that we've developed to enable us to make sense of what is happening. Our brain, especially the amygdala, is designed to recognize patterns in others and our environment for the sole purpose of keeping us safe. It is finely tuned to tell us "friend" or "foe," "safe" or "unsafe." Our brain recognizes and then reinforces us for responding to familiar scripts. That "Aha! I've figured it out" feeling literally is a chemical reward from our brain. The only hitch is this: while our brains are designed to recognize patterns or familiar maps, it's not designed to tell us whether that map is the *correct* map. For example, if you have a mind map that your boss is a difficult individual, each time you see him certain emotions may get triggered. Your brain sends a warning and interprets all of the boss's behavior through the lens of that map. In turn, your unexamined emotional response toward this boss may unwittingly give feedback that helps maintain the negative communication between you and your boss, thus reinforcing your thoughts about his difficult nature. It can be a vicious cycle. Our mind maps can be changed and adjusted, and if we do so we alter our emotional responses. Our personality type can provide a way to reposition our thinking about situations and can thereby affect our responses.

- **There is a continuum of emotional intensity with each emotion.** For example, mild anger to all-out rage is a continuum. Another kind of continuum concerns the way that emotions build on one another; for example, depending on a series of events, initial *interest* may lead to *anticipation* that results in an event that leads to *disgust* and then to *anger*. We need to map these sequences for ourselves because they vary greatly for each individual.

- **Emotions contain information.** Our goal is to identify and make sense of the information and to understand how our personality type can enable us to use this information effectively. Presumably, if we are able to translate the information correctly and if we are attuned to the role our type plays in this aspect of our experience, we can choose to respond in more effective and productive ways.

In the case of Stefan and Erica, both are aware that they've had an uncomfortable or unpleasant interaction and each has chosen to respond to this awareness in different ways. Neither has shared their thoughts or interpretation of events, and in the absence of these perceptions, they have both made conclusions that maintain the discomfort. This situation taps into two basic emotions—anger and caring—that are worth deeper exploration both in terms of the information they provide and because of the way they intersect with personality type. While exploring the nature and role of all emotions exceeds the goals of this book, some key aspects of anger and caring are provided in Tables 13 and 14.

Anger is triggered when we feel that an agreement has been violated, that an expectation was unmet, or that we have been treated improperly in some way. From a type perspective, the perception of violation or improper treatment that creates flashes of anger varies greatly by type. For example, trending type patterns by focusing on the Perceiving (Sensing or Intuiting) and Judging (Thinking or Feeling) combinations, the following triggers have been confirmed numerous times:[3]

Sensing + Thinking (ST) Triggers:
- Lack of attention to detail
- Lack of verification of information
- Failure to follow through as specifically described
- Inefficiency

Sensing + Feeling (SF) Triggers:
- Failure to respond to personal inquiry
- Failure to acknowledge hands-on efforts
- Lack of attention to personal needs

Intuiting + Feeling (NF) Triggers:
- Perceived condescension, insensitivity
- Focus on "it" or "task" rather than on the individual's needs
- Failure to acknowledge efforts
- Judgmental attitudes and statements toward others

Intuiting + Thinking (NT) Triggers:
- Incompetence
- Irrationality

- Lack of logical basis for decisions
- Failure to address incompetence after it has been identified

Stefan, with a Sensing + Thinking (ST) combination, is annoyed that Erica doesn't bother to share the details of her reactions nor provide an efficient response to his comments. Erica, with an Intuiting + Feeling (NF) combination, is irritated by Stefan's seeming insensitivity and lack of recognition of her individual needs.

It is fair to assume that, since Stefan and Erica are in a relationship, there is mutual caring, an emotion sometimes classified as affection or love. Caring promotes focus on each other's needs and prompts concern for the other's well-being. Interestingly, we often show caring for others in the very way we like to receive affection, without recognizing that the other person might experience our expressions as something else entirely. Using the same personality type combinations illustrated above, when we examine anger, we can see the different expressions of caring by type as follows:

Sensing + Thinking (ST) Ways of Showing Caring:

- Providing explicit, verifiable information to others and making no assumptions
- Efficiency

Sensing + Feeling (SF) Ways of Showing Caring:

- Attentiveness to the specific source of difficulty
- Willingness to carefully record the details of a situation

Intuiting + Feeling (NF) Ways of Showing Caring:

- Demonstrative empathy
- Active listening and emotional support

Intuiting + Thinking (NT) Ways of Showing Caring:

- Offering a strategic or "big picture" perspective on a situation
- Dialoguing about options, choices, and outcomes

Given the above differences, it is clear that Stefan's and Erica's expressions of caring are quite different and reinforce a message neither intends.

The emotions are the same but the triggers and expressions are different. In fact, the ST and NF differences seem to feed unintentionally the worst interpretations each makes about the other. What one does as an act of caring, the other experiences as a violation of trust or personal regard. What to do?

Table 13[4]
ANGER

Emotion	Secondary Feelings
Anger	Aggression, resentment, annoyance; unmet expectations and perceived violations of values or agreements; sometimes prompted by fear

When you are **angry,** your internal feedback (what you perceive) is that an individual has:

- Failed to fulfill an expectation or agreement
- Intentionally violated an important value or principle
- Created a barrier to reaching an objective
- Misused or misjudged you in some way
- Gotten in your way intentionally

This emotion serves you by:

Anger prompts your body to prepare to fight or to demonstrate protest. When you become angry, you are preparing for a physical response such as yelling or even physical contact. This emotion serves to focus attention, and when prompted for good reason, it can harness motivation to change policies and laws, or to influence others. This contributes to a state of motivated interest, even if it is negative.

Table 14
CARING

Emotion	Secondary Feelings
Caring	Concern, empathy, sympathy. Perception of another individual in physical or psychological discomfort or need

When you experience **caring,** the internal feedback (your perception) is that the relationship or other individual:

- Is important
- Is a focus of your concern
- Needs support or assistance
- Deserves your undivided attention

This emotion serves you by:

Caring deepens the bond in relationships and facilitates social responsibility. When you experience caring, you feel support and encouragement from those around you. Even in demanding situations, directing your energies toward caring eventually contributes to a state of well-being, safety, and reduced tension.

Awareness of what is at work in emotional responses and in personality type is a good start. The awareness, however, needs to bring forth recognition of the positive intent of the other before clear movement can be made to clarify what the other needs.

The tricky part is to prevent your personality type from becoming an excuse for misunderstanding or feeling stuck and unable to do anything constructive. Personality type provides clues and trends, not predictions and control. Further, and most important, the question is how to use the insights about our differences to develop behaviors essential to fostering the constructive, emotionally healthy interactions we want to have.

The Place of Most Potential

Stefan and Erica's interaction serves to illustrate the interconnections between emotions and personality type. As noted above, emotional triggers and emotional expressions are naturally engaged and demonstrated by our type. At its best, this awareness prompts questions about next steps to address and resolve these situations. Self-awareness can lead to a dead end unless we are willing to consider that some new behaviors can transform something uncomfortable into a more satisfying outcome. As a general rule, the following basic steps help us move from simple self-awareness to a more effective use of our awareness:

Internal recognition

1. Once you are aware of the way your personality type and your personal psychology affect your responses, consider that the other individual involved is acting with positive intent.
2. Consider how your behavior may have unintentionally triggered or at least facilitated the nature of the interaction.
3. Think about the desirable outcome and how you might need to behave differently to get that outcome.

External action

4. Solicit observations from the other individual—ask what he or she was experiencing, perceiving, reacting to.
5. Through active listening and paraphrasing, acknowledge the other person's perspective and ask how the situation can be improved.
6. As you discuss how to move the conversation forward, keep in mind that your filters need to be kept in check as you move toward a suitable understanding.

These suggested steps are easier written and read than achieved. It takes practice, focus, and effort to move from the automatic responses determined by our personality and personal history to more intentional responses that put our relationships in the place of most potential. It also takes being attentive to internal emotional dials and to specific demonstrated behaviors; these will ultimately determine the emotionally intelligent outcomes of your interactions. Our type preferences work as an automatic pilot guiding our perceptions and judgments, and as such they can be unintended sources of emotional triggers.

One simple intervention may be useful when caught in one of these conflicts. In multiple articles and his book *Writing to Heal*, James Pennebaker suggests that the act of writing down our emotions, stream of consciousness, raw and honest, can relieve the stress and allow us to gain a healthy objectivity on a situation. Brené Brown, in her book on resiliency, *Rising Strong*, also encourages us to write a "shitty first draft" when we feel emotionally hooked. Only then can we start to get a sense of what we're grappling with.[5] Mind you, this is not writing to share with others! In fact, just the opposite. If you'd be okay with

Table 15
INTRAPERSONAL AND INTERPERSONAL ELEMENTS OF EQ (EMOTIONAL QUOTIENT)

Intrapersonal	**Introverted Awareness and Inner Experience**
Self-Awareness	Self-confident that you can meet the challenges that arise, realistic self-assessment, recognize moods, drives; see yourself as talented and capable
Self-Regulation	Control or redirect impulses, conscientious, well-organized, fulfill obligations
Emotional Self-Control	Control emotions, suppress hostile feelings, emotional discipline; manage flow and emotional hijacking experiences
Interpersonal	**Extraverted Arena of Behavior**
Demonstrated Empathy	Understand emotional makeup of others, self; sensitivity; comfortable with personal feelings, perceptive of social nuances
Tolerance	Demonstrate patience with others' beliefs and values; fair-minded; communicate respect during discontent, conflict
Persuading	Seek to make a good impression with others; solicit others' points of view; offer ideas non-defensively; problem-solve

sharing what you've written at times like that, your writing hasn't been honest enough! It's an emotional acknowledgment exercise to accelerate movement from the amygdala "fight or flight" response, toward regaining your capacity to ask questions as suggested above (and actually hear the answers!), and to assume good intention by the others involved.

Self-awareness ("Am I triggered?"), self-regulation ("Why am I triggered? What was my part in it?"), and emotional self-control ("What can I do now that would be the most useful?") are the internal dials we need to tune up to respond in a more emotionally intelligent way. The most basic manifestation of our use of these internal emotional dials is in how we show empathy and tolerance and seek to persuade others. As our self-awareness grows, so does our capacity for empathy. As we monitor our emotional triggers and direct our emotional energies to constructive considerations, our tolerance for differences and our efforts to persuade others will improve. The reward for this effort is an emotionally healthy life.

A healthy emotional life promotes a healthy life in general, as well as satisfying relationships and an optimistic view of life events that make up the fabric of daily experience. Research suggests that the six areas of awareness or behavior noted above can lead us closer to this desired emotional state.[6] These are easily organized into intrapersonal perspectives (internal experience) and interpersonal behavior (external expressions of energy). For brevity's sake, we have blended the insights into how our emotions, emotional abilities, and type combine to affect areas considered essential to emotional competence. Table 15 provides definitions of these six areas.

The differences among the 16 types regarding these areas are explored in greater detail in Table 16. Each type varies in how it experiences these areas. We encourage you to learn your own typological trends and patterns as well as to study the trends of others. Greater awareness of the variations in perspective invites you to consider positive intention on the part of others and contributes to a greater understanding of how personality type and emotionally linked experiences are connected. And as we've suggested in other chapters in this book, use type to guide your developmental journey rather than to impale others. We find that being impaled seriously hinders development!

Summary

Stefan and Erica provide a perfect illustration of the daily interplay between individual emotions and type in what we see, how we react, and how our differing patterns potentially feed the wrong dynamics in relationships. If Stefan and Erica attended a workshop on type and emotional intelligence, they would learn how each of their automatic pilots operates and how to adjust their behaviors to achieve greater satisfaction in their relationship.

Table 16[7]
EMOTIONAL INTELLIGENCE QUALITIES OF THE 16 TYPES

ISTJ	Introverted Sensing With Extraverted Thinking
EQ Area	**Description**
Intrapersonal	**Introverted Awareness and Inner Experience**
Self-Awareness	• Confident that perceptions are realistic and logical in problem-solving • Often unaware of the effect of their behavior on group dynamics
Self-Regulation	• Control or redirect impulses, conscientious, well-organized, fulfill obligations • Sincere, dependable, and often compulsive about deadlines
Emotional Self-Control	• Often overcontrol emotions, suppress feelings • Experience flow with attention to detail or task precision and productive results • Feel emotionally hijacked when they perceive lack of loyalty from others and when they see others as too emotional, lazy, or pushing change without purpose
Interpersonal	**Extraverted Arena of Behavior**
Demonstrated Empathy	• Often do *not show* an understanding of others' emotions or the importance of emotions to an individual's experience • While pleasant and often helpful, may not be sensitive to social nuances
Tolerance	• Demonstrate patience with others' beliefs and actions • Fair-minded during discontent, conflict
Persuading	• Seek to persuade with logic and verifiable evidence • Not particularly concerned with making a good impression with others • Pursue a "no-nonsense" approach to problem-solving

ISTP	Introverted Thinking with Extraverted Sensing
EQ Area	**Description**
Intrapersonal	**Introverted Awareness and Inner Experience**
Self-Awareness	• Confident enough to be free of internal worries; see personal strengths as natural extension of an adaptive nature • Quick to focus on tasks and direction rather than emotions
Self-Regulation	• Detached nature; experience events as onlookers waiting for an opportunity to react. • Often not aware of emotional reactions until much later after an event

Table 16
EMOTIONAL INTELLIGENCE QUALITIES OF THE 16 TYPES *(Continued)*

Emotional Self-Control	• Experience flow when working calmly under pressure, especially in crisis situations; enjoy the discovery of a pragmatic solution to a problem • Feel emotionally hijacked by those they perceive as constant interrupters to activities and not bringing value to an efficient, logical analysis or action
Interpersonal	**Extraverted Arena of Behavior**
Demonstrated Empathy	• Often overlook emotional reactions of self and others, and may appear insensitive and aloof • Become emotionally engaged when logical principles are threatened
Tolerance	• Adaptable and willing to explore new situations • Less patient with emotionally related matters
Persuading	• Convince others with a storehouse of information and precise details • Logically argue for deciding on and following basic principles

ESTP	Extraverted Sensing With Introverted Thinking
EQ Area	**Description**
Intrapersonal	**Introverted Awareness and Inner Experience**
Self-Awareness	• Self-confident regarding ability to analyze and act • Realistic self-assessment of capabilities and competencies
Self-Regulation	• Activity-oriented, appearing restless at times • Lower impulse control leads to quick action
Emotional Self-Control	• Experience flow when active in physically stimulating situations • Feel emotionally hijacked by too much structure and hierarchy, and by situations that severely limit physical movement
Interpersonal	**Extraverted Arena of Behavior**
Demonstrated Empathy	• Often miss social nuances while quickly dealing with issues • May not exhibit an understanding of others' emotions or of being comfortable with personal feelings
Tolerance	• Demonstrate patience with others' beliefs and attitudes • Fair-minded but impatient with drawn-out analyses or processes designed to explore psychological meaning
Persuading	• Seek to make a good impression with others and to actively solicit others' points of view • Use logic and factual parameters as sources of influence

Table 16
EMOTIONAL INTELLIGENCE QUALITIES OF THE 16 TYPES *(Continued)*

ESTJ	Extraverted Thinking With Introverted Sensing
EQ Area	**Description**
Intrapersonal	**Introverted Awareness and Inner Experience**
Self-Awareness	• Self-confident about reaching goals but not necessarily about addressing the emotional situations that emerge when working with others • Realistic orientation toward self-assessment is directed toward competencies and capabilities
Self-Regulation	• Control impulses and direct energy toward organization and to fulfilling obligations • Dependable; "work the plan" to the degree that emotional impulses are not distracting
Emotional Self-Control	• Flow emerges from the pride of discipline and management of competencies; love meeting a challenge efficiently • Feel emotionally hijacked by individuals who appear dependent, overly sensitive, not as committed to performance, or who rely on too much processing and not enough closure for productivity
Interpersonal	**Extraverted Arena of Behavior**
Demonstrated Empathy	• Often so focused on achieving outcomes that they fail to perceive social nuances in others' reactions • Inclined toward problem-solving based on a thorough, logical analysis, which may result in inattention to others' feelings
Tolerance	• Fair-minded and open to new ideas within defined parameters • Communicate respect during discontent and conflict but often utilize a competitive strategy to resolve differences
Persuading	• More concerned with outcomes than with making a good impression on others • Solicit others' points of view when it appears practical and useful for problem-solving

ISFJ	Introverted Sensing With Extraverted Feeling
EQ Area	**Description**
Intrapersonal	**Introverted Awareness and Inner Experience**
Self-Awareness	• Confident but unassuming in fulfilling tasks and roles • Very realistic self-assessment of talents and skills
Self-Regulation	• Conscientious about helping others and collaborating • Direct energy toward obligations, traditions, and social conventions • Disciplined and focused on pragmatic tasks

Table 16
EMOTIONAL INTELLIGENCE QUALITIES OF THE 16 TYPES *(Continued)*

Emotional Self-Control	• Experience flow when steady attention focused on helping others leads to success; excel in calm and secure physical space • Feel emotionally hijacked when they sense condescension and lack of regard for their practical, steady approach
Interpersonal	**Extraverted Arena of Behavior**
Demonstrated Empathy	• Readily sympathize with others but may not naturally show insight • Acknowledge emotions and are comfortable with personal feelings • Perceptive of interpersonal nuances
Tolerance	• Demonstrate moderate patience with others' beliefs and values • Slow to engage in conflict • Tolerance decreases as uncertainty increases
Persuading	• Deliberate and careful in seeking to influence others • Expect others to understand their roles and act accordingly • Problem-solve through use of data and reliance on previous experiences

ISFP	**Introverted Feeling With Extraverted Sensing**
EQ Area	**Description**
Intrapersonal	**Introverted Awareness and Inner Experience**
Self-Awareness	• Self-confident in finding practical actions to take, though often doubting that current abilities transfer into new areas • Realistic self-assessment of moods and emotions
Self-Regulation	• Attuned to emotional energy that allows them to redirect these impulses toward helping others • Conscientious in unconventional ways, solving problems before others realize a situation is out of hand
Emotional Self-Control	• Experience flow when in quiet, fully comfortable, and private environments that are supportive and encouraging • Feel emotionally hijacked by persistent conflict, increasingly complex situations, climates of disregard, and ongoing criticism
Interpersonal	**Extraverted Arena of Behavior**
Demonstrated Empathy	• Perceptive of emotional needs and personal feelings of self and others, but may not demonstrate awareness outwardly • Show empathy by performing specific, concrete care-taking tasks

Table 16
EMOTIONAL INTELLIGENCE QUALITIES OF THE 16 TYPES *(Continued)*

Tolerance	• Wide range of openness about different views, beliefs, and values • Highly concerned with promoting independence of self and others
Persuading	• Influence through doing • Show how values and principles are to be used in addressing issues

ESFP	**Extraverted Sensing With Introverted Feeling**
EQ Area	**Description**
Intrapersonal	**Introverted Awareness and Inner Experience**
Self-Awareness	• Self-confident in dealing with others and creating harmony • Recognize moods and emotions; see self as talented and capable
Self-Regulation	• Activity-oriented and directed toward being with others • Redirect impulses toward new outlets with others
Emotional Self-Control	• Experience flow in harmonious, supportive environments where social connections are valued • Feel emotionally hijacked when in overly critical and hostile or unsupportive environments
Interpersonal	**Extraverted Arena of Behavior**
Demonstrated Empathy	• Frequently exhibit insights into emotional makeup of others • Comfortable with personal feelings, perceptive of social nuances
Tolerance	• Demonstrate patience with others' beliefs and values; fair-minded • Communicate respect during discontent, conflict
Persuading	• Seek to make a good impression on others; solicit others' points of view • Influence through facilitating decisions and actions

ESFJ	**Extraverted Feeling With Introverted Sensing**
EQ Area	**Description**
Intrapersonal	**Introverted Awareness and Inner Experience**
Self-Awareness	• Self-confident in capabilities to support and encourage others • Realistic about emotions and sympathies
Self-Regulation	• Redirect impulses toward harmony and service; may overcontrol emotions • Conscientious about giving well-organized help

Table 16

EMOTIONAL INTELLIGENCE QUALITIES OF THE 16 TYPES *(Continued)*

Emotional Self-Control	• Experience flow when actively engaged in harmonious, service-oriented activity, and when receiving recognition or appreciation • Feel emotionally hijacked when others are overly critical, unpredictable, or unstable, and when others fail to be loyal
Interpersonal	**Extraverted Arena of Behavior**
Demonstrated Empathy	• Communicate empathy with ease and sensitivity • Comfortable with personal feelings and perceptive of social nuances
Tolerance	• Reasonably patient with others' beliefs and values • Actively communicate respect during discontent, conflict
Persuading	• Seek to influence through attention to detail and procedures • Solicit others' points of view during problem-solving to earn their attention

INFJ	Introverted Intuiting With Extraverted Feeling
EQ Area	**Description**
Intrapersonal	**Introverted Awareness and Inner Experience**
Self-Awareness	• Self-confident when engaged around values and ideals • Recognize moods and usually are free of internal doubts or conflicts
Self-Regulation	• Redirect impulses toward creative outlets • Conscientious about realizing ideals and fulfilling obligations
Emotional Self-Control	• Experience flow when engaged in creative pursuits and in visualizing future creative possibilities, as well as while helping others learn • Feel emotionally hijacked by cruelty, aloofness, or insensitivity toward any living organism, and by lack of regard for privacy
Interpersonal	**Extraverted Arena of Behavior**
Demonstrated Empathy	• Understand emotional makeup of others and self; sensitive; comfortable with personal feelings, perceptive of social nuances • Reluctant to criticize or confront others and avoid giving public advice
Tolerance	• Nonjudgmental and trusting of others • Often diplomatic and patient with others' beliefs and values
Persuading	• Rely on relationships and intimate conversations for persuasion • While seeking to build rapport with individuals, may act without worry about making a good impression with others in a group

Table 16
EMOTIONAL INTELLIGENCE QUALITIES OF THE 16 TYPES *(Continued)*

INFP	Introverted Feeling With Extraverted Intuiting
EQ Area	**Description**
Intrapersonal	**Introverted Awareness and Inner Experience**
Self-Awareness	• Self-confident that ideals can be realized with time and patience • Constantly self-assess to identify important standards and aspirations
Self-Regulation	• Use emotional reactions and impulses to clarify issues of importance and at times to distract from taking action • Redirect impulses toward creative outlets
Emotional Self-control	• Experience flow when engaging in quiet, reflective considerations of ideas and actions, internal centering, and working toward authenticity • Feel emotionally hijacked when intentions are distorted, by egregious violations of values, and when they perceive maleficent actions by others toward others
Interpersonal	**Extraverted Arena of Behavior**
Demonstrated Empathy	• Understand emotional makeup of others and communicate empathy easily and naturally • Show insight and sensitivity to personal feelings
Tolerance	• Demonstrate patience with a wide range of others' beliefs and values • Communicate regard during discontent, conflict
Persuading	• More concerned with gaining commitments to reach goals related to mission than with making a good impression • Solicit others' points of view in a highly collaborative fashion

ENFP	Extraverted Intuiting With Introverted Feeling
EQ Area	**Description**
Intrapersonal	**Introverted Awareness and Inner Experience**
Self-Awareness	• Self-confident regarding abilities to be resourceful and innovative • Recognize moods and quickly identify how these affect actions
Self-Regulation	• Impulses provide a source of direction and action as well as distraction and irritation • Strive to bring negative reactions under control

Table 16

EMOTIONAL INTELLIGENCE QUALITIES OF THE 16 TYPES *(Continued)*

Emotional Self-Control	• Experience flow when freed from constraints and involved in creative activities • Feel emotionally hijacked when others are consistently critical without being appreciative (of self and others), or when they feel isolated or rejected without an opportunity to address concerns with others
Interpersonal	**Extraverted Arena of Behavior**
Demonstrated Empathy	• Expressively sensitive toward others and readily identify emotions being experienced and demonstrated • Understand the emotional makeup of others and are very comfortable with personal feelings
Tolerance	• Demonstrate openness to new ideas and others' perspectives as long as their values are not insulted • Typically avoid conflict as a way to promote harmony and social comfort
Persuading	• Persuade through relationships and sharing innovative ideas • Actively solicit others' points of view in problem-solving

ENFJ	Extraverted Feeling With Introverted Intuiting
EQ Area	**Description**
Intrapersonal	**Introverted Awareness and Inner Experience**
Self-Awareness	• Self-confident about accessing imaginative resources • Attuned to affirmations and discontent with self and others
Self-Regulation	• Redirect impulses to creative outlets • Conscientious and frequently compulsively organized
Emotional Self-Control	• Experience flow when working with individuals and negotiating understanding among groups, as well as when sharing insights • Feel emotionally hijacked by continued conflict, perceptions of mean-spiritedness and ill will, and when dealing with those who will not engage in dialogue or are disrespectful of others
Interpersonal	**Extraverted Arena of Behavior**
Demonstrated Empathy	• Exhibit insight into others' feelings and needs • Sensitive to personal feelings; are both perceptive of and responsive to social nuances
Tolerance	• Process-oriented as a way to demonstrate patience with others' beliefs and values • Communicate respect and regard of others during discontent, conflict

Table 16
EMOTIONAL INTELLIGENCE QUALITIES OF THE 16 TYPES *(Continued)*

Persuading	• Seek to make a good impression with others through building rapport and showing awareness of others' needs • Actively solicit others' points of view to creatively problem-solve

INTJ	Introverted Intuiting With Extraverted Thinking
EQ Area	**Description**
Intrapersonal	**Introverted Awareness and Inner Experience**
Self-Awareness	• Aware that the vision always exceeds the resources to realize the ideal, leading to impatience and frustration • Realistic self-assessment of motivations and reactions to situations • Actively seek feedback to check out personal sense of awareness
Self-Regulation	• Control impulses and organize efforts to fulfill obligations • While quietly spontaneous, often allow imagination to explore situations • Often have to give self-permission to "loosen up" and relax
Emotional Self-Control	• Experience flow when addressing complex and tough problems with quiet reflection or when talking with a select set of individuals • Feel emotionally hijacked when persistent irrationality and carelessness by others wastes resources
Interpersonal	**Extraverted Arena of Behavior**
Demonstrated Empathy	• May exhibit insight into others' emotional makeup • Not particularly responsive to others' personal feelings unless it serves a larger purpose
Tolerance	• Demonstrate patience with others' ideas and perspectives • Communicate respect for justice, fair-mindedness, and commitment to principles during discontent, conflict
Persuading	• Often inattentive to social shifts in interactions; usually seek to make a good impression with others in order to establish expertise • Solicit others' analytical points of view and logical problem-solving

Table 16
EMOTIONAL INTELLIGENCE QUALITIES OF THE 16 TYPES *(Continued)*

INTP	Introverted Thinking With Extraverted Intuiting
EQ Area	**Description**
Intrapersonal	**Introverted Awareness and Inner Experience**
Self-Awareness	• Self-confident regarding intellectual abilities and often engage in realistic self-assessment related to competencies and accomplishments • Often identify feelings or emotions long after an interaction or event
Self-Regulation	• Direct impulses toward intellectual pursuits; continually reflect to identify and classify emotions and impulses • Conscientious about systems, methods, and goals
Emotional Self-Control	• Experience flow when working on complex problems and identifying the most elegant, logical answer or response • Feel emotionally hijacked by faulty or nonexistent logic, persistent inconsistencies, and emotional attacks on their theories
Interpersonal	**Extraverted Arena of Behavior**
Demonstrated Empathy	• Rarely express insight or actively show understanding of emotional makeup of self and others • Not particularly comfortable or engaged with personal feelings
Tolerance	• Demonstrate patience with others' perspectives if logically and rationally presented • Fair-minded and open to debate about ideas and possibilities
Persuading	• Solicit others' points of view in service of understanding, not to make a good impression • Offer ideas non-defensively and influence through analysis when problem-solving

ENTP	Extraverted Intuiting With Introverted Thinking
EQ Area	**Description**
Intrapersonal	**Introverted Awareness and Inner Experience**
Self-Awareness	• Self-confident in analytical ability and innovative problem-solving • Often not aware of moods and emotional variations, preferring to see these as natural to human systems and processes

Table 16
EMOTIONAL INTELLIGENCE QUALITIES OF THE 16 TYPES *(Continued)*

Self-Regulation	• Relatively low impulse control, resulting in spontaneous reactions • Relentless impulse to critique to improve; constant internal "risk assessment" regarding actions and reactions
Emotional Self-Control	• Experience flow when engaged in complex challenges that solve difficult problems, include variety, and promote use of competencies • Feel emotionally hijacked by individuals who appear rigid, unable to adapt, or illogical, and by boredom and small thinking
Interpersonal	**Extraverted Arena of Behavior**
Demonstrated Empathy	• Due to quick response and critiquing style, may not show sensitivity to others on a consistent basis • Perceptive of social nuances but do not consistently check out interpretations of interpersonal shifts with others
Tolerance	• Demonstrate patience with others' beliefs and values • Conflict situations tend to initiate a competitive rather than cooperative response
Persuading	• Solicit others' points of view and articulate logical positions and possibilities; assertively engage dialogue • Actively problem-solve through generating new ideas and possibilities

ENTJ	Extraverted Thinking With Introverted Intuiting
EQ Area	**Description**
Intrapersonal	**Introverted Awareness and Inner Experience**
Self-Awareness	• Self-confident and often realistic about competencies and capacities • Clear about the drive to compete and achieve • May not recognize moods and can dismiss feelings as not valuable
Self-Regulation	• Control impulses and make a conscious effort to direct attention • Inclined to trust hunches and be activity-oriented
Emotional Self-Control	• Experience flow when applying creative and logical solutions to complex problems • Feel emotionally hijacked by those who appear incompetent, who allow emotions to "overly" influence their views, and who are indecisive

Table 16
EMOTIONAL INTELLIGENCE QUALITIES OF THE 16 TYPES *(Continued)*

Interpersonal	**Extraverted Arena of Behavior**
Demonstrated Empathy	• Have a working "theory" about emotions and how they influence behavior • May not show sensitivity to the emotional needs of others and are often uncomfortable with expressions of personal feelings • Perceptive of social nuances but may not act on this awareness
Tolerance	• Demonstrate patience with others' beliefs and values if these seem orderly and subject to reasoned analysis • Fair-minded; communicate respect of others during discontent, conflict • Impatient with the pace of others
Persuading	• Seek to make a good impression on others • Solicit others' points of view • Problem-focused rather than person-focused

ESFP	**Extraverted Sensing With Introverted Feeling**
EQ Area	**Description**
Intrapersonal	**Introverted Awareness and Inner Experience**
Self-Awareness	• Self-confident in dealing with others and creating harmony • Recognize moods and emotions; see self as talented and capable
Self-Regulation	• Activity-oriented and directed toward being with others • Redirect impulses toward new outlets with others
Emotional Self-Control	• Experience flow in harmonious, supportive environments where social connections are valued • Feel emotionally hijacked when in overly critical and hostile or unsupportive environments
Interpersonal	**Extraverted Arena of Behavior**
Demonstrated Empathy	• Frequently exhibit insights into emotional makeup of others • Comfortable with personal feelings, perceptive of social nuances
Tolerance	• Demonstrate patience with others' beliefs and values; fair-minded • Communicate respect during discontent, conflict
Persuading	• Seek to make a good impression on others; solicit others' points of view • Influence through facilitating decisions and actions

Table 16
EMOTIONAL INTELLIGENCE QUALITIES OF THE 16 TYPES *(Continued)*

ESFJ	Extraverted Feeling With Introverted Sensing
EQ Area	**Description**
Intrapersonal	**Introverted Awareness and Inner Experience**
Self-Awareness	• Self-confident in capabilities to support and encourage others • Realistic about emotions and sympathies
Self-Regulation	• Redirect impulses toward harmony and service; may overcontrol emotions • Conscientious about giving well-organized help
Emotional Self-Control	• Experience flow when actively engaged in harmonious, service-oriented activity, and when receiving recognition or appreciation • Feel emotionally hijacked when others are overly critical, unpredictable, or unstable, and when others fail to be loyal
Interpersonal	**Extraverted Arena of Behavior**
Demonstrated Empathy	• Communicate empathy with ease and sensitivity • Comfortable with personal feelings and perceptive of social nuances
Tolerance	• Reasonably patient with others' beliefs and values • Actively communicate respect during discontent, conflict
Persuading	• Seek to influence through attention to detail and procedures • Solicit others' points of view during problem-solving to earn their attention
INFJ	**Introverted Intuiting With Extraverted Feeling**
EQ Area	**Description**
Intrapersonal	**Introverted Awareness and Inner Experience**
Self-Awareness	• Self-confident when engaged around values and ideals • Recognize moods and usually are free of internal doubts or conflicts
Self-Regulation	• Redirect impulses toward creative outlets • Conscientious about realizing ideals and fulfilling obligations
Emotional Self-Control	• Experience flow when engaged in creative pursuits and in visualizing future creative possibilities, as well as while helping others learn • Feel emotionally hijacked by cruelty, aloofness, or insensitivity toward any living organism, and by lack of regard for privacy

Table 16

EMOTIONAL INTELLIGENCE QUALITIES OF THE 16 TYPES *(Continued)*

Interpersonal	**Extraverted Arena of Behavior**
Demonstrated Empathy	• Understand emotional makeup of others and self; sensitive; comfortable with personal feelings, perceptive of social nuances • Reluctant to criticize or confront others and avoid giving public advice
Tolerance	• Nonjudgmental and trusting of others • Often diplomatic and patient with others' beliefs and values
Persuading	• Rely on relationships and intimate conversations for persuasion • While seeking to build rapport with individuals, may act without worry about making a good impression with others in a group

INFP	**Introverted Feeling With Extraverted Intuiting**
EQ Area	**Description**
Intrapersonal	**Introverted Awareness and Inner Experience**
Self-Awareness	• Self-confident that ideals can be realized with time and patience • Constantly self-assess to identify important standards and aspirations
Self-Regulation	• Use emotional reactions and impulses to clarify issues of importance and at times to distract from taking action • Redirect impulses toward creative outlets
Emotional Self-control	• Experience flow when engaging in quiet, reflective considerations of ideas and actions, internal centering, and working toward authenticity • Feel emotionally hijacked when intentions are distorted, by egregious violations of values, and when they perceive maleficent actions by others toward others
Interpersonal	**Extraverted Arena of Behavior**
Demonstrated Empathy	• Understand emotional makeup of others and communicate empathy easily and naturally • Show insight and sensitivity to personal feelings
Tolerance	• Demonstrate patience with a wide range of others' beliefs and values • Communicate regard during discontent, conflict
Persuading	• More concerned with gaining commitments to reach goals related to mission than with making a good impression • Solicit others' points of view in a highly collaborative fashion

Table 16
EMOTIONAL INTELLIGENCE QUALITIES OF THE 16 TYPES *(Continued)*

ENFP	Extraverted Intuiting With Introverted Feeling
EQ Area	**Description**
Intrapersonal	**Introverted Awareness and Inner Experience**
Self-Awareness	• Self-confident regarding abilities to be resourceful and innovative
	• Recognize moods and quickly identify how these affect actions
Self-Regulation	• Impulses provide a source of direction and action as well as distraction and irritation
	• Strive to bring negative reactions under control
Emotional Self-Control	• Experience flow when freed from constraints and involved in creative activities
	• Feel emotionally hijacked when others are consistently critical without being appreciative (of self and others), or when they feel isolated or rejected without an opportunity to address concerns with others
Interpersonal	**Extraverted Arena of Behavior**
Demonstrated Empathy	• Expressively sensitive toward others and readily identify emotions being experienced and demonstrated
	• Understand the emotional makeup of others and are very comfortable with personal feelings
Tolerance	• Demonstrate openness to new ideas and others' perspectives as long as their values are not insulted
	• Typically avoid conflict as a way to promote harmony and social comfort
Persuading	• Persuade through relationships and sharing innovative ideas
	• Actively solicit others' points of view in problem-solving

ENFJ	Extraverted Feeling With Introverted Intuiting
EQ Area	**Description**
Intrapersonal	**Introverted Awareness and Inner Experience**
Self-Awareness	• Self-confident about accessing imaginative resources
	• Attuned to affirmations and discontent with self and others
Self-Regulation	• Redirect impulses to creative outlets
	• Conscientious and frequently compulsively organized
Emotional Self-Control	• Experience flow when working with individuals and negotiating understanding among groups, as well as when sharing insights
	• Feel emotionally hijacked by continued conflict, perceptions of mean-spiritedness and ill will, and when dealing with those who will not engage in dialogue or are disrespectful of others

Table 16

EMOTIONAL INTELLIGENCE QUALITIES OF THE 16 TYPES *(Continued)*

Interpersonal	**Extraverted Arena of Behavior**
Demonstrated Empathy	• Exhibit insight into others' feelings and needs • Sensitive to personal feelings; are both perceptive of and responsive to social nuances
Tolerance	• Process-oriented as a way to demonstrate patience with others' beliefs and values • Communicate respect and regard of others during discontent, conflict
Persuading	• Seek to make a good impression with others through building rapport and showing awareness of others' needs • Actively solicit others' points of view to creatively problem-solve

INTJ	**Introverted Intuiting With Extraverted Thinking**
EQ Area	**Description**
Intrapersonal	**Introverted Awareness and Inner Experience**
Self-Awareness	• Aware that the vision always exceeds the resources to realize the ideal, leading to impatience and frustration • Realistic self-assessment of motivations and reactions to situations • Actively seek feedback to check out personal sense of awareness
Self-Regulation	• Control impulses and organize efforts to fulfill obligations • While quietly spontaneous, often allow imagination to explore situations • Often have to give self-permission to "loosen up" and relax
Emotional Self-Control	• Experience flow when addressing complex and tough problems with quiet reflection or when talking with a select set of individuals • Feel emotionally hijacked when persistent irrationality and carelessness by others wastes resources
Interpersonal	**Extraverted Arena of Behavior**
Demonstrated Empathy	• May exhibit insight into others' emotional makeup • Not particularly responsive to others' personal feelings unless it serves a larger purpose
Tolerance	• Demonstrate patience with others' ideas and perspectives • Communicate respect for justice, fair-mindedness, and commitment to principles during discontent, conflict
Persuading	• Often inattentive to social shifts in interactions; usually seek to make a good impression with others in order to establish expertise • Solicit others' analytical points of view and logical problem-solving

Table 16
EMOTIONAL INTELLIGENCE QUALITIES OF THE 16 TYPES *(Continued)*

INTP	Introverted Thinking With Extraverted Intuiting
EQ Area	**Description**
Intrapersonal	**Introverted Awareness and Inner Experience**
Self-Awareness	• Self-confident regarding intellectual abilities and often engage in realistic self-assessment related to competencies and accomplishments • Often identify feelings or emotions long after an interaction or event
Self-Regulation	• Direct impulses toward intellectual pursuits; continually reflect to identify and classify emotions and impulses • Conscientious about systems, methods, and goals
Emotional Self-Control	• Experience flow when working on complex problems and identifying the most elegant, logical answer or response • Feel emotionally hijacked by faulty or nonexistent logic, persistent inconsistencies, and emotional attacks on their theories
Interpersonal	**Extraverted Arena of Behavior**
Demonstrated Empathy	• Rarely express insight or actively show understanding of emotional makeup of self and others • Not particularly comfortable or engaged with personal feelings
Tolerance	• Demonstrate patience with others' perspectives if logically and rationally presented • Fair-minded and open to debate about ideas and possibilities
Persuading	• Solicit others' points of view in service of understanding, not to make a good impression • Offer ideas non-defensively and influence through analysis when problem-solving

ENTP	Extraverted Intuiting With Introverted Thinking
EQ Area	**Description**
Intrapersonal	**Introverted Awareness and Inner Experience**
Self-Awareness	• Self-confident in analytical ability and innovative problem-solving • Often not aware of moods and emotional variations, preferring to see these as natural to human systems and processes
Self-Regulation	• Relatively low impulse control, resulting in spontaneous reactions • Relentless impulse to critique to improve; constant internal "risk assessment" regarding actions and reactions

Table 16

EMOTIONAL INTELLIGENCE QUALITIES OF THE 16 TYPES *(Continued)*

Emotional Self-Control	• Experience flow when engaged in complex challenges that solve difficult problems, include variety, and promote use of competencies • Feel emotionally hijacked by individuals who appear rigid, unable to adapt, or illogical, and by boredom and small thinking
Interpersonal	**Extraverted Arena of Behavior**
Demonstrated Empathy	• Due to quick response and critiquing style, may not show sensitivity to others on a consistent basis • Perceptive of social nuances but do not consistently check out interpretations of interpersonal shifts with others
Tolerance	• Demonstrate patience with others' beliefs and values • Conflict situations tend to initiate a competitive rather than cooperative response
Persuading	• Solicit others' points of view and articulate logical positions and possibilities; assertively engage dialogue • Actively problem-solve through generating new ideas and possibilities

ENTJ	**Extraverted Thinking With Introverted Intuiting**
EQ Area	**Description**
Intrapersonal	**Introverted Awareness and Inner Experience**
Self-Awareness	• Self-confident and often realistic about competencies and capacities • Clear about the drive to compete and achieve • May not recognize moods and can dismiss feelings as not valuable
Self-Regulation	• Control impulses and make a conscious effort to direct attention • Inclined to trust hunches and be activity-oriented
Emotional Self-Control	• Experience flow when applying creative and logical solutions to complex problems • Feel emotionally hijacked by those who appear incompetent, who allow emotions to "overly" influence their views, and who are indecisive
Interpersonal	**Extraverted Arena of Behavior**
Demonstrated Empathy	• Have a working "theory" about emotions and how they influence behavior • May not show sensitivity to the emotional needs of others and are often uncomfortable with expressions of personal feelings • Perceptive of social nuances but may not act on this awareness

Table 16
EMOTIONAL INTELLIGENCE QUALITIES OF THE 16 TYPES *(Continued)*

Tolerance	• Demonstrate patience with others' beliefs and values if these seem orderly and subject to reasoned analysis
	• Fair-minded; communicate respect of others during discontent, conflict
	• Impatient with the pace of others
Persuading	• Seek to make a good impression on others
	• Solicit others' points of view
	• Problem-focused rather than person-focused

ESFP	Extraverted Sensing With Introverted Feeling
EQ Area	**Description**
Intrapersonal	**Introverted Awareness and Inner Experience**
Self-Awareness	• Self-confident in dealing with others and creating harmony
	• Recognize moods and emotions; see self as talented and capable
Self-Regulation	• Activity-oriented and directed toward being with others
	• Redirect impulses toward new outlets with others
Emotional Self-Control	• Experience flow in harmonious, supportive environments where social connections are valued
	• Feel emotionally hijacked when in overly critical and hostile or unsupportive environments
Interpersonal	**Extraverted Arena of Behavior**
Demonstrated Empathy	• Frequently exhibit insights into emotional makeup of others
	• Comfortable with personal feelings, perceptive of social nuances
Tolerance	• Demonstrate patience with others' beliefs and values; fair-minded
	• Communicate respect during discontent, conflict
Persuading	• Seek to make a good impression on others; solicit others' points of view
	• Influence through facilitating decisions and actions

ESFJ	Extraverted Feeling With Introverted Sensing
EQ Area	**Description**
Intrapersonal	**Introverted Awareness and Inner Experience**
Self-Awareness	• Self-confident in capabilities to support and encourage others
	• Realistic about emotions and sympathies
Self-Regulation	• Redirect impulses toward harmony and service; may overcontrol emotions
	• Conscientious about giving well-organized help

Table 16

EMOTIONAL INTELLIGENCE QUALITIES OF THE 16 TYPES *(Continued)*

Emotional Self-Control	• Experience flow when actively engaged in harmonious, service-oriented activity, and when receiving recognition or appreciation • Feel emotionally hijacked when others are overly critical, unpredictable, or unstable, and when others fail to be loyal
Interpersonal	**Extraverted Arena of Behavior**
Demonstrated Empathy	• Communicate empathy with ease and sensitivity • Comfortable with personal feelings and perceptive of social nuances
Tolerance	• Reasonably patient with others' beliefs and values • Actively communicate respect during discontent, conflict
Persuading	• Seek to influence through attention to detail and procedures • Solicit others' points of view during problem-solving to earn their attention

INFJ	**Introverted Intuiting With Extraverted Feeling**
EQ Area	**Description**
Intrapersonal	**Introverted Awareness and Inner Experience**
Self-Awareness	• Self-confident when engaged around values and ideals • Recognize moods and usually are free of internal doubts or conflicts
Self-Regulation	• Redirect impulses toward creative outlets • Conscientious about realizing ideals and fulfilling obligations
Emotional Self-Control	• Experience flow when engaged in creative pursuits and in visualizing future creative possibilities, as well as while helping others learn • Feel emotionally hijacked by cruelty, aloofness, or insensitivity toward any living organism, and by lack of regard for privacy
Interpersonal	**Extraverted Arena of Behavior**
Demonstrated Empathy	• Understand emotional makeup of others and self; sensitive; comfortable with personal feelings, perceptive of social nuances • Reluctant to criticize or confront others and avoid giving public advice
Tolerance	• Nonjudgmental and trusting of others • Often diplomatic and patient with others' beliefs and values
Persuading	• Rely on relationships and intimate conversations for persuasion • While seeking to build rapport with individuals, may act without worry about making a good impression with others in a group

Table 16
EMOTIONAL INTELLIGENCE QUALITIES OF THE 16 TYPES *(Continued)*

INFP	Introverted Feeling With Extraverted Intuiting
EQ Area	**Description**
Intrapersonal	**Introverted Awareness and Inner Experience**
Self-Awareness	• Self-confident that ideals can be realized with time and patience • Constantly self-assess to identify important standards and aspirations
Self-Regulation	• Use emotional reactions and impulses to clarify issues of importance and at times to distract from taking action • Redirect impulses toward creative outlets
Emotional Self-control	• Experience flow when engaging in quiet, reflective considerations of ideas and actions, internal centering, and working toward authenticity • Feel emotionally hijacked when intentions are distorted, by egregious violations of values, and when they perceive maleficent actions by others toward others
Interpersonal	**Extraverted Arena of Behavior**
Demonstrated Empathy	• Understand emotional makeup of others and communicate empathy easily and naturally • Show insight and sensitivity to personal feelings
Tolerance	• Demonstrate patience with a wide range of others' beliefs and values • Communicate regard during discontent, conflict
Persuading	• More concerned with gaining commitments to reach goals related to mission than with making a good impression • Solicit others' points of view in a highly collaborative fashion

ENFP	Extraverted Intuiting With Introverted Feeling
EQ Area	**Description**
Intrapersonal	**Introverted Awareness and Inner Experience**
Self-Awareness	• Self-confident regarding abilities to be resourceful and innovative • Recognize moods and quickly identify how these affect actions
Self-Regulation	• Impulses provide a source of direction and action as well as distraction and irritation • Strive to bring negative reactions under control

Table 16

EMOTIONAL INTELLIGENCE QUALITIES OF THE 16 TYPES *(Continued)*

Emotional Self-Control	• Experience flow when freed from constraints and involved in creative activities • Feel emotionally hijacked when others are consistently critical without being appreciative (of self and others), or when they feel isolated or rejected without an opportunity to address concerns with others
Interpersonal	**Extraverted Arena of Behavior**
Demonstrated Empathy	• Expressively sensitive toward others and readily identify emotions being experienced and demonstrated • Understand the emotional makeup of others and are very comfortable with personal feelings
Tolerance	• Demonstrate openness to new ideas and others' perspectives as long as their values are not insulted • Typically avoid conflict as a way to promote harmony and social comfort
Persuading	• Persuade through relationships and sharing innovative ideas • Actively solicit others' points of view in problem-solving

ENFJ	Extraverted Feeling With Introverted Intuiting
EQ Area	**Description**
Intrapersonal	**Introverted Awareness and Inner Experience**
Self-Awareness	• Self-confident about accessing imaginative resources • Attuned to affirmations and discontent with self and others
Self-Regulation	• Redirect impulses to creative outlets • Conscientious and frequently compulsively organized
Emotional Self-Control	• Experience flow when working with individuals and negotiating understanding among groups, as well as when sharing insights • Feel emotionally hijacked by continued conflict, perceptions of mean-spiritedness and ill will, and when dealing with those who will not engage in dialogue or are disrespectful of others
Interpersonal	**Extraverted Arena of Behavior**
Demonstrated Empathy	• Exhibit insight into others' feelings and needs • Sensitive to personal feelings; are both perceptive of and responsive to social nuances
Tolerance	• Process-oriented as a way to demonstrate patience with others' beliefs and values • Communicate respect and regard of others during discontent, conflict

Table 16
EMOTIONAL INTELLIGENCE QUALITIES OF THE 16 TYPES *(Continued)*

| Persuading | • Seek to make a good impression with others through building rapport and showing awareness of others' needs
• Actively solicit others' points of view to creatively problem-solve |

INTJ	**Introverted Intuiting With Extraverted Thinking**
EQ Area	**Description**
Intrapersonal	**Introverted Awareness and Inner Experience**
Self-Awareness	• Aware that the vision always exceeds the resources to realize the ideal, leading to impatience and frustration • Realistic self-assessment of motivations and reactions to situations • Actively seek feedback to check out personal sense of awareness
Self-Regulation	• Control impulses and organize efforts to fulfill obligations • While quietly spontaneous, often allow imagination to explore situations • Often have to give self-permission to "loosen up" and relax
Emotional Self-Control	• Experience flow when addressing complex and tough problems with quiet reflection or when talking with a select set of individuals • Feel emotionally hijacked when persistent irrationality and carelessness by others wastes resources
Interpersonal	**Extraverted Arena of Behavior**
Demonstrated Empathy	• May exhibit insight into others' emotional makeup • Not particularly responsive to others' personal feelings unless it serves a larger purpose
Tolerance	• Demonstrate patience with others' ideas and perspectives • Communicate respect for justice, fair-mindedness, and commitment to principles during discontent, conflict
Persuading	• Often inattentive to social shifts in interactions; usually seek to make a good impression with others in order to establish expertise • Solicit others' analytical points of view and logical problem-solving

INTP	**Introverted Thinking With Extraverted Intuiting**
EQ Area	**Description**
Intrapersonal	**Introverted Awareness and Inner Experience**
Self-Awareness	• Self-confident regarding intellectual abilities and often engage in realistic self-assessment related to competencies and accomplishments • Often identify feelings or emotions long after an interaction or event

Table 16

EMOTIONAL INTELLIGENCE QUALITIES OF THE 16 TYPES *(Continued)*

Self-Regulation	• Direct impulses toward intellectual pursuits; continually reflect to identify and classify emotions and impulses • Conscientious about systems, methods, and goals
Emotional Self-Control	• Experience flow when working on complex problems and identifying the most elegant, logical answer or response • Feel emotionally hijacked by faulty or nonexistent logic, persistent inconsistencies, and emotional attacks on their theories
Interpersonal	**Extraverted Arena of Behavior**
Demonstrated Empathy	• Rarely express insight or actively show understanding of emotional makeup of self and others • Not particularly comfortable or engaged with personal feelings
Tolerance	• Demonstrate patience with others' perspectives if logically and rationally presented • Fair-minded and open to debate about ideas and possibilities
Persuading	• Solicit others' points of view in service of understanding, not to make a good impression • Offer ideas non-defensively and influence through analysis when problem-solving

ENTP	Extraverted Intuiting With Introverted Thinking
EQ Area	**Description**
Intrapersonal	**Introverted Awareness and Inner Experience**
Self-Awareness	• Self-confident in analytical ability and innovative problem-solving • Often not aware of moods and emotional variations, preferring to see these as natural to human systems and processes
Self-Regulation	• Relatively low impulse control, resulting in spontaneous reactions • Relentless impulse to critique to improve; constant internal "risk assessment" regarding actions and reactions
Emotional Self-Control	• Experience flow when engaged in complex challenges that solve difficult problems, include variety, and promote use of competencies • Feel emotionally hijacked by individuals who appear rigid, unable to adapt, or illogical, and by boredom and small thinking
Interpersonal	**Extraverted Arena of Behavior**
Demonstrated Empathy	• Due to quick response and critiquing style, may not show sensitivity to others on a consistent basis • Perceptive of social nuances but do not consistently check out interpretations of interpersonal shifts with others

Table 16
EMOTIONAL INTELLIGENCE QUALITIES OF THE 16 TYPES *(Continued)*

Tolerance	• Demonstrate patience with others' beliefs and values
	• Conflict situations tend to initiate a competitive rather than cooperative response
Persuading	• Solicit others' points of view and articulate logical positions and possibilities; assertively engage dialogue
	• Actively problem-solve through generating new ideas and possibilities

ENTJ	Extraverted Thinking With Introverted Intuiting
EQ Area	**Description**
Intrapersonal	**Introverted Awareness and Inner Experience**
Self-Awareness	• Self-confident and often realistic about competencies and capacities
	• Clear about the drive to compete and achieve
	• May not recognize moods and can dismiss feelings as not valuable
Self-Regulation	• Control impulses and make a conscious effort to direct attention
	• Inclined to trust hunches and be activity oriented
Emotional Self-Control	• Experience flow when applying creative and logical solutions to complex problems
	• Feel emotionally hijacked by those who appear incompetent, who allow emotions to "overly" influence their views, and who are indecisive
Interpersonal	**Extraverted Arena of Behavior**
Demonstrated Empathy	• Have a working "theory" about emotions and how they influence behavior
	• May not show sensitivity to the emotional needs of others and are often uncomfortable with expressions of personal feelings
	• Perceptive of social nuances but may not act on this awareness
Tolerance	• Demonstrate patience with others' beliefs and values if these seem orderly and subject to reasoned analysis
	• Fair-minded; communicate respect of others during discontent, conflict
	• Impatient with the pace of others
Persuading	• Seek to make a good impression on others
	• Solicit others' points of view
	• Problem-focused rather than person-focused

Table 16

EMOTIONAL INTELLIGENCE QUALITIES OF THE 16 TYPES *(Continued)*

ESFP	Extraverted Sensing With Introverted Feeling
EQ Area	**Description**
Intrapersonal	**Introverted Awareness and Inner Experience**
Self-Awareness	• Self-confident in dealing with others and creating harmony • Recognize moods and emotions; see self as talented and capable
Self-Regulation	• Activity-oriented and directed toward being with others • Redirect impulses toward new outlets with others
Emotional Self-Control	• Experience flow in harmonious, supportive environments where social connections are valued • Feel emotionally hijacked when in overly critical and hostile or unsupportive environments
Interpersonal	**Extraverted Arena of Behavior**
Demonstrated Empathy	• Frequently exhibit insights into emotional makeup of others • Comfortable with personal feelings, perceptive of social nuances
Tolerance	• Demonstrate patience with others' beliefs and values; fair-minded • Communicate respect during discontent, conflict
Persuading	• Seek to make a good impression on others; solicit others' points of view • Influence through facilitating decisions and actions

ESFJ	Extraverted Feeling With Introverted Sensing
EQ Area	**Description**
Intrapersonal	**Introverted Awareness and Inner Experience**
Self-Awareness	• Self-confident in capabilities to support and encourage others • Realistic about emotions and sympathies
Self-Regulation	• Redirect impulses toward harmony and service; may overcontrol emotions • Conscientious about giving well-organized help
Emotional Self-Control	• Experience flow when actively engaged in harmonious, service-oriented activity, and when receiving recognition or appreciation • Feel emotionally hijacked when others are overly critical, unpredictable, or unstable, and when others fail to be loyal

Table 16

EMOTIONAL INTELLIGENCE QUALITIES OF THE 16 TYPES *(Continued)*

Interpersonal	**Extraverted Arena of Behavior**
Demonstrated Empathy	• Communicate empathy with ease and sensitivity • Comfortable with personal feelings and perceptive of social nuances
Tolerance	• Reasonably patient with others' beliefs and values • Actively communicate respect during discontent, conflict
Persuading	• Seek to influence through attention to detail and procedures • Solicit others' points of view during problem-solving to earn their attention

INFJ	**Introverted Intuiting With Extraverted Feeling**
EQ Area	**Description**
Intrapersonal	**Introverted Awareness and Inner Experience**
Self-Awareness	• Self-confident when engaged around values and ideals • Recognize moods and usually are free of internal doubts or conflicts
Self-Regulation	• Redirect impulses toward creative outlets • Conscientious about realizing ideals and fulfilling obligations
Emotional Self-Control	• Experience flow when engaged in creative pursuits and in visualizing future creative possibilities, as well as while helping others learn • Feel emotionally hijacked by cruelty, aloofness, or insensitivity toward any living organism, and by lack of regard for privacy
Interpersonal	**Extraverted Arena of Behavior**
Demonstrated Empathy	• Understand emotional makeup of others and self; sensitive; comfortable with personal feelings, perceptive of social nuances • Reluctant to criticize or confront others and avoid giving public advice
Tolerance	• Nonjudgmental and trusting of others • Often diplomatic and patient with others' beliefs and values
Persuading	• Rely on relationships and intimate conversations for persuasion • While seeking to build rapport with individuals, may act without worry about making a good impression with others in a group

Table 16

EMOTIONAL INTELLIGENCE QUALITIES OF THE 16 TYPES *(Continued)*

INFP	Introverted Feeling With Extraverted Intu
EQ Area	**Description**
Intrapersonal	**Introverted Awareness and Inner Experience**
Self-Awareness	• Self-confident that ideals can be realized with time and patience
	• Constantly self-assess to identify important standards and aspirations
Self-Regulation	• Use emotional reactions and impulses to clarify issues of importance and at times to distract from taking action
	• Redirect impulses toward creative outlets
Emotional Self-control	• Experience flow when engaging in quiet, reflective considerations of ideas and actions, internal centering, and working toward authenticity
	• Feel emotionally hijacked when intentions are distorted, by egregious violations of values, and when they perceive maleficent actions by others toward others
Interpersonal	**Extraverted Arena of Behavior**
Demonstrated Empathy	• Understand emotional makeup of others and communicate empathy easily and naturally
	• Show insight and sensitivity to personal feelings
Tolerance	• Demonstrate patience with a wide range of others' beliefs and values
	• Communicate regard during discontent, conflict
Persuading	• More concerned with gaining commitments to reach goals related to mission than with making a good impression
	• Solicit others' points of view in a highly collaborative fashion

ENFP	Extraverted Intuiting With Introverted Feeling
EQ Area	**Description**
Intrapersonal	**Introverted Awareness and Inner Experience**
Self-Awareness	• Self-confident regarding abilities to be resourceful and innovative
	• Recognize moods and quickly identify how these affect actions
Self-Regulation	• Impulses provide a source of direction and action as well as distraction and irritation
	• Strive to bring negative reactions under control

Table 16
EMOTIONAL INTELLIGENCE QUALITIES OF THE 16 TYPES *(Continued)*

Emotional Self-Control	• Experience flow when freed from constraints and involved in creative activities • Feel emotionally hijacked when others are consistently critical without being appreciative (of self and others), or when they feel isolated or rejected without an opportunity to address concerns with others
Interpersonal	**Extraverted Arena of Behavior**
Demonstrated Empathy	• Expressively sensitive toward others and readily identify emotions being experienced and demonstrated • Understand the emotional makeup of others and are very comfortable with personal feelings
Tolerance	• Demonstrate openness to new ideas and others' perspectives as long as their values are not insulted • Typically avoid conflict as a way to promote harmony and social comfort
Persuading	• Persuade through relationships and sharing innovative ideas • Actively solicit others' points of view in problem-solving

ENFJ	**Extraverted Feeling With Introverted Intuiting**
EQ Area	**Description**
Intrapersonal	**Introverted Awareness and Inner Experience**
Self-Awareness	• Self-confident about accessing imaginative resources • Attuned to affirmations and discontent with self and others
Self-Regulation	• Redirect impulses to creative outlets • Conscientious and frequently compulsively organized
Emotional Self-Control	• Experience flow when working with individuals and negotiating understanding among groups, as well as when sharing insights • Feel emotionally hijacked by continued conflict, perceptions of mean-spiritedness and ill will, and when dealing with those who will not engage in dialogue or are disrespectful of others
Interpersonal	**Extraverted Arena of Behavior**
Demonstrated Empathy	• Exhibit insight into others' feelings and needs • Sensitive to personal feelings; are both perceptive of and responsive to social nuances
Tolerance	• Process-oriented as a way to demonstrate patience with others' beliefs and values • Communicate respect and regard of others during discontent, conflict

Table 16
EMOTIONAL INTELLIGENCE QUALITIES OF THE 16 TYPES *(Continued)*

Persuading	• Seek to make a good impression with others through building rapport and showing awareness of others' needs • Actively solicit others' points of view to creatively problem-solve

INTJ	**Introverted Intuiting With Extraverted Thinking**
EQ Area	**Description**
Intrapersonal	**Introverted Awareness and Inner Experience**
Self-Awareness	• Aware that the vision always exceeds the resources to realize the ideal, leading to impatience and frustration • Realistic self-assessment of motivations and reactions to situations • Actively seek feedback to check out personal sense of awareness
Self-Regulation	• Control impulses and organize efforts to fulfill obligations • While quietly spontaneous, often allow imagination to explore situations • Often have to give self-permission to "loosen up" and relax
Emotional Self-Control	• Experience flow when addressing complex and tough problems with quiet reflection or when talking with a select set of individuals • Feel emotionally hijacked when persistent irrationality and carelessness by others wastes resources
Interpersonal	**Extraverted Arena of Behavior**
Demonstrated Empathy	• May exhibit insight into others' emotional makeup • Not particularly responsive to others' personal feelings unless it serves a larger purpose
Tolerance	• Demonstrate patience with others' ideas and perspectives • Communicate respect for justice, fair-mindedness, and commitment to principles during discontent, conflict
Persuading	• Often inattentive to social shifts in interactions; usually seek to make a good impression with others in order to establish expertise • Solicit others' analytical points of view and logical problem-solving

Table 16
EMOTIONAL INTELLIGENCE QUALITIES OF THE 16 TYPES *(Continued)*

INTP	Introverted Thinking With Extraverted Intuiting
EQ Area	**Description**
Intrapersonal	**Introverted Awareness and Inner Experience**
Self-Awareness	• Self-confident regarding intellectual abilities and often engage in realistic self-assessment related to competencies and accomplishments • Often identify feelings or emotions long after an interaction or event
Self-Regulation	• Direct impulses toward intellectual pursuits; continually reflect to identify and classify emotions and impulses • Conscientious about systems, methods, and goals
Emotional Self-Control	• Experience flow when working on complex problems and identifying the most elegant, logical answer or response • Feel emotionally hijacked by faulty or nonexistent logic, persistent inconsistencies, and emotional attacks on their theories
Interpersonal	**Extraverted Arena of Behavior**
Demonstrated Empathy	• Rarely express insight or actively show understanding of emotional makeup of self and others • Not particularly comfortable or engaged with personal feelings
Tolerance	• Demonstrate patience with others' perspectives if logically and rationally presented • Fair-minded and open to debate about ideas and possibilities
Persuading	• Solicit others' points of view in service of understanding, not to make a good impression • Offer ideas non-defensively and influence through analysis when problem-solving

ENTP	Extraverted Intuiting With Introverted Thinking
EQ Area	**Description**
Intrapersonal	**Introverted Awareness and Inner Experience**
Self-Awareness	• Self-confident in analytical ability and innovative problem-solving • Often not aware of moods and emotional variations, preferring to see these as natural to human systems and processes

Table 16
EMOTIONAL INTELLIGENCE QUALITIES OF THE 16 TYPES *(Continued)*

Self-Regulation	• Relatively low impulse control, resulting in spontaneous reactions • Relentless impulse to critique to improve; constant internal "risk assessment" regarding actions and reactions
Emotional Self-Control	• Experience flow when engaged in complex challenges that solve difficult problems, include variety, and promote use of competencies • Feel emotionally hijacked by individuals who appear rigid, unable to adapt, or illogical, and by boredom and small thinking
Interpersonal	**Extraverted Arena of Behavior**
Demonstrated Empathy	• Due to quick response and critiquing style, may not show sensitivity to others on a consistent basis • Perceptive of social nuances but do not consistently check out interpretations of interpersonal shifts with others
Tolerance	• Demonstrate patience with others' beliefs and values • Conflict situations tend to initiate a competitive rather than cooperative response
Persuading	• Solicit others' points of view and articulate logical positions and possibilities; assertively engage dialogue • Actively problem-solve through generating new ideas and possibilities

ENTJ	Extraverted Thinking With Introverted Intuiting
EQ Area	**Description**
Intrapersonal	**Introverted Awareness and Inner Experience**
Self-Awareness	• Self-confident and often realistic about competencies and capacities • Clear about the drive to compete and achieve • May not recognize moods and can dismiss feelings as not valuable
Self-Regulation	• Control impulses and make a conscious effort to direct attention • Inclined to trust hunches and be activity oriented
Emotional Self-Control	• Experience flow when applying creative and logical solutions to complex problems • Feel emotionally hijacked by those who appear incompetent, who allow emotions to "overly" influence their views, and who are indecisive

Table 16
EMOTIONAL INTELLIGENCE QUALITIES OF THE 16 TYPES *(Continued)*

Interpersonal	**Extraverted Arena of Behavior**
Demonstrated Empathy	• Have a working "theory" about emotions and how they influence behavior • May not show sensitivity to the emotional needs of others and are often uncomfortable with expressions of personal feelings • Perceptive of social nuances but may not act on this awareness
Tolerance	• Demonstrate patience with others' beliefs and values if these seem orderly and subject to reasoned analysis • Fair-minded; communicate respect of others during discontent, conflict • Impatient with the pace of others
Persuading	• Seek to make a good impression on others • Solicit others' points of view • Problem-focused rather than person-focused

ESFP	**Extraverted Sensing With Introverted Feeling**
EQ Area	**Description**
Intrapersonal	**Introverted Awareness and Inner Experience**
Self-Awareness	• Self-confident in dealing with others and creating harmony • Recognize moods and emotions; see self as talented and capable
Self-Regulation	• Activity-oriented and directed toward being with others • Redirect impulses toward new outlets with others
Emotional Self-Control	• Experience flow in harmonious, supportive environments where social connections are valued • Feel emotionally hijacked when in overly critical and hostile or unsupportive environments
Interpersonal	**Extraverted Arena of Behavior**
Demonstrated Empathy	• Frequently exhibit insights into emotional makeup of others • Comfortable with personal feelings, perceptive of social nuances
Tolerance	• Demonstrate patience with others' beliefs and values; fair-minded
Persuading	• Communicate respect during discontent, conflict • Seek to make a good impression on others; solicit others' points of view • Influence through facilitating decisions and actions

Table 16
EMOTIONAL INTELLIGENCE QUALITIES OF THE 16 TYPES *(Continued)*

ESFJ	Extraverted Feeling With Introverted Sensing
EQ Area	**Description**
Intrapersonal	**Introverted Awareness and Inner Experience**
Self-Awareness	• Self-confident in capabilities to support and encourage others • Realistic about emotions and sympathies
Self-Regulation	• Redirect impulses toward harmony and service; may overcontrol emotions • Conscientious about giving well-organized help
Emotional Self-Control	• Experience flow when actively engaged in harmonious, service-oriented activity, and when receiving recognition or appreciation • Feel emotionally hijacked when others are overly critical, unpredictable, or unstable, and when others fail to be loyal
Interpersonal	**Extraverted Arena of Behavior**
Demonstrated Empathy	• Communicate empathy with ease and sensitivity • Comfortable with personal feelings and perceptive of social nuances
Tolerance	• Reasonably patient with others' beliefs and values • Actively communicate respect during discontent, conflict
Persuading	• Seek to influence through attention to detail and procedures • Solicit others' points of view during problem-solving to earn their attention

INFJ	Introverted Intuiting With Extraverted Feeling
EQ Area	**Description**
Intrapersonal	**Introverted Awareness and Inner Experience**
Self-Awareness	• Self-confident when engaged around values and ideals • Recognize moods and usually are free of internal doubts or conflicts
Self-Regulation	• Redirect impulses toward creative outlets • Conscientious about realizing ideals and fulfilling obligations
Emotional Self-Control	• Experience flow when engaged in creative pursuits and in visualizing future creative possibilities, as well as while helping others learn • Feel emotionally hijacked by cruelty, aloofness, or insensitivity toward any living organism, and by lack of regard for privacy

Table 16
EMOTIONAL INTELLIGENCE QUALITIES OF THE 16 TYPES *(Continued)*

Interpersonal	**Extraverted Arena of Behavior**
Demonstrated Empathy	• Understand emotional makeup of others and self; sensitive; comfortable with personal feelings, perceptive of social nuances • Reluctant to criticize or confront others and avoid giving public advice
Tolerance	• Nonjudgmental and trusting of others • Often diplomatic and patient with others' beliefs and values
Persuading	• Rely on relationships and intimate conversations for persuasion • While seeking to build rapport with individuals, may act without worry about making a good impression with others in a group

INFP	**Introverted Feeling With Extraverted Intuiting**
EQ Area	**Description**
Intrapersonal	**Introverted Awareness and Inner Experience**
Self-Awareness	• Self-confident that ideals can be realized with time and patience • Constantly self-assess to identify important standards and aspirations
Self-Regulation	• Use emotional reactions and impulses to clarify issues of importance and at times to distract from taking action • Redirect impulses toward creative outlets
Emotional Self-control	• Experience flow when engaging in quiet, reflective considerations of ideas and actions, internal centering, and working toward authenticity • Feel emotionally hijacked when intentions are distorted, by egregious violations of values, and when they perceive maleficent actions by others toward others
Interpersonal	**Extraverted Arena of Behavior**
Demonstrated Empathy	• Understand emotional makeup of others and communicate empathy easily and naturally • Show insight and sensitivity to personal feelings
Tolerance	• Demonstrate patience with a wide range of others' beliefs and values • Communicate regard during discontent, conflict
Persuading	• More concerned with gaining commitments to reach goals related to mission than with making a good impression • Solicit others' points of view in a highly collaborative fashion

Table 16

EMOTIONAL INTELLIGENCE QUALITIES OF THE 16 TYPES *(Continued)*

ENFP	Extraverted Intuiting With Introverted Feeling
EQ Area	**Description**
Intrapersonal	**Introverted Awareness and Inner Experience**
Self-Awareness	• Self-confident regarding abilities to be resourceful and innovative
	• Recognize moods and quickly identify how these affect actions
Self-Regulation	• Impulses provide a source of direction and action as well as distraction and irritation
	• Strive to bring negative reactions under control
Emotional Self-control	• Experience flow when freed from constraints and involved in creative activities
	• Feel emotionally hijacked when others are consistently critical without being appreciative (of self and others), or when they feel isolated or rejected without an opportunity to address concerns with others
Interpersonal	**Extraverted Arena of Behavior**
Demonstrated Empathy	• Expressively sensitive toward others and readily identify emotions being experienced and demonstrated
	• Understand the emotional makeup of others and are very comfortable with personal feelings
Tolerance	• Demonstrate openness to new ideas and others' perspectives as long as their values are not insulted
	• Typically avoid conflict as a way to promote harmony and social comfort
Persuading	• Persuade through relationships and sharing innovative ideas
	• Actively solicit others' points of view in problem-solving

ENFJ	Extraverted Feeling With Introverted Intuiting
EQ Area	**Description**
Intrapersonal	**Introverted Awareness and Inner Experience**
Self-Awareness	• Self-confident about accessing imaginative resources
	• Attuned to affirmations and discontent with self and others
Self-Regulation	• Redirect impulses to creative outlets
	• Conscientious and frequently compulsively organized
Emotional Self-control	• Experience flow when working with individuals and negotiating understanding among groups, as well as when sharing insights
	• Feel emotionally hijacked by continued conflict, perceptions of mean-spiritedness and ill will, and when dealing with those who will not engage in dialogue or are disrespectful of others

Table 16
EMOTIONAL INTELLIGENCE QUALITIES OF THE 16 TYPES *(Continued)*

Interpersonal	**Extraverted Arena of Behavior**
Demonstrated Empathy	• Exhibit insight into others' feelings and needs • Sensitive to personal feelings; are both perceptive of and responsive to social nuances
Tolerance	• Process-oriented as a way to demonstrate patience with others' beliefs and values • Communicate respect and regard of others during discontent, conflict
Persuading	• Seek to make a good impression with others through building rapport and showing awareness of others' needs • Actively solicit others' points of view to creatively problem-solve

INTJ	**Introverted Intuiting With Extraverted Thinking**
EQ Area	**Description**
Intrapersonal	**Introverted Awareness and Inner Experience**
Self-Awareness	• Aware that the vision always exceeds the resources to realize the ideal, leading to impatience and frustration • Realistic self-assessment of motivations and reactions to situations • Actively seek feedback to check out personal sense of awareness
Self-Regulation	• Control impulses and organize efforts to fulfill obligations • While quietly spontaneous, often allow imagination to explore situations • Often have to give self-permission to "loosen up" and relax
Emotional Self-Control	• Experience flow when addressing complex and tough problems with quiet reflection or when talking with a select set of individuals • Feel emotionally hijacked when persistent irrationality and carelessness by others wastes resources
Interpersonal	**Extraverted Arena of Behavior**
Demonstrated Empathy	• May exhibit insight into others' emotional makeup • Not particularly responsive to others' personal feelings unless it serves a larger purpose
Tolerance	• Demonstrate patience with others' ideas and perspectives • Communicate respect for justice, fair-mindedness, and commitment to principles during discontent, conflict
Persuading	• Often inattentive to social shifts in interactions; usually seek to make a good impression with others in order to establish expertise • Solicit others' analytical points of view and logical problem-solving

Table 16
EMOTIONAL INTELLIGENCE QUALITIES OF THE 16 TYPES *(Continued)*

INTP	Introverted Thinking With Extraverted Intuiting
EQ Area	**Description**
Intrapersonal	**Introverted Awareness and Inner Experience**
Self-Awareness	• Self-confident regarding intellectual abilities and often engage in realistic self-assessment related to competencies and accomplishments • Often identify feelings or emotions long after an interaction or event
Self-Regulation	• Direct impulses toward intellectual pursuits; continually reflect to identify and classify emotions and impulses • Conscientious about systems, methods, and goals
Emotional Self-Control	• Experience flow when working on complex problems and identifying the most elegant, logical answer or response • Feel emotionally hijacked by faulty or nonexistent logic, persistent inconsistencies, and emotional attacks on their theories
Interpersonal	**Extraverted Arena of Behavior**
Demonstrated Empathy	• Rarely express insight or actively show understanding of emotional makeup of self and others • Not particularly comfortable or engaged with personal feelings
Tolerance	• Demonstrate patience with others' perspectives if logically and rationally presented • Fair-minded and open to debate about ideas and possibilities
Persuading	• Solicit others' points of view in service of understanding, not to make a good impression • Offer ideas non-defensively and influence through analysis when problem-solving

ENTP	Extraverted Intuiting With Introverted Thinking
EQ Area	**Description**
Intrapersonal	**Introverted Awareness and Inner Experience**
Self-Awareness	• Self-confident in analytical ability and innovative problem-solving • Often not aware of moods and emotional variations, preferring to see these as natural to human systems and processes

Table 16
EMOTIONAL INTELLIGENCE QUALITIES OF THE 16 TYPES *(Continued)*

Self-Regulation	• Relatively low impulse control, resulting in spontaneous reactions • Relentless impulse to critique to improve; constant internal "risk assessment" regarding actions and reactions
Emotional Self-Control	• Experience flow when engaged in complex challenges that solve difficult problems, include variety, and promote use of competencies • Feel emotionally hijacked by individuals who appear rigid, unable to adapt, or illogical, and by boredom and small thinking
Interpersonal	**Extraverted Arena of Behavior**
Demonstrated Empathy	• Due to quick response and critiquing style, may not show sensitivity to others on a consistent basis • Perceptive of social nuances but do not consistently check out interpretations of interpersonal shifts with others
Tolerance	• Demonstrate patience with others' beliefs and values • Conflict situations tend to initiate a competitive rather than cooperative response
Persuading	• Solicit others' points of view and articulate logical positions and possibilities; assertively engage dialogue • Actively problem-solve through generating new ideas and possibilities

ENTJ	Extraverted Thinking With Introverted Intuiting
EQ Area	**Description**
Intrapersonal	**Introverted Awareness and Inner Experience**
Self-Awareness	• Self-confident and often realistic about competencies and capacities • Clear about the drive to compete and achieve • May not recognize moods and can dismiss feelings as not valuable
Self-Regulation	• Control impulses and make a conscious effort to direct attention • Inclined to trust hunches and be activity oriented
Emotional Self-Control	• Experience flow when applying creative and logical solutions to complex problems • Feel emotionally hijacked by those who appear incompetent, who allow emotions to "overly" influence their views, and who are indecisive

Table 16
EMOTIONAL INTELLIGENCE QUALITIES OF THE 16 TYPES *(Continued)*

Interpersonal	**Extraverted Arena of Behavior**
Demonstrated Empathy	• Have a working "theory" about emotions and how they influence behavior • May not show sensitivity to the emotional needs of others and are often uncomfortable with expressions of personal feelings • Perceptive of social nuances but may not act on this awareness
Tolerance	• Demonstrate patience with others' beliefs and values if these seem orderly and subject to reasoned analysis • Fair-minded; communicate respect of others during discontent, conflict • Impatient with the pace of others
Persuading	• Seek to make a good impression on others • Solicit others' points of view • Problem-focused rather than person-focused

Extracting the elements of emotional intelligence is a bit like trying to identify specific vitamins in food by taste. We know the working parts but not necessarily how they blend together. In much the same way, the abilities, patterns of Perception and Judgment, and behaviors that combine to make up emotionally intelligent responses are inseparable, self-reinforcing partners. For pragmatic purposes, the goal of this chapter is to give us a view into how our personality type links with emotional intelligence. We hope it will provide a kind of inoculation against judging others' behavior prematurely and that it will free us to move beyond our own habits and hang-ups to engage fearlessly with others for the good of all.

Self-Report on Basic EQ Abilities

Using a five-point scale, rate each of the following statements.

Circle your response: 1 = rarely, 2 = sometimes, 3 = often, 4 = frequently, 5 = always

	Statements	1	2	3	4	5
A	1. I am aware of how often I am angry.	1	2	3	④	5
	2. I easily use feeling words (e.g., *happy, irritated*) to describe my emotions.	1	2	3	④	5
	3. I am aware of what triggers my different emotional reactions.	1	2	3	④	5

	Statements	1	2	3	4	5
B	1. I am aware of which situations prompt feelings of comfort or discomfort.	1	2	3	④	5
	2. I am attuned to how to change my emotional responses by altering my context.	1	2	③	4	5
	3. I am aware of how relationships vary in emotional tone.	1	2	3	④	5

	Statements	1	2	3	4	5
C	1. I quickly and accurately read others' facial expressions.	1	2	3	④	5
	2. I am aware of how body language reflects different moods or reactions.	1	2	3	④	5
	3. I actively look for clues about others' emotional responses.	1	2	3	4	⑤

	Statements	1	2	3	4	5
D	1. When I enter situations, I anticipate how others will react.	1	2	③	4	5
	2. I am careful to present information in non-emotional terms.	1	2	③	4	5
	3. It is easy for me to change the emotional climate in a conversation.	1	2	③	4	5

	Statements	1	2	3	4	5
E	1. I easily identify what others are feeling in a situation.	1	2	3	④	5
	2. I can quickly express and name others' emotional reactions.	1	2	3	④	5
	3. I regularly show an interest in others' feelings.	1	2	3	4	⑤

	Statements	1	2			
F	1. When I sense frustrating circumstances, I diffuse the situation by taking perspective.	1	2	3		
	2. When I get angry, I find a way to "talk through it."	1	2	3		
	3. When I feel excited, I direct energy into constructive action.	1	2	3	4	5

	Statements	1	2	3	4	5
G	1. I can readily identify the emotional aspects of relationships.	1	2	3	4	5
	2. I clarify emotional reactions through active listening.	1	2	3	4	5
	3. I assess the emotional intensity of interactions.	1	2	3	4	5

	Statements	1	2	3	4	5
H	1. My first response is to demonstrate empathetic understanding during interactions.	1	2	3	4	5
	2. When others are upset, I actively work to calm everyone down.	1	2	3	4	5
	3. I am careful to use positive emotional words to promote constructive action.	1	2	3	4	5

INTERPRETING YOUR RESULTS

Skill Dimension—Total the points and circle your result for each category

	Develop	Enrich	Effective
A: Recognizing your emotions	3–7	7–12	13–15
B: Identifying the context of your emotions	3–7	7–12	13–15
C: Recognizing others' emotions	3–7	7–12	13–15
D: Anticipating others' emotions	3–7	7–12	13–15
E: Identifying emotional responses	3–7	7–12	13–15
F: Matching emotions with situations	3–7	7–12	13–15
G: Evaluating the emotional needs of others	3–7	7–12	13–15
H: Demonstrating appropriate responses	3–7	7–12	13–15

ACTING ON YOUR RESULTS

Develop	This reflects a need to pay careful attention to this area of EQ. Become more observant and solicit information from those who appear to be effective with this behavior.
Enrich	This reflects a need to become more intentional about this area of EQ.
Effective	This reflects frequent use of this area of EQ. You can be a model for others.

Getting There from Here

INCREASING PERSONAL EFFECTIVENESS
AT WORK AND AT HOME

A t the heart of our daily to-do list is a presumption that if we finish tasks on the list, we are making progress. Personal effectiveness is sometimes measured by how successful we are at things like picking up groceries and remembering to return a call. Getting things done on the daily list often gives satisfaction and a feeling of movement. Many of us also have a larger to-do list that is related to health, career, and personal satisfaction as we work through life changes, manage stress, and seek resolutions to the conflicts and problems that make up the broad strokes of life. Understanding personality type, our own and others', can aid us in designing tactics and strategies to manage our time and tasks in ways that enrich our experience and increase our overall effectiveness—turning life's "to-dos" into joyful "ta-das!"

Effectiveness means knowing what to do and doing it. To "know" what to do requires that we appraise a situation, then align our understanding with actions designed to produce constructive outcomes. For example, if we perceive that an individual is behaving in a problematic way and we decide to engage in a solution-oriented discussion, we are seeking a constructive outcome. Each aspect of effectiveness is influenced by our personality type, which in turn can enhance or impede our efforts to move toward a more satisfying state of affairs in any life arena. A full understanding of how type plays into these arenas allows for more conscious choices about living intentionally and with increasing levels of effectiveness. In this chapter, we explore effectiveness related to career choices, health issues, and important relationships.

As we examine these links, we will see that working on our type development in general enhances effectiveness across all of the arenas outlined. Type development means having clarity about our type patterns and being agile enough to stretch beyond our preferences to engage other type processes so that we can successfully address an issue. For example, if your preferences are INFJ, you may need to "stretch" to become more expressive (Extraverted), pragmatic (Sensing), analytical (Thinking), and questioning (Perceiving) from time to time. Being agile within your personality type means that while you know and trust your typical automatic responses, you also know how to respond differently when the situation requires it.

Given the above definition of effectiveness, a very practical way of thinking about type is to consider how the mental processes (as defined by type) affect your "knowing" and "doing" in numerous ways. Table 17 outlines the role of the core mental processes in how we perceive (know) and act (do) related to life's challenges. Recall that the richness of type lies in how these eight processes are used dynamically to generate patterns of Perception (the first aspect of "knowing") and Judgment (the first aspect of "doing").

We certainly recognize that "knowing" and "doing" are considerably more complicated than outlined above. We've noted many times that, while type has an important role on our behavior, it's not the only player on the field. Our goal is to provide you with a pragmatic handle on leveraging the mental processes that reside at the core of personality type. Of course, when we combine the perceiving and the acting functions of type with the knowing and doing behaviors of effectiveness, the links are pretty clear. For example, the individual who prefers to "know" by cataloguing facts (Sensing that is Introverted) and "do" through logical action (Thinking that is Extraverted) may use those gifts very effectively when solving a math problem. Though we know some of you may find it hard to believe, life is not one big math problem. If this same individual does not access some Intuiting perceptions (seeing links and possibilities) and Feeling-related actions (attending to personal alignment), she may run into trouble when trying to solve interpersonal relationship issues (which typically aren't like math problems).

Having clearer perceptions requires that we intentionally explore four kinds of knowing:

- Factual, verifiable data (Se)
- Patterns and associations that make up context (Ne)
- Cataloged, historical information (Si)
- Scenarios and possible outcomes (Ni)

Acting with an expectation of effectively achieving a result requires being intentional about four kinds of judgment:

- Critiquing options, looking at pros/cons, evaluating options (Te)
- Analyzing underlying principles or logic, driving toward precision (Ti)

- Aligning needs, values, people with desirable outcomes (Fe)
- Evaluating the acceptability of options as related to ideals and holistic criteria (Fi)

If we turn these categories of perceptions and judgments into questions for evaluating a course of action we are about to take, we are most likely going to make a better decision, and a more effective outcome will follow. So when considering how you are going to respond to a situation, ponder these eight questions:

Table 17[1]
TYPE MENTAL PROCESSES AND EFFECTIVENESS: GENERAL TRENDS

Function/Mental Process	Knowing	Doing
Sensing that is Introverted (Si)	• Verifying information • Cataloguing details	
Sensing that is Extraverted (Se)	• Reacting to changing conditions • Focusing precisely on the immediate environment	
Intuiting that is Introverted (Ni)	• "Seeing" scenarios • Creating novel links to information	
Intuiting that is Extraverted (Ne)	• Seeing interconnections • Identifying trends quickly	
Thinking that is Introverted (Ti)		• Analyzing choices • Seeking precision
Thinking that is Extraverted (Te)		• Critiquing options • Generating logical outcomes
Feeling that is Introverted (Fi)		• Evaluating alignment with ideals • Judging the "fit" of action with intention
Feeling that is Extraverted (Fe)		• Finding links between individuals • Aligning and harmonizing needs with relationships

1. Do I have sufficient concrete, practical, and verifiable data on the situation and on options under consideration? (Se)
2. Do I have a full understanding of the contextual factors in this situation? (Ne)
3. Do I understand the historical trends that are relevant in this situation? (Si)
4. Have I given due consideration to possible scenarios that can also explain what has happened or what could happen? (Ni)
5. Have I created (in my mind's eye, if not on paper) a grid of options, criteria, and ways to evaluate the logical merits of the situation and available options? (Te)
6. Am I clear about underlying principles and factors that affect the situation? (Ti)
7. When I take action, will I be pleased with the effect the outcomes have on those around me? Will the action represent the qualities of the relationships I want to foster? (Fe)
8. Have I adequately evaluated the alignment between the proposed courses of action and the ideals I feel are so important to uphold and value? (Fi)

Attending to these considerations will result in a more comprehensive and well-balanced decision-making process, whether you are dealing with matters at home or at work. Consider the eight mental processes as silent partners on your own personal board of directors. You can tap their wisdom more effectively by considering the questions above.

A "thought experiment" will make the point. Think about the last time you were in a conflict with someone at work and the outcome wasn't good. Apply the questions above to this situation and identify the root problem—incomplete information, incomplete scenario planning, failure to connect key dots, or simply ignoring how to link your ideals with those of the other person? How would covering these considering the eight questions individually and collaboratively have helped the situation? Usually, when you apply these questions you will see immediately what wasn't given enough attention and how that contributed to the unsatisfactory outcome. You also come to a clearer understanding of what you need to do to address the situation in the future.

Thinking about effectiveness at its most basic level, psychological type provides a framework for evaluating both the range of information we need for managing situations and the decision processes we tend to apply to those situations. Knowing and doing are the essential requirements for individual effectiveness, whether you are deciding and implementing a recycling plan at home or creating a long-term financial plan.

Being Effective in Your Career

For many people, career decisions create a complex and important list of to-dos that can greatly affect their quality of life over the span of their careers. Fortunately, psychological type can help when exploring career choices and when making decisions about how to be successful in a career.

Throughout this book we've tried to correct the common misconception that there is a direct link between type preferences (e.g., Extraversion, Sensing, Thinking) and an aptitude for various skills. For example, those who have not read this book nor had an accurate education in type theory will often assume that those with a Sensing preference are "good at" detail work such as accounting, nursing, or mechanical engineering. It's true that those with a Sensing preference are often attracted to these fields and often have strong enough interests to build skills in these areas. But this is not the same as saying that we naturally have a certain skill because of our preference or that we should "do what we are." There are no data to support a singular predictive, aptitude-driven interpretation of type preferences. Some will offer that as a criticism of the MBTI. Those people don't understand the underlying theory and model of psychological type.

The elements that go into career decisions are so complex that we discourage anyone from using type as the sole source of information when deciding on a career or when making any other kind of decision that links type preference to competencies. All types can be found in all jobs, though at different frequencies of attraction and interest. When we've interviewed different types for a given job, we have found that the primary motivation and passion for the work is type related, but that does not equate to being good at a given job. To illustrate the point, refer to Table 18, which considers trends in types, jobs, and work-related motivation.

There are several important takeaways from these trends. We can see how type preferences appear to "pull" individuals to specific kinds of jobs. *Trends are not predictions, make no assessment of aptitude, and should be seen only as clues and suggestions when considering personal work fit.* In fact, career planning is best thought of as a process similar to puzzle-working. Puzzles have a number of important parts, as characterized in Illustration 1 on page 166.

When considering careers, it is important to think about the ideal work function, work level, work competencies, and the environment (physical and mental) that are important to success. For an individual to "fit" with these other pieces, he must consider carefully his interests, working and learning style, values, achievement and affiliation needs, development and network opportunities, stressors, and personality type.[2]

Table 18
TYPES, JOBS, AND ATTRACTION—TRENDS AND PATTERNS

Type	Attracted to	Less Attracted to	Work-Related Motivation
ISTJ	Accountant	Psychotherapist	Enjoy verifiable, fact-based problem-solving
ISTP	Safety engineer	Schoolteacher	Enjoy pragmatic action with specific, useful outcomes
ESTP	Salesperson	Librarian	Enjoy action-oriented rewards
ESTJ	Bank or general project manager	Abstract sciences teacher, such as physics professor	Enjoy organizing projects, seeing productive results
ISFJ	Health services worker	Science teacher	Enjoy "hands-on" activity
ISFP	School counselor	Engineer	Enjoy encouraging others and creating comfort
ESFP	Retail manager	Laboratory aid	Enjoy personal involvement and providing immediate solutions
ESFJ	Human resources manager	Scientific researcher	Enjoy helping solve individuals' problems
INFJ	Minister or related role	School administrator	Enjoy blending ideals with helpful action
INFP	Artist or writer	Engineer	Enjoy creative expression
ENFP	Training specialist	Elementary schoolteacher	Enjoy engaging others, brainstorming ideas
ENFJ	Psychotherapist	Laboratory researcher	Enjoy facilitating personal growth
INTJ	Strategic planner	Elementary schoolteacher	Enjoy solving problems with a long-term impact
INTP	College professor	Public relations specialist	Enjoy abstract and theoretical issues, problems to solve

Table 18

TYPES, JOBS, AND ATTRACTION—TRENDS AND PATTERNS *(Continued)*

ENTP	Analyst, broker	Personnel director	Enjoy entrepreneurial activities, finding innovative solutions
ENTJ	Manager in company or other organization	Human resources worker	Enjoy complexity and solving systems problems

Make sure to connect with a career planning professional when working through these considerations. When using personality type as part of the career development puzzle, think of these applications.

- Use Table 18 to make sure you are taking into account all of the key factors in each area of the puzzle.
- Identify the attraction of your type to the career that interests you. If your type is infrequently attracted to that career, then you are likely to bring a fresh and different perspective. You are also likely to experience stressors different from those of your peers in the job. For example, the ISTJ high school counselor may find that many of her colleagues prefer ENFP, and both types can be quite successful in different ways. The ISTJ may find that she isn't stressed much by those issues that bother the ENFP (e.g., extensive documentation), while, conversely, many likely stressors for the ISTJ (e.g., emotional processes) may not be experienced as intensely by the ENFPs. Chapter 3 provides insight and suggestions as to how to be attuned to growing pressures and how to respond to them. Keep in mind that any type can be successful in any job, even while approaching the work differently; success may come *because* you approach it differently. Note that individuals who are drawn to a career and who persist in that work tend to develop deep skills and competencies in that career. Some individuals find that the work is no longer satisfying over time and seek to explore parallel work opportunities. For a handy and deeper dive into the type, college major, and career choice linkages, using an iPad application like Careerfitosity gives you critical and comprehensive type and career information at your fingertips.
- Clarify your motivations for the kind of work you want to do and focus on those things that will reinforce your sense of accomplishment and add value to your organization.

It will become critical to manage your stressors as you become aware of just how much your strategy differs from the strategies of those who are inclined

Illustration 1
THE CAREER PUZZLE

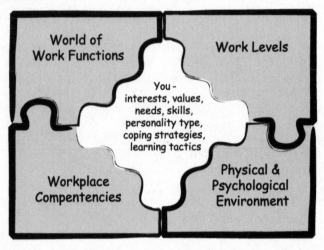

to the job by type. Later, we will look at some stress management strategies to apply at work and at home. The primary point here is discerning appropriate ways to use type to *inform* career choices, and to beware of using it as the sole data point related to your career choice. Use personality type to help navigate toward your career—not to determine your career.

For those individuals already settled in a career, the question becomes how to increase overall long-term effectiveness at work. In a major study conducted using a global corporation that systematically collected verified type data on its employees, researchers analyzed key type-related trends among the twenty-one competencies the company identified as critical to its mission. For the purposes of this chapter, only those managers who rated as high performers were included in this analysis. Therefore, though in any finite list there must be a top and bottom three competencies, in an absolute sense all are highly rated behaviors. These data points provide guidance as to the typical talents and the potential development challenges of these managers, given their types. The top and bottom three behaviors are listed in Table 19. Note that this is one of many studies that forms the basis of the Pearman Personality Integrator.

These trends, sorted by whole type, are indicative of those behaviors most frequently observed as most and least effective by colleagues who work with these individuals on a daily basis. These ratings are anonymous and were given by those who work closely with these managers—bosses, peers, direct reports, and customers. Raters are reporting what they "see" in terms of the effectiveness, rather than the frequency, of the behaviors being displayed.

Feedback from numerous sources helps to clarify the effect of our behavior on others. Knowing how our talents are received is affirming and knowing those things that others would like to see more or less of can enrich our sense of control over our destiny. It is beyond the scope of this book to give specific development strategies by type; a critical starting point is to understand the power of the trends in behavior. (Two resources, *DIY: Develop It Yourself*[3] and *YOU: Being More Effective in Your MBTI Type,*[4] can aid you in understanding these competencies and provide you with the best learning strategies for development; they can be found at the bookstore at leadership-systems.com.) Given the amount of time we spend in our work-related activities, we should make effective use of personality type as a tool to help identify areas of enrichment and satisfaction. That said, keep in mind that to be most effective we need more than our inborn preferences to find natural expression in our work; we need to use the whole array of Perceiving (knowing) and Judging (doing) processes.

Table 19[5]

TOP AND BOTTOM THREE BEHAVIOR RATINGS FOR EACH TYPE

The top-rated behaviors for each type appear in italic type; the bottom-rated behaviors appear in roman type.

ISTJ	ISFJ	INFJ	INTJ
Getting organized	*Understanding business*	*Caring about others*	*Understanding business*
Understanding business	*Getting organized*	*Relating skills*	*Getting organized*
Relating skills	*Caring about others*	*Being open and receptive*	*Making complex decisions*
Managing up	Managing up	Dealing with trouble	Creating new/ different possibilities
Inspiring others	Dealing with trouble	Making tough people calls	Delegating work
Creating new/ different possibilities	Inspiring others	Managing up	Inspiring others

ISTP	ISFP	INFP	INTP
Understanding business	*Relating skills*	*Caring about others*	*Understanding business*
Keeping on point	*Caring about others*	*Relating skills*	*Making complex decisions*
Focusing on the bottom line	*Being open and receptive*	*Understanding business*	*Keeping on point*
Demonstrating flexibility	Dealing with trouble	Managing up	Delegating work
Delegating work	Inspiring others	Dealing with trouble	Managing up
Inspiring others	Creating new/ different possibilities	Inspiring others	Inspiring others

Table 19
TOP AND BOTTOM THREE BEHAVIOR RATINGS FOR EACH TYPE *(Continued)*

ESTP	ESFP	ENFP	ENTP
Relating skills	*Relating skills*	*Relating skills*	*Relating skills*
Understanding business	*Caring about others*	*Caring about others*	*Being open and receptive*
Being open and receptive	*Being open and receptive*	*Being open and receptive*	*Understanding business*
Delegating work	Managing work processes	Dealing with trouble	Delegating work
Inspiring others	Inspiring others	Managing work processes	Making tough people calls
Creating new/ different possibilities	Creating new/ different possibilities	Making tough people calls	Inspiring others

ESTJ	ESFJ	ENFJ	ENTJ
Understanding business	*Relating skills*	*Relating skills*	*Getting organized*
Relating skills	*Caring about others*	*Caring about others*	*Understanding business*
Getting organized	*Understanding business*	*Being open and receptive*	*Relating skills*
Demonstrating flexibility	Making complex decisions	Inspiring others	Creating new/ different possibilities
Making tough people calls	Making tough people calls	Managing work processes	Dealing with trouble
Creating new/ different possibilities	Creating new/ different possibilities	Dealing with trouble	Demonstrating flexibility

Note: high and low ratings are within each type but not across the 16 types.

Constant Alarm

If our work life reflects the economic realities that affect most people today, gaining greater control over our careers is critical. Experiencing a good fit with work and knowing how to leverage our strengths and to attend to those areas that require more intentional effort means navigating "white water" regularly—white water is a rafting term that describes periods of turbulence on a river where large amounts of water are being forced through a narrow pass with multiple rocks in the way. Sound like your life? Gone are the days when our nine-to-five jobs had predictability and economic certainty. We now must bring a host of competencies to work, including being our own "brand" manager for "Me, Inc." We have to take care of this brand at the core, which means dealing with the stressors of change, ambiguity, and a host of other pressures coming at us. How we manage stress in our lives affects our performance and fulfillment at work and at home.

Whether or not we are conscious of it, our bodies are constantly monitoring, managing, and too often storing, our stress. Stress is merely the body's reaction to demands placed upon it. For example, if a job requires you to lift thirty pounds of material every twenty-five minutes, the lifting stresses the body. If you are in conflict with your romantic partner, that psychological situation stresses the body. The body's only response to stress is to dump hormones into the bloodstream to power a basic fight-or-flight response, though neither of these responses is usually productive in today's world. Our bodies keep pumping the chemicals into our systems with each stressor. The result is that we are stewing in our own juices. Literally, our internal organs are being saturated daily with chemicals they don't need at levels that are generally not conducive to good lifelong health.

Our type is relevant at a couple of levels to the stress we experience. How we perceive a stressor affects our response. For example, consider the differences in perception of a discussion between two people. Some people who observe a given discussion may perceive an intense emotional conflict between the individuals involved, while others perceive a dialogue between individuals with different opinions. Those who experience the discussion as an emotional conflict are likely to have stress responses triggered. Another important stressor is being in a role or engaged in activities that are constantly working against what is comfortable. Introverted Thinkers get worn out when they have to constantly be an expressive supporter of a team. Gaining insight on how much demand on you works against what is most comfortable leads to the nature question of identifying sources of restoration. The Pearman Personality Integrator expressly looks at this problem and its impact on well-being. Advice on learning to flex is critical to using your type effectively in this kind of stressful dynamic.

There are several levels on which we can attack the stress in our lives. First, the kind of "self-talk" we do when we experience a stressor is an initial line of attack. Second, using a range of coping resources, as identified in Table 20, to deal with the stress is vital. Finally, taking time to learn from the experience so that we can reduce the power of the stressor in the future is a longer-term prevention strategy.

Everyone, regardless of type, engages in self-talk. This is the conversation we have with ourselves in which we ask *What should I do?* or *Who should I talk* to *about this situation?* Sometimes, during our self-talk, we blame ourselves or others for our stress or our uncomfortable situation, which only compounds bad feelings. And it will not surprise anyone who has read this far that some of the self-talk is type related. For example, ST (Sensing plus Thinking) types often internalize specifics about how to do something procedurally different next time. SF (Sensing plus Feeling) types tend to reflect on whether anyone was distressed by the situation at hand. NF (Intuiting plus Feeling) types have internal talk about alignment of the situation with what they ideally want to have happen. NT (Intuiting plus Thinking) types carry on an internal discussion about the competence of themselves and others in a given situation. Add an emotional valence to this self-talk, and the stress response is triggered. These internal messages tend to elevate discomfort and simply increase the agitation you experience.

Stress is a biological reality. Using stress for helpful outcomes often means doing something different from what you used to do. As a friend of ours likes to say, "It's not about getting rid of the butterflies in your stomach, it's about making them fly in formation." In Table 20, you can see the rank order the cognitive functions of the types (i.e., ST, SF, NF, NT) give to the typical coping strategies we have available to us.

Table 20
Ranking of Coping Strategies of the Types by Cognitive Functions

	ST	SF	NF	NT
	Sensing+Thinking	Sensing+Feeling	Intuiting+Feeling	Intuiting+Thinking
1st Rank	Physical activity	Accessing others	Philosophical/ Spiritual reflection	Thinking through
2nd Rank	Thinking through	Emotions management	Emotions management	Philosophical/ Spiritual reflection
3rd Rank	Accessing others	Philosophical/ Spiritual reflection	Accessing others	Accessing others
4th Rank	Philosophical/ Spiritual reflection	Physical activity	Thinking through	Physical activity
5th Rank	Emotions management	Thinking through	Physical activity	Emotions management

All five strategies are important to draw on; however, individuals tend to lean on a strategy or two while ignoring the others. Each strategy has been shown to positively affect stress levels in the body, so a more complete strategy involves covering all the bases. As you think about your own stress management method, ask yourself: *Do I attend to all the coping strategies available to me?* These include:

- Physical activity that gives your body sufficient movement to clean your lymph system. This can be accomplished by a brisk forty-minute walk.
- Thinking through a situation to make sure you reflect on alternative meanings, factors, and options that will help you address similar situations in the future.
- Accessing others as a sounding board to share your concerns and worries, and when appropriate soliciting advice about finding solutions. See Brené Brown's research on shame and the power of reaching out when we're in a shame storm. "Shame hates being spoken. Empathy is the antidote to shame."[6]
- Philosophical or spiritual reflection to give you a new perspective. What story is your brain feeding you in an effort to keep you safe? Is it true or merely familiar? Usually, this reflective mode invites considering alternative assumptions and motives for the situation at hand. It might generate questions you need clearer answers to before taking action. "What did you mean by that?" is a constantly useful one!
- Emotions management, which means being thoughtful about your emotions, understanding the "information" in emotions, and using that information in constructive ways.[7]

These tactics and coping strategies can make a positive difference toward feeling good about your work and relationships and in maintaining your health. The demonstrable link between bad stress management and poor health makes the argument pretty easy: to heal thyself, use a range of strategies like those suggested above, and use them often.

Since first publishing this book in 1996, the mindfulness movement has gathered momentum and positive force in the United States and globally. Many important volumes citing research and lived experience are available in all the usual places. We recommend starting with the work of Kristin Neff, the pioneer and still at the forefront of the mindfulness research. She is the cofounder of the Center for Mindful Self-Compassion, where she and others are finding a powerful set of connections between self-compassion, mindfulness, and compassion for others. Layering in your type insights with a self-compassion practice is a powerful strategy for self-care in all its forms. With regular practice, stress reduction is a high-probability outcome! There is now a published compendium of professional juried research on the power of mindfulness practices on overall well-being.[8]

A set of contrasting illustrations makes the point. Jerry, an ESTJ manager, and his boss, Shari, INFJ, were talking about a new product line in their company. Jerry brought forth reams of evidence to support his suggestions for the product launch. Shari was more concerned about who was on the product launch team and whether or not effective teamwork was likely. The more Jerry focused on the numbers and Shari focused on the details of the team, the more they both felt misheard, misaligned, and thoroughly irritated. Jerry spent an extra hour at the gym working off his agitation while Shari called a peer to talk about this ongoing conflict. Of course, Jerry could have benefited from getting others' opinions and perspectives, and Shari could have benefited from thinking through the dynamics of what was happening.

Contrast this with Robert, ESTJ, and Wendy, ENFJ, in a similar product launch situation. Robert has his reams of information, and Wendy has her people concerns. Both have learned about type preferences, and both said, "Let's have a type time-out and talk about what we have here." They took time to work through the eight questions provided earlier in this chapter and realized they each had important parts of the puzzle but not the whole puzzle. This was nonetheless a high-energy situation for them both, requiring some attention to their own stress levels. Both Robert and Wendy engaged in physical exercise, met different colleagues for drinks to talk about the product launch, and reflected on the depth of knowledge and importance of their collaboration. And, most important, both returned to work the next day with a refreshed and regenerated perspective on the task at hand.

We, too, can live our lives more refreshed and regenerated on a daily basis by making sure that we use a variety of coping strategies, adjust our self-talk, and actively learn from our experiences. Using the eight questions listed on page 162 of this chapter as a debrief checklist will prove beneficial in virtually any situation you need to address.

The "There"

In the way we live our lives, we inch, slouch, or run toward our futures. We need to face a key question that matters: Will the future be what we choose rather than just what happens to us? A created life or a reported-on life? Becoming more intentional about our choices, particularly concerning career and stress management issues, is a key benefit to understanding type. With personality type, we have questions to consider that, when asked and answered, give us a more complete picture of the situations in which we find ourselves. We get glimpses into the trends and patterns that many individuals of our type find satisfying and fulfilling. And just as type provides clues about how we come to know something and how we act on our knowledge, our type approach to stress management can be unveiled for what it brings to our strategies, as well as how it may limit them.

As we suggested at the start of this chapter, being more effective is knowing what to do and doing it. With the items outlined throughout, the knowing seems pretty evident. The doing is now up to you. What will you choose?

Us: Using Personality Type to Maximize Our Collective Strengths

"Kindness is the language which the deaf can hear and the blind can see."[1]

—Mark Twain

This section examines how to apply type when communicating with others and in valuing human differences, especially as played out in generational and cultural dimensions.

8 Pathways of Communication
Type as a Lantern on the Path to Understanding
reminds us how to use type with the most important communication principles currently known.

9 Valuing Differences
Making Diversity Work
takes a look at the valuing strategies of the types and how we can use these insights to communicate greater regard for those around us.

10   What's Up, Pops?
Exploring Type and Generational Differences

challenges our assumptions about the generations and links to personality differences.

11   Across the Ponds
Using Type to Reach across Cultural Boundaries

reminds us of the complexity of culture and how type maximizes some differences while minimizing others.

Pathways of Communication

TYPE AS A LANTERN ON THE PATH TO UNDERSTANDING

Olivia Pearman, 6 years old at the time, asked her dad, Roger (coauthor of this book), a simple question: "When do I get to be a person?" Shocked, he began to wonder where he had gone wrong. After years of training in psychology and education, staying home to raise his infant children, and spending untold hours focused on his daughter's development, he found her question unthinkable. How could she doubt she was a person? Bending down to look his daughter in the face, tears welling in his eyes, he asked, "What do you mean, Olivia?" She said, "When do I get to make decisions that count?" Roger asked again, "What do you mean? What kinds of decisions would you like to make?" Olivia, looking him straight in the eye, replied, "I want a calendar and a clock!" Roger understood immediately. She had heard him make appointments and schedule meetings, so this must be what real people do—they get to use calendars and clocks! So father and daughter got in the car, drove to the nearest store, and selected a clock and calendar. Olivia still uses them daily. She would tell you that learning to schedule and manage her time enabled her to put her talents to work and graduate Phi Beta Kappa and summa cum laude from Clemson University. She earned a graduate degree from Yale and is working on a PhD. This example illustrates the communication processes with which we all live. A person gives us information and we attach certain meanings to it depending on our own experience. Until we ask for clarification from the person who sent the message, however, we cannot be sure what it really means. The swift and fluid interchange that we euphemistically call communication creates both bridges and chasms between human beings. The simple task of exchanging ideas, information, or experiences so that each person knows what the other really means turns out to be a rather complex business.

To fully understand this complexity, we must begin with the proposition that a successful communicator can communicate beyond his or her own gender, race, age, and culture, or those of the audience. Of course, these factors influence how we communicate because they affect how certain words and expressions are interpreted. Yet truly successful communication depends on taking the time to establish and agree upon certain common experiences and common interpretations of those experiences. When Olivia initiated communication with her father, each had very different experiences in mind when using the phrase "to be a person." Only when Roger took the time to find out what Olivia meant—to reach an agreement with her about the experience they were discussing—did a satisfactory outcome for the interaction become possible. The expression of information, a critical part of this dynamic, is heavily influenced by a person's psychological type and by what the person has learned.

What We All Want

Whatever the job, situation, or relationship, we all face the problems and pleasures of communication. From our research and that of many other experts in the field, and from our own personal experiences, we feel comfortable asserting that there are certain qualities in communication that most reasonable, interpersonally healthy people want to experience when they interact with others.

First, we generally want people to be trustworthy and to perceive us as being trustworthy. We also want honesty from others and the space and security within a relationship to be more honest. We want few barriers built and a joint commitment to remove any existing barriers. We want to hear from others about those things that truly interest them, and in turn we want to experience interest from others. Finally, we want to have our communication treated as it was intended—specifically, we want it understood that our constructive problem-solving is not a personal attack. As illustrated in the opening example, this wish list in communication does not always fit so easily within our communication processes. Just when we think we have given a message of trust, we learn that it has been received with doubt. When we have tried to communicate a description, we learn it has been heard as slanted in favor of a particular view. When we have tried to keep silent so that another may have space to speak of his life's interests, we learn we have been perceived as dull and uninterested.

The trick is to learn to communicate in such a way as to keep the flow of information "clean." This means being aware of how we express our thoughts and ideas as well as becoming aware of how others may express themselves.

Psychological Type as a Handle

Psychological type gives us a handle on how healthy, normal individuals usually interpret and express themselves about events. Though type preferences are not all there is to the communication equation, understanding the concepts of type provides an excellent start toward making the most of our efforts. Psychological type will give us these insights if we can begin to understand the basic elements of attention and decision-making. When efforts are made to communicate, type offers us a path toward greater understanding of people and their probable intentions. Because it is part of the fabric of everyday life, psychological type provides a rational way for individuals to reach agreement about a shared experience.

Typical patterns of attending to and deciding about information affect everything about the way individuals are attracted to, interpret, and eventually attempt to express their responses to experiences. Type furnishes us with a model for understanding those patterns; it gives us a different ear for listening and a different voice for sharing our thoughts and feelings, and it helps us gain a new perspective on some of the most difficult aspects of misunderstandings in communication.

For those seeking a quick handle on framing messages clearly to individuals whose psychological type is different, consider the iPad applications Teamosity and Relate!, which use type as the basis for enhancing communication between all type pairs. These applications take the insights from this book and extend them into very specific environments where you deal with individuals.

We Are Always Communicating Messages

We must accept that when in the presence of others, we are communicating messages all the time. Like it or not, we have no exit, no reprieve from the awareness of the other person. You can convey the message "leave me alone" or "you seem interesting" to total strangers in a theater line without a word ever being spoken. Among healthy, normal adults, whether you intend it or not, if another person believes you sent a message, then you have.* You could be minding your own business in an elevator when a dust mote irritates your

---

* Let's be clear, we are not speaking of unbalanced or predatory people who make the serendipitous eye contact of another person mean aggression or invitation. No one who has experienced unwanted attention or violence from another person "asked for it." In this context we are simply acknowledging the fact that normal functioning humans are communicating all the time and the meaning of the message is in the receiver of the message. Understanding those patterns enhances our ability to communicate more effectively.

contact lens. Completely unaware of those around you, you breathe a sigh, wink, and roll the irritated eye heavenward, all the while twitching your face in search of relief. This arouses empathy in one fellow passenger who herself is aggravated by lingering smoke on someone's coat and attributes your behavior to the same. But another passenger experiences disdain and some anxiety about riding in an elevator with someone so disturbed as to have lost control of his facial muscles. He noticed the office sign of a criminal psychologist in the building and is wondering if you are a client. Both leave your presence confident they have understood something about you, yet neither one realized that your contact lens was the source of it all. In the preconceived notions of the observer, you have been understood.

Projection Is at the Heart of It

In general terms, the word *projection* is used in psychology when discussing unconscious scripts that are brought to life on—projected onto—external circumstances. For example, if after meeting a person you begin to feel this person is unacceptable and unlikable, and if there is no basis for the feeling, you are likely to be experiencing a projection based on qualities about yourself that you dislike. When you perceive those same unacceptable qualities in the other person, your unconscious mind sees that projection (watches that movie, if you will) and swiftly informs you that you do not like that person.[1] All of this goes on unconsciously, making it difficult to immediately recognize or address.

A classic example might be the person already a bit aggravated about having to do housework who suddenly trips over his spouse's shoe in the middle of the floor. In a fit of self-righteousness, he marches out of the room to confront her over her slovenliness but finds himself facedown on the floor, toes throbbing—he's tripped over another shoe, this one his own! Part of his irrational anger over a simple shoe left on the floor is really anger at recognizing his own behavior and seeing how unattractive it is. But projection has a broader meaning than just seeing your own habits in others—it is at the core of all interactional dynamics.

Projection in this context means that each of us takes the words we hear and the actions we see and overlays our own experiences on them. For example, the word *fish* may prompt some to remember fishing by a lake, others to imagine visiting an aquarium, and still others to think about eating at a seafood restaurant. We hear the word and immediately put our experience onto it. Unless we ask the speaker for more information, our projection may give an entirely different meaning than what was intended.

Projection is a useful term because it implies connecting experience and emotion in such a way as to create meaning. Association and recognition are not the same as projection; they imply somewhat more cognitive and conscious processes. Projection is the unconscious process whereby individuals create meaning from their experiences, especially in interactions. Note, however, that the same process is at work when we are quietly alone reflecting on ideas, comments, or experiences. Projection is happening whenever we are faced with experiences, be they interactions among people or purely one-way interactions, as when reading a book, watching television, walking on the beach, or seeing a play. Projection is not always negative—far from it. It simply exists, and it must be understood if there is any hope of improving our communications.

Neuroscientists have pointed out that "words" trigger biological, neurological-based emotional reactions. These can be either positive or negative emotional moments, and, as such, the key is in how we manage these. The most powerful question we can ask ourselves is why certain words or situations prompt emotional reactions, and what does this say about us and what we need from others.

Misunderstanding Is More Than Word Confusion

Communication usually becomes an issue when there is a misunderstanding. As we have illustrated, sometimes the misunderstanding results from not having a shared meaning of the words or the tone used. More often than not, when conflict occurs due to miscommunication, we fear there is something deeper. Because of the intensity of these conflicts, it is important to find a neutral and constructive model for unraveling them. Type is such a model, and, by first looking at primary sources of misunderstanding, the usefulness of type in communication is plain to see.

Prejudice, preconception, and emotional reactions are the opposite sides of the coins of appreciation, acceptance, and positive feelings, all of which result from projections. Prejudice, preconception, and emotional reactions are the sources of misunderstanding. Prejudice, the irrational judgment of other people or situations, leads to stereotyping. We project our questions and doubts about a whole group onto any individual from that group whom we encounter. It is as if all the unique attributes of individuals within a specified group have been lumped into a chemist's beaker and cooked out; only a hard and lifeless residue remains, obstructing the flow of information, ideas, and events so that real dialogue can never take place.

Preconception, the assumption of what will be, leads to our paying attention to only the information that supports our presumed truth. Preconception is a self-congratulatory attitude that assumes rightness and knowledge. When a new situation bears any similarity to previous experience, we project our earlier learning onto it with unshakable certitude. Again, this is largely driven by a primitive brain function trying to keep us safe and rewarding us for a

181

story/pattern it recognizes. Then, because we think we know what's going on, we stop attending to any new information that could dissuade us. Sleight-of-hand artists rely on this habit in audience members to create their illusions.

Emotional reactions are those gut responses to events that bend our rationality like a prism bends light. As illustrated in chapter 6, our type plays an integral part in our emotional triggers. This distortion compromises our usual reliance on factual information to the point where the rules of fair play often become swords of righteousness. Negative emotional reactions are often the result of old, unconscious fears being projected onto new situations. For example, after a childhood of being taunted about being chubby, a father may respond emotionally and withdraw his son from a soccer team when the coach makes an offhand remark about flabby kids needing to do more work.

Prejudice, preconception, and emotional reactions are repeatedly at the heart of communication gone wrong. And, predictably, because type is foremost about cognitive style, each type is inclined toward patterns in bias and reactivity. Knowing these predictable patterns invites the possibility that we can understand their automaticity in our lives and invite alternative choices in how we react. In short, we are in psychological chains until we understand and free ourselves from the power of these biases.

Type Offers a New Language for Communicating with the World

Today, an awareness of the interdependent nature of the world calls for a new way of communication. Certainly wars still exist—more than a hundred at any given time around the globe, on average—and these are stark reminders that ancient prejudice, preconception, and emotionality are still strong and compelling in human behavior. But we know now that distant wars have local consequences; our interdependent economies require us to confront the fact that we cannot escape communicating with those who are different. As we work through these ideas, it becomes clear that psychological type offers a constructive way to communicate and to understand communication within our own culture *and across cultures* (explored more closely in chapter 11).

Type shows us new ways to speak and new ways to listen, but learning any new way of communication requires patience, awareness of communication mechanisms, and a willingness to be open to new insights. The insights of psychological type inform us of both the ways we misunderstand and of the ways we may eventually communicate more constructively. Type teaches us to apply the old carpenters' rule—measure twice, cut once—to interactions. In other words, we must be very sure what other people mean when they use a given word or phrase, and only take action after we've reached a mutual understanding.

Through development of a mature understanding of our own processes and of the complexity of life, we are able to escape the narrow confines of the boundaries cast by prejudice, preconception, and emotionality. But to bring light to the darkness inherent in unconscious processes, we must be willing to expose them, recognize them, integrate them, and move on to develop other parts of ourselves. Our emergence and our struggle throughout life depend on the drive to specialize, to become so good at what we do that we do it with grace and ease. One outcome of this emergence, of this specialization, is the further development of type preferences and behaviors.

Preferences Lead to Focus

Preferences for left- or right-handedness, for certain colors, or for certain foods all serve the individual. These preferences allow for specialization, for focus. In the same way, psychological type is the by-product of preferences and habits of mind that mold our expressions. In the first part of this book, we argued that psychological type is another example of the evolution of the human psyche. As basic as collecting energy, sorting perceptions, and making judgments may be, these are also the mechanisms that forge, among many human qualities, our prejudices, preconceptions, and emotions.

An Argument

The scene: two men are having an argument. One is very tough-minded, logical, impersonal, objective, and arrogant. The other is very accommodating, responsive, personal, and somewhat subservient. Their differences are so striking that they seem funny.

The action: suddenly, the second man hits and knocks out the arrogant logician. Everyone applauds the gentle man for clobbering the logician, but he is filled with remorse for harming another human being. He quickly departs but returns with a gift and an apology for his victim. However, the tough man states that he was satisfied that they had settled the issue like men. He rejects the other's "pity" and protests the insult. Stunned, the accommodating character leaves, stuttering, disoriented, and disbelieving that his motive could be so misunderstood.

The explanation: though not delivered here with clever dialogue and exaggerated antics, this scene from a recent situation comedy captures a number of very important issues in communication. The interpersonal styles of the characters are so different that they are disgusted with each other. It did not appear that the events of the scene should lead to violence and misunderstanding, but when both men unwittingly projected their various meanings onto the events the result was virtually inescapable.

We constantly live out the idea that what we believe to be true actually is true—our perceptions become our realities—and as rational human beings we take action based on reality. Because each perceived the other as the enemy, both men generated a great deal of emotional heat between them. The fight was perceived by one as the just settlement of their disagreement, while the other saw it as a demoralizing event. The gift was a peace offering to the one giving it, pity to the recipient. These two men were both raised in the same culture, even attended the same schools, but are as different as people from separate countries. They do not see the world the same way. Messages were sent but not received in the manner in which they were intended.

Our Precarious Balance

As in the sitcom scene, there is a precarious balance in every interaction. Whether we like it or not, we are sending messages all the time. Some we intend, others we are unaware of. Most projections are created by integrating verbal content, tone, emotional expression, appearance, and delivery. Simply being in a room with another person is going to send a message, so learning how to appropriately direct the message is very important. We make a serious error when we assume that the person we are talking to is indeed receiving the exact message we intended to send.

Useful Utterances

Every day we assume our utterances are understood. Like the habits of mind that make up our psychological type, we unconsciously assume people know what we mean when we are sharing information. By watching how people respond to or act on our words, we get feedback that the message was received and understood. But what of the messages from which we get no feedback?

Which aspects of our communication style trigger another's reaction that leads to a misunderstanding? How about our interpretation of others' messages? How often do we check them out? How aware are we of our own reactions and of how these reactions affect our judgments? The proliferation of communication platforms over the years since the first edition of this book was published only add to this dilemma. Years ago in the early days of email, we did a conference presentation entitled "Your Technologies Are Communicating, How About Your People? Is Faster Always Better?" Little did we know then the avalanche of "communication" tools in the mountain of snow above our heads!

Fortunately, psychological type can help us unravel many issues and encourages us to develop a constructive interpersonal style that avoids unnecessary misunderstandings—and possibly a few broken noses! For if communication begins with internal projection, we need to know what signals are hitting the screen, so to speak. Psychological type suggests that we can identify, understand, and constructively use differences among the types in communication patterns. Through type we can get a handle on some of the typical prejudices, preconceptions, and emotional "buttons" of most people. In short, we have a pathway to understand the kinds of images and associations different types tend to make, which in turn lead to the projection of meaning in communication. So we have a cycle: we project what we learn, we learn from what we are, we are at least partly the outcome of the preferences we live out in daily life—and the way we live feeds what we learn. And so it goes, on and on.

If, for example, we learn at an early age that people are to be mistrusted and treated with suspicion, we tend to see others' behaviors as having bad intentions and ulterior motives. Consequently, we withhold information from people and protect ourselves in ways that are likely to elicit responses that support our suppositions. If our preference is for Extraversion, we may express our distrust energetically; if we are Introverted, we may simply become too anxious around others to engage them. In either case, the results are the same: we project certain meaning onto another person's behavior, we behave ourselves in a way that supports our assumptions, and we receive confirmation that our projection was correct.

Obviously relationships are never this simple, and the cycle is often transformed. This usually comes about through people changing their projections. One way this occurs is by observing others and seeing the outcomes of their different behavior. Another is when the process and projections are exposed and individuals look at their behavior and decide to change it. Bringing light to the darkness, as Jung put it, is a difficult process but very productive for personal growth and relationship enrichment.[2] See the writing process suggestion in chapter 6 for capturing our own cycle of internal dialogue with the hope of taking a different look at it, once it's on the page.

What We Learn

To enrich the communication cycle, we must first acknowledge we are in it, identify other ways to react, and consciously seek those lessons we have avoided. For example, if you have avoided learning about communication skills because you thought they were soft disciplines, chances are you think of yourself as tough-minded and are drawn to things that reinforce your perception. You would certainly be startled if, after twenty years of marriage, your spouse were to say that communication with you has been nearly impossible and, as a result, wants to leave the relationship. Whatever lessons we avoid along the way usually become more costly lessons later. So if only for efficiency's sake, as you study the following pages on the communication issues of the 16 types and again in chapter 9, when valuing differences is explored, you might ask yourself what lessons you have been avoiding.

In the pages ahead we look at the general communication style of each of the preferences and then of the 16 whole types. We reflect on the lessons each is drawn to and on those typically avoided in communications with others. Before we can see the positive contributions of those whose preferences are different from our own, we must first understand the component parts and then the dynamic whole of each type. Understanding, however, is not the same as valuing; this issue is covered in the next chapter.

What We Are

So far, we have asserted that: (1) when two or more people are together, communication is an ongoing fact, whether we are trying to send messages or not; (2) projection is at the root of all communication—we hear or see something and project our meaning onto it; (3) most misunderstandings occur because of prejudice, preconception, and emotional reactivity, which are opposite the honesty, candor, and openness we generally want in relationships; (4) how we express ourselves, what we project, and part of our prejudices, preconceptions, and emotional reactions are related to our psychological type; and (5) psychological type can help us rationally understand our expressions and projections in constructive ways and can also help us listen to others more effectively.

Remembering that type is all about how we usually attend to information, what we attend to, how we decide, and how we act on what we believe to be true, we will explore type's contribution to communication first by exploring the preferences singly and then by studying the more important and complex effects of type dynamics.

We assert that the richness of the whole type (e.g. INFP) is vital in getting to the deep roots of effective communication. It is understandable that the general approach to looking at type is at a basic preference (e.g. E or I, S or N, etc) level provides a foundation of understanding. Note that the following dimensions common to most psychological type inventories, which are primarily based on Jung's theory, are simply the first steps in getting to the richness of type differences in communication:

- Extraverting: Seeking and initiating in the environment
- Introverting: Receiving and reflecting on the environment
- Sensing: Attraction to data from present-oriented experiences, often seeking pragmatic and realistic information
- Intuiting: Attraction to ideas about future possibilities, seeing patterns, seeking abstract and theoretical information
- Thinking: Deciding by logical arguments; often critical and analytical
- Feeling: Deciding by value, relational arguments; often accommodating

- Judging: Acting in a decisive way, either in an analytical or a value-oriented way
- Perceiving: Acting in an emergent, go-with-the-flow way; primarily conscious of either the present or the imagined future

Communication Effects of Extraversion/Introversion

By habit, Extraverts tend to express themselves freely. They are so comfortable initiating in their environment that they assume everyone else is, too. Further, a lack of immediate reaction from Extraverts usually occurs when they do not trust a situation (or person) or when they feel incapable of making a reasonable response. Aware of this personal discomfort, they often assume that when they see someone else who is not immediately responsive, or who appears cautious, that person must also be uncomfortable, worried, and possibly slow or only moderately competent in the situation.

Notice the ease with which the Extravert's experience becomes the baseline for judging others' reactions. This is the nature of projection. It is an unconscious process that colors our understanding. It may well be the Extravert's first unspoken prejudice; understanding is based on what the Extravert is comfortable with, rather than what may be true for an Introvert.

For example, a consultant we know had been working with a group of managers on a regular basis over several months. On a break during one session, the supervisor of the group approached the consultant with a smug grin and said, "You know, John, I've finally figured out why I don't trust people like you!" Somewhat taken aback, John nonetheless remembered his own lessons well enough to ask, "What do you mean by that?" The supervisor said, "I've been watching you for all these months now, and I've finally figured it out. Whenever one of my managers asks you a question, you always pause before you respond. I can see the gears turning in your head, and that pausing tells me you're withholding information from my people. I don't trust anyone who doesn't tell me all they know." This was all John needed to understand what was going on. He said, "George, if I ask you a question and you pause before responding, could I trust your response to be the whole truth?" George replied quickly, "Absolutely not. If I can't answer immediately, that means I have a hidden agenda to sort through before I can formulate a verbal response." "Aha!" John said. "Just because that's true for you doesn't mean it is for me. Remember our sessions on type a few months ago? As I recall, your preference is for Extraversion. Mine is for Introversion. All I can tell you is that when someone asks me a question, it's like a marble being dropped into one of those multilevel puzzles with holes in each layer. It starts rolling around, finds the hole and drops to the next layer, finds the hole there and drops through to the next layer, and

187

so forth until it falls out the bottom. When it falls out, I have a response. I am not consciously withholding anything. Nor am I stupid or slow. I simply prefer to process internally before I respond. In fact, if I respond too quickly, it may mean I have a prefabricated answer that has been designed to cover something up!" As the truth of this explanation dawned on him, George began to turn very pale. John touched him on the arm and asked what was wrong. George whispered, ashamed, "I can't tell you how many people I've fired because I thought I couldn't trust them."

Consider the converse situation, in which a person with Introverted preference observes an Extravert initiating and moving through many interactions in a short period of time. The Introvert may view such behavior as superficial. Keep in mind that an Introvert engaged in this behavior may indeed feel shallow and, therefore, assumes others would feel the same. The Introvert's baseline is all wrong for making sense of the Extravert's behavior.

Missed Associations

Whatever a person's preference, the behavior of a person with the opposite preference can seem inconsistent and out of sync with our experience. Never mind that the associations being made by both parties may be all wrong. It's no wonder such a situation can lead to complete misjudgments. Given the studies showing that we assess and make up our minds about people within thirty seconds of meeting them, it seems important to keep this kind of cross-preference projection in mind. It is most pronounced between Extraversion and Introversion, but missed associations happen at every level between individual preferences and among whole types. It is therefore vital to know that the message you intend to send may not be reaching your audience.

With Extraverts' typical hunger for pace, variation, and expressive engagement, it is easy to see how they can get into trouble with other types in important relationships at work or at home. The energy Extraverts put into engaging in the world may be interpreted by Introverts in their life as leaving little energy for them. Likewise, the Extravert may feel that the energy an Introverted partner puts into internal analysis denies him the important insights needed to solve the problem before them.

It is safe to assume that people engaged in the environment and interacting with others are expressing Extraversion. In that mode, their comments may simply be the beginning or middle of a thought, not the end. They may be probing for reactions, and if so their comments may have no more significance than to simply spur the conversation. Extraverts are constantly misunderstood as meddling, opinionated, and forceful, but if you listen carefully and keep your judgments in check, you may hear information that reveals richness of thought and the intent of the message.

When individuals are observant, are careful about word choice, and seem somewhat disengaged, it is reasonable to assume they are expressing Introversion. In this mode, their comments are usually the end parts of their thoughts. Unless they tell you otherwise, what comes out verbally is typically their most complete thought on the topic for the time being. Receptive and appearing cautious, they are simply trying to create space in their environment to let their heads work. Typically oblivious to being seen as guarded, their pace may simply allow their minds to be undistracted as they sort through their experiences. They generally share what is important to them, and if you listen carefully you will get a very good idea of their mind-set and perspective. They are not holding back, necessarily; they are simply sorting through all the internal static to become clear on what to finally say. Often misunderstood as aloof, condescending, and anxious, Introverts are actually creating the time and space needed to respond to the experience they are having.

Communication Effects of Sensing and Intuiting

If the differences between Extraversion and Introversion lead to misunderstandings about the value and meaningfulness of shared information, the differences between Sensing and Intuiting hit at the heart of trust and honesty. There is no more profound difference in communication than the projections developed by these preferences, because they are at the root of building our understanding of reality.

The Essence of Sensing

Sensing, by its nature, finds the information of the moment clear, concise, and concrete. A person with this preference is likely to have an appreciation for brief statements describing the who, what, where, when, how, why, and relative status of the situation. Studies of military personnel consistently show that a large proportion of them report having a Sensing preference: order, precision, focus, and immediate action are hallmark qualities.[3] Military forms must be filled out with exact information; they do not ask what you think was going on in the heads of folks involved in an incident. Fidelity to the facts of the present is bedrock Sensing.

Contrasting Intuiting

Nothing could be further from the primary attention of Intuiting than fidelity to facts. For Intuiting, a fact only begins to have meaning in the context of situations; thus, from the Intuitive perspective, the interpretation of a fact may change as the context shifts, and more often than not focusing on facts creates·

189

barriers to new ideas. Those with an Intuitive preference are more inclined to imagine potential outcomes, extrapolate about events and people's motives, and look for information that confirms the reigning theory (about people, situations, or other things). More important to such folks than facts is whether certain perceived principles were honored.

Imagine a meeting of a business team in which three members have a Sensing preference and two have an Intuitive preference. The discussion could be filled with a considerable amount of conflict if one cluster wants to focus on the realistic, present-oriented, concrete elements of a problem and the other two seek to develop multiple alternatives to solve the problem at some point in the future. The abstraction and theoretical interests of the Intuitive will be evident in the language and the questions used during the discussion. Depending on how critical the situation is, these pressures could drive these two groups into heated and difficult conflict as each group believes the other is focusing on the wrong set of issues.

A sense of the pragmatic versus a sense of the possible will always stymie interactions between Sensing and Intuitive types until they are cognizant of each other. In fact, each can easily begin to believe the other is idiotic. Sensing types are often baffled at the language used by Intuitives and at their apparent focus on the future, the theoretical, and the abstract. "How can a simple question generate so much stuff?" Sensing types often wonder. "Why can't they see more in this information, see its paradoxical meaning?" say Intuitives about Sensing types. Because the influence of perception is the fountainhead to the operation of the psyche, these differences are profound. And the profound nature of these differences can be seen in the speed with which distrust can be created among people of goodwill.

Communication Effects of Thinking and Feeling

If Sensing and Intuiting perceptions are at the heart of trust in communication, then Thinking and Feeling are critical to the communication of mutual respect. Thinking types often show their interest and enthusiasm by critiquing their experiences and the information put in front of them. Feeling types, by contrast, show their interest and enthusiasm by identifying and expressing appreciation for important aspects of their experiences and the information put before them.

"Stepping Out" for Clarity

Trying to step out of the situation in which they find themselves in order to gain clarity, individuals with a Thinking preference seek to find criteria that can frame information and experience in such a way that there is a sense of objective analysis. It seems objective because of the logical, orderly manner in which situations are reviewed. Folks with a Thinking preference put enormous effort into looking at the pros and cons of a situation, analyzing how things are related, and proposing principles to guide their thoughts.

"Stepping In" for Awareness

Those with a Feeling preference want to step into a situation and gain a very specific awareness of how people in the situation are affected. Feeling types immediately focus on the consequences of contemplated actions or real choices in terms of the people involved. Acutely aware that reasoned criteria are valuable for decisions, those with a Feeling preference have an automatic personal value system that places specific human well-being above any externally imposed system of analysis. Knowing full well the argument that decisions are made in business to ensure the well-being of the greatest number of employees, the Feeling type's concern for the outcomes on individual human beings nevertheless remains undaunted.

There is often the danger, when exploring Thinking and Feeling, of people taking the definitions too far. Thinking types have feelings and values that inform their analysis; Feeling types use reason and logic to assist their judgment. But the primary basis of the judgment they use is profoundly different.

Define Conflict and Give Three Examples

When people grouped together by preference along this dimension are asked to define conflict and give three examples, they consistently respond in the following general ways.

Thinking types: Conflict exists whenever two or more people disagree for so long that emotions get involved. It is often very productive and useful and enables us to get to the heart of issues and make better decisions. Take, for example, some wars that are very useful, some corporate actions that are critical to competitiveness, and even some vigorous arguments at home that clear the air.

Feeling types: Conflict exists when we disagree. It is often avoided because of the discomfort it creates. It is rarely useful and gets in the way. A clear example is the conflict evident when people argue or debate.

Can individual realities be so different? Driven by a framework of fair play, those with a Thinking preference are inclined to assume that everyone values that playing field. Focused on a value of avoiding harm to others, those with a Feeling preference naturally assume that anyone choosing to make others uncomfortable simply does not honor other people over their need to be right or correct. Consider this dialogue:

Teacher:	I had to fail three students last year in my English class. I've seen those kids since then and I worry about their self-esteem.
Principal:	You shouldn't worry about them. They chose not to do the work. We need to be careful not to let our emotions override standards for performance.
Teacher:	First of all, I said they failed, so my standards are very much in place. Second, my emotions are not involved with these students, as you're suggesting, but they are getting involved with this discussion.
Principal:	I was merely trying to make the point that standards are important.
Teacher:	I was merely pondering whether we are attending to the self-esteem of these kids so they will grow up to be caring and productive adults! I don't need to justify my feelings or my standards.

Potential Loss of Respect

The teacher's comments are a fairly typical Feeling reaction, and the principal's responses are a fairly typical Thinking reaction. This type of interaction leads to the false conclusion that one does not really respect the other. It would be easy for either one to walk away with the awareness of being misunderstood and perhaps even feeling unappreciated. And as we noted at the beginning of this section, this dimension has the greatest effect on the sense of mutual respect between people during interactions. Often the source of considerable interpersonal pain and discomfort, the language of Thinking and Feeling prompts deeply felt reactions.

If the role of projection is as critical as it seems, the loss of respect between persons with these differences is understandable. Because the Thinking type judgment process relies on logic, it quickly and constructively responds to a logical presentation of information. Thinking types tend to communicate respect to a person whose presentation is elegantly logical, that is, with the conclusion following efficiently from the premise without the static of interpersonal overtones or caveats. We know that a Thinking type is dedicated to and even passionate about things when he or she thoroughly critiques them. Thinking types report that they know a person respects them when they receive thorough and constructive feedback about what they can do to improve the next presentation or project.

On the other hand, Feeling types have enormous energy associated with the awareness of accepting and being accepted. They tend to communicate respect through acceptance. Often what Feeling types most want in an interaction, before continuing a discussion, is an initial indication that the other individual finds them acceptable as a person.

Feeling types say that they know a person respects them when the feedback is initially about the importance of the individual contribution and effort before discussing the range of improvements that could be made in a presentation or project.

Communication Effects of Judgment and Perception

Isabel Briggs Myers carried Jung's theory of types to its fullest extension by focusing on the dynamic within each type. As discussed earlier, we Extravert either Judgment or Perception and Introvert the opposite of what is Extraverted. Myers had to struggle with how to get at such subtle distinctions when constructing the MBTI inventory. We developed the following material about her Judging-Perceiving dimension to identify the preferred mental function in the Extraverted mode. For example, Myers's assumption is that an ENFP Extraverts Intuiting and Introverts Feeling. But like the other dimensions at the core of psychological type, this carries with it another layer of interactional issues. With this exploration we begin wading into the dynamics of the types.

Judgment in the Extraverted mode, whether Thinking or Feeling, is an orientation toward observable decision-making. The attraction of closure is strong for those who Extravert their Judgment function. Often desirous of a methodical and systematic approach, those who sort Judgment on the Myers-Briggs Type Indicator instrument are indicating that you are likely to see and hear decisive action from them.[4] The message often received by others who run into Extraverted Judgment is one of eagerness to decide and make progress and bare tolerance of anything that slows down the action.

Decision Now or Later

Those who Extravert Perception give the message that they are concerned about the negative consequences of making premature decisions. Preferring to trust information whether it is data specific or impressionistic, they find almost any information useful and tend to seek out interactions that move among several different topics before settling on any given one. This often annoys those who are ready to make something happen now by making a decision.

Unfortunately, given the speed with which decisions about other people are made upon first meeting them, this observable behavior can trigger all kinds of preconceptions. Extraverted Perceptive types often see those with Extraverted Judgment as rigid, dogmatic, and pushy; Extraverted Judgers often see those with Extraverted Perception as ineffectual, inefficient laggards. For example, in a committee meeting where a person who Extraverts Judgment (ET, EF) wants a time limit for discussion on each topic, often the Extraverted Perceiver (EN, ES) will object that doing so feels confining and could cause the group to lose out on important late-breaking information. When the Extraverted Perceiver wants to keep the discussion going past the agreed-upon time, often the Extraverted Judger feels that the other person is wasting time, looking at irrelevant material, and waiting too long to act.

Value of Type Dynamics in Communication

This look at the dimensions of type—Extraversion, Introversion, Sensing, Intuiting, Thinking, Feeling, and Myers's Judgment and Perception qualities—leads to the core issue in using type constructively in communication: the dynamics of the types. While the broad necessities of communication—trust, honesty, and respect—are certainly influenced by the expression of the preferences, the more complex and often truer examination of communication is discovered by analyzing the types' dynamics.

In case you have skipped ahead to this chapter without reviewing the basics, here is a brief review: each of the 16 types is a combination of the uses of Extraverted and Introverted Judgment and Perception. For easy reference, the constellation of types follows. Keep in mind that the Extraverted functions play the most observable initial role in our efforts to communicate with others.

	Lead Function	Support Function
ISTJ	Introverted Sensing (S i)	Extraverted Thinking (T e)
ISFJ	Introverted Sensing (S i)	Extraverted Feeling (F e)
INFJ	Introverted Intuiting (N i)	Extraverted Feeling (F e)
INTJ	Introverted Intuiting (N i)	Extraverted Thinking (T e)
ISTP	Introverted Thinking (T i)	Extraverted Sensing (S e)
ISFP	Introverted Feeling (F i)	Extraverted Sensing (S e)
INFP	Introverted Feeling (F i)	Extraverted Intuiting (N e)
INTP	Introverted Thinking (T i)	Extraverted Intuiting (N e)
ESTP	Extraverted Sensing (S e)	Introverted Thinking (T i)
ESFP	Extraverted Sensing (S e)	Introverted Feeling (F i)
ENFP	Extraverted Intuiting (N e)	Introverted Feeling (F i)
ENTP	Extraverted Intuiting (N e)	Introverted Thinking (T i)
ESTJ	Extraverted Thinking (T e)	Introverted Sensing (S i)
ESFJ	Extraverted Feeling (F e)	Introverted Sensing (S i)
ENFJ	Extraverted Feeling (F e)	Introverted Intuiting (N i)
ENTJ	Extraverted Thinking (T e)	Introverted Intuiting (N i)

Informational Projections as Influenced by Type

By now you have sorted yourself several times while reading this book, and perhaps you have completed a psychological type inventory; thus you have some initial hypothesis of your type preferences. If we want to learn how to listen closely to other people, and in so doing learn the general content of their thought and the intent of their communication, we need to know the way information is generally sorted and saved. For example, if I know you are attracted to information that is testable and verifiable, and that you associate precision in details with clarity of judgment, it would benefit our interaction for me to strive to express information in those ways. Further, if you tend to express or react in a calm, unassuming manner, chances are good that attempting to wow you with status, credentials, and prestige will not be effective in establishing credibility.

Credibility is established through the verifiable and precise data presented in the interaction. Table 21 reviews the information attractive to, associations made by, and expressions common to each of the 16 types. Specifically, we explore the role of the types' dynamics in basic informational projections, preferred relationship qualities, typical emotional buttons, and constructive reframing of communications. These are the bases by which people make projections on the information they get while interacting with others.

As you review the expressions of the types, consider both your type and the expressions of those with whom you interact every day. The information individuals find interesting is likely to be part of their outlook and conversations. Associations individuals make about their experience determine a good deal about what they are willing to listen to in conversations and presentations. Finally, how people express themselves is unique to the individual, but there is enough consistency among same-type individuals to free us from instantly judging the intent of their remarks. Table 21 is based on four decades of questioning and listening to hundreds of each of the 16 types.

TABLE 21
TYPE PATTERNS OF INFORMATION PROJECTIONS

ISTJ	
Introverted Sensing with Extraverted Thinking	
Information attracted to	Tested and verifiable data that are easily analyzed
Associations made	Precision in detail leads to clarity of thought
Expressions offered	Generally present oneself in an unassuming manner, preferring to express information in a calm, careful way

TABLE 21
TYPE PATTERNS OF INFORMATION PROJECTIONS *(Continued)*

ISFJ

Introverted Sensing with Extraverted Feeling

Information attracted to	Consistent and reliable data that aid people
Associations made	Steady and realistic information leads to loyalty
Expressions offered	Generally fastidious, careful, preferring to express information about people in an unhurried fashion

INFJ

Introverted Intuiting with Extraverted Feeling

Information attracted to	Ideas related to people; idealistic belief in theory
Associations made	Actions reflect motives
Expressions offered	Generally appreciative in comments and, though often appearing somewhat scholarly, are quite inclusive and warm

INTJ

Introverted Intuiting with Extraverted Thinking

Information attracted to	Theories supported by analytical thought and systematic evidence examined by a variety of sources
Associations made	Reasonableness and mental versatility lead to real contributions
Expressions offered	Usually observations contain a formula about their experiences; action-oriented comments are quite systematic

ISTP

Introverted Thinking with Extraverted Sensing

Information attracted to	Present, thorough data that show who, what, when, where, and how
Associations made	Detached analysis focused on practical issues leads to clarity about what should be done when
Expressions offered	Often quiet organizers of data, they ask questions to get specificity about the situation they are in; when talking, they make practical observations

TABLE 21
TYPE PATTERNS OF INFORMATION PROJECTIONS *(Continued)*

INTP

Introverted Thinking with Extraverted Intuiting

Information attracted to	Theories, models, and imaginative connections among ideas
Associations made	Independent skeptical thought will provide a better analysis of a situation
Expressions offered	Initially critical and skeptical in comments; detachedly curious about situations

---

ISFP

Introverted Feeling with Extraverted Sensing

Information attracted to	Pragmatic information that is related to other people
Associations made	Thorough, reliable information will provide for realistic action
Expressions offered	Warmth and good-natured conversation seem easy; comments are gentle, factual, realistic

---

INFP

Introverted Feeling with Extraverted Intuiting

Information attracted to	Drawn to information that is reflective of values
Associations made	Introspective consideration of circumstances will lead to ideas that promote harmony and innovation
Expressions offered	Often deferent in interactions; comments seem unconventional; identify and express complex ideas

ESTP

Extraverted Sensing with Introverted Thinking

Information attracted to	Present-oriented, practical data that aids action now
Associations made	Reliable and thorough action now will secure a realistic future in relationships and work
Expressions offered	Generally engaging with practical suggestions, though critical and forceful comments may be made

TABLE 21
TYPE PATTERNS OF INFORMATION PROJECTIONS *(Continued)*

ESFP

Extraverted Sensing with Introverted Feeling

Information attracted to	Data about people and their situations
Associations made	Knowing who, what, where, and when will show care and concern for the well-being of others
Expressions offered	Energetic observations about people and how to aid them in taking the next practical action

ENFP

Extraverted Intuiting with Introverted Feeling

Information attracted to	Ideas that promote selected values
Associations made	Active, enthusiastic sharing is resourceful
Expressions offered	Verbally fluent information that is friendly and directed toward harmonious interaction

ENTP

Extraverted Intuiting with Introverted Thinking

Information attracted to	Ideas that are fresh and original
Associations made	Uninhibited analysis will lead to resourceful and adaptable choices
Expressions offered	Independent-minded, imaginative, and clever comments; like to question situations but ultimately look for a strategy to competently adapt

ESTJ

Extraverted Thinking with Introverted Sensing

Information attracted to	Verifiable data collected in a systematic way
Associations made	Logical and tested options provide for practical action
Expressions offered	Energetic, analytical observations that are practical and critical and show concern for realistic action

TABLE 21
TYPE PATTERNS OF INFORMATION PROJECTIONS *(Continued)*

ENTJ

Extraverted Thinking with Introverted Intuiting

Information attracted to	Analytical information derived from systematic observation
Associations made	Conceptual frameworks that make sense of experience are indicative of a resourceful mind
Expressions offered	Critical about situations and options; often seem impatient to others; value intellectual matters, leading to comments that give formula-like responses

ESFJ

Extraverted Feeling with Introverted Sensing

Information attracted to	Data connecting with people issues and problems
Associations made	Sociable and friendly comments promote cooperation and realistic action
Expressions offered	Often expressive and affiliative in interaction; sympathetic but cooperative action-oriented remarks

ENFJ

Extraverted Feeling with Introverted Intuiting

Information attracted to	Ideas and abstractions that help make people understandable
Associations made	Warm, caring people who are idealistic can make important social contributions
Expressions offered	Expressive and sociable in interactions, but some formality in comments; appreciative of others; often make comments that get at the heart of the issue

This information about the way type influences communication gives us an extraordinary opportunity to listen anew to comments made by others. It's a mine-free, efficient pathway to understand the differences between people that so often lead relationships into trouble. With some patience—a mental counting to ten—we can avoid unnecessary confusion in our efforts to communicate. The hints listed above give us a way, based on psychological type, to present and hear information without blame or judgment. At the very least we can see that there are so many differences it would behoove us to take the time to ask, "What did you mean by that?" and then *really listen to the response.*

Preferred Relationship Qualities as Influenced by Type

Assuming that most normal, healthy relationships have trustful, honest, and nonjudgmental aspects to them, it would be valuable to know how people with vastly different habits of mind experience these qualities. Such insight makes it easier to communicate in ways that promote mutual understanding.

When we have the experience of being told we are untrustworthy, and there is no basis for this observation, it is surprising and often disquieting to us. One of our working assumptions is that normal people like to be seen as trustworthy and that there is bewilderment at being seen otherwise. In a similar fashion, people like to be thought of as honest. Being honest means that your comments do not conceal your agenda. Additionally, most people like their comments to be heard as perceptions based on their experience rather than accusations or judgments about others. We may be stunned to learn that a comment intended as a statement of how we see a situation was instead taken personally. Table 22 lists how the types experience these three qualities. It is important and exciting to report that exploring these qualities with people with whom you have relationships can dramatically aid in actually creating trust, honesty, and nonjudgmental communication.

TABLE 22
TYPE PATTERNS IN KEY RELATIONSHIP QUALITIES

	ISTJ
Introverted Sensing with Extraverted Thinking	
Trust	Information shared over time that is consistent
Honesty	Precision, accuracy, and timeliness
Nonjudgmental	Direct, concise, descriptive comments
	ISFJ
Introverted Sensing with Extraverted Feeling	
Trust	People who are reliable and who do what they say they will do
Honesty	Show me and tell me and I'll know your honest feelings
Nonjudgmental	Sympathetic expressions of practical, hands-on caring

TABLE 22
TYPE PATTERNS IN KEY RELATIONSHIP QUALITIES *(Continued)*

INFJ	
Introverted Intuiting with Extraverted Feeling	
Trust	Values that promote human well-being
Honesty	Recognize the effects of their comments on individuals
Nonjudgmental	Feelings and ideas that are persistently applied

INTJ	
Introverted Intuiting with Extraverted Thinking	
Trust	Analytical frameworks freely offered and based on data
Honesty	Connecting actions, motives, and outcomes in situations
Nonjudgmental	Specific observations about patterns and how these affect systems

ISTP	
Introverted Thinking with Extraverted Sensing	
Trust	Information derived from experience
Honesty	Precise observations about current situations
Nonjudgmental	Candid statement about what is currently happening

INTP	
Introverted Thinking with Extraverted Intuiting	
Trust	Good sound theory supported by analytical observations
Honesty	Find paradox more honest than factual accounts
Nonjudgmental	Critical review of models and information that is validating

TABLE 22
TYPE PATTERNS IN KEY RELATIONSHIP QUALITIES *(Continued)*

	ISFP
	Introverted Feeling with Extraverted Sensing
Trust	Actions that help people
Honesty	Show intentions in actions, not in words
Nonjudgmental	Lessons on how to care successfully

	INFP
	Introverted Feeling with Extraverted Intuiting
Trust	Personal Intuitings about people and situations
Honesty	Reflective summary of thoughts and ideas
Nonjudgmental	Actions that avoid causing harm may result in not sharing data

	ESTP
	Extraverted Sensing with Introverted Thinking
Trust	Precision in the moment; concise interactions
Honesty	Good-natured interactions recognizing the pace of change
Nonjudgmental	Focus on the moment by attending to specifics

	ESFP
	Extraverted Sensing with Introverted Feeling
Trust	Consistent sharing over time
Honesty	Telling the facts, tempered with concern for others' reactions
Nonjudgmental	Caring for others, enjoying the moment, arousing liking in people

	ENFP
	Extraverted Intuiting with Introverted Feeling
Trust	Enthusiastic engagement related to selective values
Honesty	Sharing the big picture, touching on the human side of the image
Nonjudgmental	Perpetual innovation as a resourceful act

TABLE 22
TYPE PATTERNS IN KEY RELATIONSHIP QUALITIES *(Continued)*

ENTP	
Extraverted Intuiting with Introverted Thinking	
Trust	Consistent competent analysis
Honesty	Acknowledging the complexity of information without simplifying
Nonjudgmental	Critique as part of the analysis needed to adapt

ESTJ	
Extraverted Thinking with Introverted Sensing	
Trust	Tested data presented in a realistic manner
Honesty	Careful but often direct feedback
Nonjudgmental	Critique and analysis as a way to develop loyalty

ENTJ	
Extraverted Thinking with Introverted Intuiting	
Trust	Energetic critical analysis that is theory-based
Honesty	Expressive about perceived motives and theoretical thoroughness
Nonjudgmental	Reasonable and mentally versatile critiquing to achieve results

ESFJ	
Extraverted Feeling with Introverted Sensing	
Trust	Friendly and inclusive interactions addressing human concerns
Honesty	Unassuming descriptions that support conventions
Nonjudgmental	Exploring ideas through facts as a way to get cooperative action

TABLE 22
TYPE PATTERNS IN KEY RELATIONSHIP QUALITIES *(Continued)*

	ENFJ
	Extraverted Feeling with Introverted Intuiting
Trust	Cooperative interactions that are sympathetic to people
Honesty	Sharing the way information and reactions support or discount others
Nonjudgmental	Expressiveness and gregariousness as a way to gain information

The Only Way We Know How

The way we express trust and what we seek out as trusting are essentially the same. Those who trust information that has been consistent over time are also likely not to trust so easily those who innovate, where little is consistent over time. The reverse is also true: those who trust innovation are less likely to feel particularly trusting of those who recite the same facts repeatedly. Gaining clarity about what we easily trust informs us as to what we might mistake as untrustworthy.

In a similar vein, we are honest in the only way we know how to be. If you consider honesty to be accurate and precise information, you are less likely to trust people who focus on global impressions. What one person reveals as part of what he or she considers an honest discussion, another may consider inappropriate and raise doubts about the judgment of the person who is trying to communicate.

Finally, the way we behave during interactions is rarely ever intended to send a message that is judgmental. We want to be heard for what we mean without being seen as judgmental; thus, when we are direct or sympathetic with the situation of another person, we are telling the truth as we see it without blaming.

With these thoughts in mind, consider the descriptions in Table 22 for the 16 types that respond to these questions and statements: "What do they trust?"; "Expresses honesty through… or experiences honesty in others who…?"; and finally, "Is being nonjudgmental when offering…." Note that the lead or dominant preference is listed first, and the supporting or auxiliary preference is second.

Most of us wish we experienced more trust, honesty, and nonjudgmental qualities in our relationships. However, given the pace of today's work and home life, it's often difficult to find the time to foster and develop these qualities in relationships. Using the advantage that type provides, we can get closer to establishing those qualities we most earnestly desire in interactions with others.

Typical Prejudices, Preconceptions, and Emotional Hot Buttons

Along with discomfort about trust, honesty, and judgment, we are vulnerable to other interactional discomforts. Because of the speed of communication today and the demands of the moment, we are unlikely to recognize what's happening when somebody pushes our emotional buttons. Everyone has them; they simply vary depending upon personality type. We forget about them until they're pushed, but then they trigger emotions that may be experienced as internal disgust or external agitation. Why do we forget about them? Because human beings are creatures of comfort, and we move away from discomfort as quickly as possible. But knowing what bothers us most gives us an unusual opportunity to recognize misplacement of our energy and to redirect our communications in a way that utilizes our strengths.

Table 23 lists the most common prejudices, preconceptions, and emotional hot buttons of each of the 16 types, once again based on the responses that people of all types gave to related questions. Insofar as we are able to get a handle on prejudices, preconceptions, and hot buttons, we have a chance to understand some of the reactions we give to or get from people during conversations. We are all surprised now and then by our own reactions to certain discussion topics, and by the way some of our innocently meant comments seem to bother others. We have an opportunity here to learn to be more forgiving of ourselves and others by understanding that emotional triggers affect everyone; they do so because they impinge, in one way or another, on something we hold dear—perhaps even on one of the reasons we get up in the morning, get to the meeting on time, or keep trying to improve our individual and collective opportunities.

TABLE 23
TYPE PATTERNS IN PREJUDICES, PRECONCEPTIONS, AND HOT BUTTONS

	ISTJ
	Introverted Sensing with Extraverted Thinking
Prejudices	Impressionistic data are worthless; tell what you see, not what you think
Preconceptions	Competence is related to precision of analysis; concise statements reflect clear thinking
Hot buttons	Challenge to either the competency or the factual basis of an analysis

TABLE 23
TYPE PATTERNS IN PREJUDICES, PRECONCEPTIONS, AND HOT BUTTONS *(Continued)*

ISFJ

Introverted Sensing with Extraverted Feeling

Prejudices	Theory without practice has little value
Preconceptions	Service to people or institutions has inherent value and virtue
Hot buttons	Debate, argument, or sustained disagreement

INFJ

Introverted Intuiting with Extraverted Feeling

Prejudices	Fostering human growth begins with an inner vision
Preconceptions	Details get in the way of working with ideas
Hot buttons	Loss of private space, incomplete issues in interactions

---

INTJ

Introverted Intuiting with Extraverted Thinking

Prejudices	Analytical decisions provide useful information for action
Preconceptions	Introspection promotes theory and encourages thorough analysis
Hot buttons	Loss of autonomy through structure, undervaluing intellectual development

---

ISTP

Introverted Thinking with Extraverted Sensing

Prejudices	Theory gets in the way of practical action
Preconceptions	Skeptical analysis is reliable and thorough
Hot buttons	Group work that tolerates philosophical discussion and loses sight of tangible goals

---

INTP

Introverted Thinking with Extraverted Intuiting

Prejudices	Thoroughly analyze quietly before you talk; only independent and autonomous people are imaginative
Preconceptions	Somebody else's model is more complete because it is so critical and analytical
Hot buttons	Poor logical arguments; doubts about the integrity of one's own analysis

TABLE 23

TYPE PATTERNS IN PREJUDICES, PRECONCEPTIONS, AND HOT BUTTONS *(Continued)*

ISFP

Introverted Feeling with Extraverted Sensing

Prejudices	Noisy people don't reflect very much and therefore cannot be thorough when attending to details
Preconceptions	Knowing the details—who, where, what, when—helps you know and care for people
Hot buttons	Negative feedback, loss of collaboration among people

---

INFP

Introverted Feeling with Extraverted Intuiting

Prejudices	Conventional thinking leads to poor problem-solving due to the lack of innovation and flexible resources
Preconceptions	Interpersonal harmony is more valuable than conflict; introspective reflection is more effective than group problem-solving
Hot buttons	Assertions of a lack of caring, questioning of motives, being seen as touchy and interpersonally suspicious

---

ESTP

Extraverted Sensing with Introverted Thinking

Prejudices	Past is dead, future can't be predicted, so focus on now
Preconceptions	Knowing specifics will lead to practical action
Hot buttons	Unrealistic and impractical suggestions

ESFP

Extraverted Sensing with Introverted Feeling

Prejudices	Good-natured people are reliable and thorough
Preconceptions	Being practical makes sense in helping people; having a great deal of energy reflects a person's action orientation
Hot buttons	Unkind critical comments; people who detach from a situation

---

ENFP

Extraverted Intuiting with Introverted Feeling

Prejudices	Closed-minded people; slow and unenthusiastic interactions suggest an unadaptable mind-set
Preconceptions	If they generate lots of ideas, people will not mind implementing them; being friendly and adaptable means you agree

TABLE 23
TYPE PATTERNS IN PREJUDICES, PRECONCEPTIONS, AND HOT BUTTONS *(Continued)*

Hot buttons	Questioning beliefs or values, challenging ideas put forth, managing implementation procedures

ENTP

Extraverted Intuiting with Introverted Thinking

Prejudices	Being verbally fluent and adaptable means you are resourceful; analysis and intellectual development are best
Preconceptions	Good thinking leads to good action; being adaptable means you will have more opportunities
Hot buttons	Questioning depth and competence; suggesting responsibility for the effects of remarks

ESTJ

Extraverted Thinking with Introverted Sensing

Prejudices	Reasonable and analytical people are more resourceful
Preconceptions	Once the data are verified, act quickly for best results; only action-oriented people who are analytical get things done
Hot buttons	Disloyal, disorganized, dreamy people

ENTJ

Extraverted Thinking with Introverted Intuiting

Prejudices	Mentally versatile people make real contributions; proactive and systematic decision-making leads to the best conclusions
Preconceptions	Action-oriented, fast-paced, aspirational, and analytical people are intelligent and more capable than others at getting things done
Hot buttons	Non–team players, people who are not bright, people who have no critical or analytical conversation skills

ESFJ

Extraverted Feeling with Introverted Sensing

Prejudices	Friendly and sympathetic people are loyal and inclusive
Preconceptions	Only through strong relationships can you really get things done
Hot buttons	Cool, detached people who are more interested in their own thoughts than in sharing with others

TABLE 23

TYPE PATTERNS IN PREJUDICES, PRECONCEPTIONS, AND HOT BUTTONS *(Continued)*

	ENFJ
	Extraverted Feeling with Introverted Intuiting
Prejudices	Warm, responsive people are likely to work cooperatively
Preconceptions	Being sympathetic and idealistic are the best qualities for working with people
Hot buttons	People who exclude others and who are detached from sharing; withdrawn people who show no appreciation

To move beyond simple recognition that our emotional buttons have an orderly basis, and to use the same basis to reframe our experiences, is a step toward constructive communication with others. Gaining knowledge about informational patterns, sources of preferred qualities in communication, and sources of bias in communication gives us insight into the complexity of human interchange. But our exploration of this complexity would be incomplete if we failed to look at how we typically reframe information to aid our understanding. Further, we need to consider the overall style of the 16 types; this gives us the best impression of their efforts to communicate.

Constructive Reframing of Communications

After years of interactions, most of us are aware when our messages are not being received or understood. In response, we frequently attempt to rephrase what we said in a way that we hope will clarify it. Most often, though, our rephrasing is simply an enlargement of the original. When, for example, we explain the concept of time to a child by using a broad focus, if the child doesn't understand at first we may shift to an even broader focus. Only after several unsuccessful attempts with that strategy might it occur to us to try a different method entirely—concrete examples, perhaps. Conversely, someone who begins with concrete examples may eventually resort to using broad concepts to get the point across.

Such a new strategy is simply a different cut of prior effort; taking a new angle in this way is called reframing. Whenever you hear yourself with a hint of frustration in your voice begin a new sentence with words such as, "Okay— let me try to explain it another way," you are attempting to reframe the concept or issue at hand. The impulse is good—reframing attempts to find the words that allow all parties to be winners.

In our effort to share information, to be understood, and to make a contribution, we rely on our past experiences. Our general interactive style is reinforced and encouraged partly due to our biases for certain information. But in the end, our style and our expressions come from the heart of who we are. If we are ever going to be able to move from old modes of interaction to new and more effective ways to communicate, we need to own our role in creating the message. Our habits of mind collude with our expressions to make up the core of our interpersonal efforts in communication.

Table 24 gives descriptors of the patterns each type employs to clarify and reframe messages. First is a statement about the type's general style, which sets the context for how that type clarifies and then reframes a message. Then comes a description of the typical clarification effort, followed by a suggested reframing strategy for that type based on the kinds of information they may be inclined to overlook.

Our efforts to reframe experience and to regroup in conversations are reflective of the impulse to understand what is put before us. The tools we have to make sense of our experiences are a combination of our natural gifts, our wits at the time, and the lessons we have learned. In communicating, we are likely to rely on what is nearest to who we are, for it is the script we know best. The unconscious competence of our habits of mind is exhibited in most of our conversations. We can become more in tune with these habits by knowing how we listen to ourselves, how we reframe, and how we generally communicate.

TABLE 24
TYPE PATTERNS IN CLARIFYING COMMUNICATIONS

ISTJ	
Introverted Sensing with Extraverted Thinking	
General style	Usually so quiet and reserved it is difficult to know how information personally affects them; share logical, factual perspectives in an unhurried and careful manner
Clarification	Attempt understanding by gathering facts and asking questions
Reframing	May need to identify themes and share personal reactions

ISFJ	
Introverted Sensing with Extraverted Feeling	
General style	Empathetic with those around them, warm and thoughtful about others, careful and studied comments about people and situations that are reliable statements of any current situation
Clarification	Calmly go about doing what they think helpful, rarely assert own needs, often test ideas with facts
Reframing	May need to ask about larger issues than those in the present, share critiques

TABLE 24
TYPE PATTERNS IN CLARIFYING COMMUNICATIONS *(Continued)*

	INTJ
	Introverted Intuiting with Extraverted Thinking
General style	Often collect theories and ideas, can react to most any situation competently, systematic in gathering information, often seem critical and questioning; drive for independence and autonomy, seem cool and detached
Clarification	Want interactions to make sense in the big picture, and so ask tougher and more comprehensive questions
Reframing	May need to share thoughtful personal reactions in seeking to be friendly and to test theories with facts
	INFJ
	Introverted Intuiting with Extraverted Feeling
General style	Appreciative in comments, find that interactions suggest the motives and values of conversants, value information about people for its own sake and therefore seem somewhat scholarly— reserved, idealistic, formal
Clarification	Seek to understand motives and personal frameworks for decisions
Reframing	May need to ask about verifiable facts and realistic choices
	ISTP
	Introverted Thinking with Extraverted Sensing
General style	Somewhat detached and independent but good-natured style; often imaginative in responses yet questioning seems unconventional and betrays the organized analysis used to make sense of the world
Clarification	Pursue practical and realistic discussion about action to take today, seem skeptical and unconcerned about personal outcomes
Reframing	May need to show more interest in effects of situations on others and to express inclusion of others in conversations
	INTP
	Introverted Thinking with Extraverted Intuiting
General style	Can be very satisfied as detached onlookers, ask only questions sufficient to address gaps in the logic of those engaged in discussions; appear adaptable but skeptical and critical

TABLE 24
TYPE PATTERNS IN CLARIFYING COMMUNICATIONS *(Continued)*

Clarification	Ask more questions, analyze more circumstances, and organize more ideas
Reframing	May need to show more inclusion of and interest in others

ISFP

Introverted Feeling with Extraverted Sensing

General style	Often so introspective that actions of care and concern speak more than words; share practical and reliable information
Clarification	Show interest and concern by becoming more deferent; want to understand by knowing the specifics
Reframing	May need to consider the overall framework and be critical questioners of situations

INFP

Introverted Feeling with Extraverted Intuiting

General style	Introspective and gentle; often say whatever will harmonize the conversation or situation; appear adaptable
Clarification	Pursue wider frames of meaning, connect the conversation to larger contexts
Reframing	May need to look at the facts and attend to the current circumstance regardless of its personal meaning

ESTP

Extraverted Sensing with Introverted Thinking

General style	Action orientation captured in excitable and energetic attention to the who, what, where, and when of a situation; critical nature overshadowed by ability to ease tensions in the present
Clarification	Focus on the action now and forcefully get at the facts
Reframing	May need to show empathy and ask about personal values

ESFP

Extraverted Sensing with Introverted Feeling

General style	Active, practical, and realistic responses to situations likely to reflect enjoyment of other people; creative at finding hands-on solutions; arouse liking and acceptance
Clarification	Focus on the here-and-now aspects of situations; express and show concern for others
Reframing	May need to be more questioning of the motives and contexts of interactions

TABLE 24
TYPE PATTERNS IN CLARIFYING COMMUNICATIONS *(Continued)*

	ENTP

Extraverted Intuiting with Introverted Thinking

General style	Energetically engage in conversation, asking imaginative questions; generally resist conventional actions, prefer original, almost irreverent responses; seem adaptable but in fact go along for the ride to collect more information for analysis
Clarification	Ask more skeptical questions and provide more statements of reasonable, logical options
Reframing	May need to step back and observe others, make personal connections before theorizing

	ENFP

Extraverted Intuiting with Introverted Feeling

General style	Communicate enthusiasm and energy, seem adaptable and open to possibilities, seem to work in spurts but in fact reflect on connection of current situation to similar previous circumstances; friendly and verbally fluent about values
Clarification	Seek more possibilities and more ideas to address a situation
Reframing	May need to focus on one option, collecting sufficient facts to test the strength of an idea

	ESTJ

Extraverted Thinking with Introverted Sensing

General style	High energy, hard-hitting interactions where practical and realistic action endorsed; fluent about loyalties; may appear so convinced of a formula for making things make sense that they have no patience for other views
Clarification	More facts and more logical analysis
Reframing	May need to ask more about values and themes, and seek to be more empathetic

	ENTJ

Extraverted Thinking with Introverted Intuiting

General style	Expressive and fluent about analysis, seek to show resourcefulness for helping address a situation; prefer a fast-paced interaction that provides theory, analysis, action
Clarification	Seek understanding by being more critical, more analytical, and more systematic

TABLE 24
TYPE PATTERNS IN CLARIFYING COMMUNICATIONS *(Continued)*

Reframing	May need to show appreciation and express more concern for people involved in a given interaction

ESFJ

	Extraverted Feeling with Introverted Sensing
General style	Warm and outgoing, loyal and unassuming conversationalists, often inclusive of others; test ideas with facts; careful about actions to ensure no one will be left out; often thorough about facts and fastidious about actions
Clarification	Express more empathy and inclusion to gain cooperation
Reframing	May need to express more ideas and be more critical about the logic of others' analyses

ENFJ

	Extraverted Feeling with Introverted Intuiting
General style	Engaging socially, outgoing and gregarious, often show appreciation and sympathetic understanding, like ideas and enjoy interactions that add knowledge to personal libraries of possibilities to explore
Clarification	Express more personal meaning and seek out more personal information during interactions
Reframing	May need to verify facts and test ideas

In gaining such clarity, we have the benefit of learning to listen more acutely to others and to what they have to offer.

Engaging the Expressions

To understand others fully requires us first to understand ourselves. Being aware of and acknowledging our individual psychology—habits of perception and judgment, including type, personal history, lessons learned, and responses—is first on the list of ways that lead to communicating well. When we are clear about the typical responses we give, we can then focus more clearly on the expressions others provide. Paradoxical as it might seem, we may become better at listening to others when we know more about our own patterns of communication.

The reason is that if we come to expect certain patterns, we need not project unnecessary (even incorrect) meaning onto other people's comments. For example, knowing that an Extraverted Thinker provides criticism as a basic way to communicate means that one needn't presume that the critique signifies lack of respect. Understanding type allows us to be able to hear people's expressions without unwarranted blame or judgment.

When we stop assuming that what we hear or see is something we know, we have a clean slate that enables us to ask other people what they really mean when we feel we have missed their true meaning the first time around. Remember the story at the beginning of this chapter? Roger had to ask Olivia what she meant twice before he discerned her needs. So it is with everyone: asking and listening generates more effective communication.

Of course, there are times when new learning does not simplify our lives at the outset. Psychological type informs us that interactions are rarely simple, and therefore our efforts to improve communication will likely fail if we look only at male-female socialization, cultural differences, or historical developments. To move forward, we must recognize the full complexity of the individual.

Valuing Differences

MAKING DIVERSITY WORK

A corporate vice president of operations, age 53, was discussing the promotion of several staff members with the company president when he said about one candidate, "I really can't figure out how his mind works. He's a good 'A-plus producer' but he's unconventional and has a really different perspective. I'm not sure we can risk moving him to the new position."

Perceptions of difference often lead to judgments that limit careers or even have more physically harmful outcomes, as in the following scenario: as the chains and belts beat the legs and back of a boy who happened upon a group of teenagers beneath the stands at a high school football game, he cried out, "Why are you doing this to me?"

They screamed back, "Because you're different from us!"

Perhaps the major psychological challenge of our time is that of developing the capacity to value human differences. It seems that no matter where we look, people are in conflict, even at war, because their beliefs are different, their roots are different, or their history is different. Such conflict is inevitable when the underlying assumption of either party is that being different means one side is better, the other worse; one valued, the other worthless; one more important, the other secondary at best. At its extreme, such belief leads to the conclusion that those who are different have no rights—not even the right to live. Even in democracies where difference is supposed to be tolerated, we find enormous rifts among various groups due to perceived differences and antagonistic interpretations of those differences.

Some differences are far more obvious and painful than others, but at the root of our responses to all of them are individual psychological differences. Even observable differences such as race or physical disability wouldn't separate people unnecessarily if not for the psychology of the observer. Individuals who believe that other races are inferior or untrustworthy, or who believe they have nothing in common with people who have a disability, often simply avoid interacting with them. These beliefs, attitudes, and expectations about others are all part of our individual perspectives, and they contribute to how we manage our daily interactions.

Troubling Differences

Certainly some differences are troubling. Individuals who hear voices from God giving them permission to break every human law, or people who feel compelled for whatever reason to destroy others, are different in ways that civilized society has declared intolerable. Such differences in behavior and ideas are clearly recognized as unacceptable. In the 24 years since this book was originally published, we've all seen horrendous examples of this, from genocides in African nations and Eastern Europe to suicide bombings around the world, to the World Trade Center attack on September 11, 2001. The current generation of high school students have grown up with an endless string of mass shootings in schools, churches, synagogues, restaurants and places once thought safe for entertainment. With each such event, trust and tolerance levels around the world run the risk of becoming more depleted. In the 10 years since the publication of the second edition of this book, the United States has seen this play out on the national stage as individuals have been pitted against one another by divisive factions fanning the flames that differences can't be tolerated. It is easy to see worldwide what happens when this goes so far as one group being unable to tolerate the very existence of another group.

Imagine a tolerance continuum. The low end, a position for those who have no tolerance, is occupied by people who commit heinous crimes against other people because they have no tolerance for differences. The high end is populated by those with absolute openness to other points of view—so confident and comfortable are they with their own values that they feel no threat whatsoever and thus remain completely open to others.

The vast majority of people—those of us who work to improve our lives, raise our families, and contribute to the general welfare—fall in the midrange between these two extremes. It would be nice if there were only a few differences that each of us found unacceptable. The world would be a far different place if there was a long distance between most of us and an absence of tolerance. But that is rarely the case. Human nature seems to be such that once we have declared *some* differences unacceptable, we extend that reaction to many other differences.

The differences we see immediately are gender and race. Sometimes clothes pinpoint differences in social status. These differences have their own place in the history of human struggle and are beyond the scope of this book. But the differences represented in personality, though more subtle, are subject

218

to the same forces as those in gender, race, or religion. For example, in organizations where we have been able to collect personality type preference data
on the executives, managers, associates, and newly selected supervisors of the
same company, we found that executives tend to select managers and supervisors who are like themselves. The results were both statistically significant and
practically significant. These are not random results. Like our earlier story of
the manager who fired people he thought he couldn't trust, the data suggest
that executives develop intolerance for those who think and behave differently.[1]

Preferred Flocks

Any way you look at it, we usually like people who are like ourselves. We are
more comfortable with them and more accepting of their foibles. The tendency
to join together with those who share interests, worldviews, political attitudes,
and general outlooks on life is basic. It is rooted in the need to socialize with
those who support and affirm our needs and experiences. At its most primitive core, it's a matter of survival. Humans are wired for connection. When
we stretch ourselves, or ask others to stretch themselves psychologically to
embrace difference at any level, we are asking a great deal. From the outset, we
are somewhat programmed to avoid prolonged dealings with those who are
really different. This is the first hurdle when addressing the topic of valuing
differences.

A second problem arises when we mistakenly equate "understanding"
with "valuing." It is a drastic flaw in logic to conclude that if you are understood, then you are also valued. Understanding that a woman earns seventy
cents while a man doing the same job makes a dollar does not change the fact,
nor does it mean that women are valued in any sense more than they are paid.
Children often make the mistake of assuming that a parent's understanding
of a behavior means permission has been granted to do it. Quickly, however,
kids learn that parental understanding of what, when, why, and how does not
necessarily mean acceptance of a proposed activity. Understanding is not valuing; understanding is a process in its own right and is a necessary first step in
the valuing process.

Understand Me

There is a global "understand me" craze evident in the numerous diversity
training programs throughout industry and government. It is sadly ironic that
so many people spend long hours in workshops listening to the stories of others but come away valuing others no more and behaving just as hurtfully as
before. We've heard of more than one instance where these kinds of training experiences actually cause the opposite reaction: "Yeah, I understand the

situation now—and I understand why I don't like [fill in the blank] and never will. I understand all that a lot better now. Thanks." Understanding the plight of minorities in our society has done little to change social attitudes toward valuing the contribution they could make to overall society. Seeking to understand is valuable in its own right; the error is in believing that it automatically creates a valuing of those who are different.

We will go so far as to say that those who settle for understanding and being understood have less than fully developed their communication potential. Jung suggested that the notion of being understood really means to be embraced, to be interpreted correctly. Those who have a passion to be understood are merely seeking satisfaction for the most basic impulses—to be embraced and comforted. The only person who really comes close to understanding us in this sense is, in most cases, if we're lucky, our mother. So we might consider that to seek only to be understood is to seek the embrace of Mother.[2] While that embrace is temporarily satisfying, it fails the test of maturity. It fails to acknowledge the critical task of a mature human being, which is to develop interdependencies with those who neither understand us nor wish to support us in our quests. Learning to value difference and to act upon that understanding may be one of the developmental tasks of adulthood that leads to wisdom.

A Language for Valuing

If liking those who are like ourselves and wanting simply to be understood make getting at the central nature of valuing difficult, consider a third issue: we do not have an easy language for valuing. Many of our ideas about valuing are like those of children who think that being understood and valued means getting your way. Clearly, being valued for your differences does not imply that being different guarantees getting your way. Valuing is awkward to describe and analyze. It is difficult to get our minds around the importance of valuing. Like equatorial natives who have no word for snow, maybe we have so few experiences of being valued that our language fails us. We propose that valuing begins with learning about differences and then acting in ways so that those who are different can experience being valued.

The language difficulty is obvious, for example, on the internet. Surf it sometime and try to find material on valuing. You will find little discussion except about financial matters—evaluation of companies or properties people wish to sell. When we checked recently, nine of the top ten Google suggestions for "valuing" were about valuing a business, intellectual property, warrants, donations for tax purposes, and so on. Only one of the ten was "valuing diversity." Type in "values" and you get a little closer to the topic. Only a few suggestions for business surfaced, along with one for the values of various mathematical concepts. Perhaps to our point, the remainder focused on values clarification—getting clear about what our values are. Nothing was listed about expressing value for others. Yet on any number of topics such as communication or values there are hundreds of entries. Read some of them and you will find that people are struggling with valuing differences.

Psychological Type Extends Beyond Understanding

Psychological type provides a model to understand and value difference. Type presumes that all preferences for mental processes, for taking in energy, perceiving information, and making decisions are present in every normally functioning individual. We all have the capacity, if not the inclination, to do all of it. These functions enable us to adapt and respond to our daily challenges with more ease and effectiveness. Thus a difference in response to situations is really less about "rightness" and more about judgment and choices.

Type offers a rational way to understand the differences in the ways people respond to events. With the expressions inherent in Extraverted or Introverted Perception and Judgment, we have observable differences in behavior. Once we understand the source and nature of these differences, we can reject the notion that they are a threat to our way of seeing the world. As we have seen throughout this book, psychological type provides insights into the way our minds work and the way we respond as a result of these mental habits. Furthermore, type preferences provide a pathway to valuing differences.

Given the Difference, So What?

The hard truth is that the act of valuing means determining a degree of importance, a measure of worth of a thing, a contribution, or an experience. When a situation arises in which we start wondering and get curious about how to measure the worth of something, a valuing process is what we use. That curiosity is necessary but hardly sufficient to push us toward behaviors of valuing.

Why should we tolerate differences? Why go through the trouble of understanding and then trying to develop behaviors that express our valuing of others? Why is it worth the effort? The answer to all these questions is that valuing personality differences, and being able to demonstrate that valuing, has a major impact on relationships, interactions, decision-making, and human development. Understanding the reasonable and real variations of "normal" allows us to make more conscious choices about giving and receiving messages of all kinds, which in turn makes us more effective. Valuing differences is both a moral decision and a pragmatic decision. It may be a true measure of love—to love someone because of their differences rather than in spite of them,

221

a crucial element in successful partnerships of all kinds, certainly is connected to the concept of being valued. The interdependent nature of life means our ability to survive and adapt is directly tied to our ability to manage differences. This is true in one-on-one relationships as well as on a global level. The model of psychological type provides a path of insight for asking better questions and making better choices toward valuing others.

An Old, Wise Story

"Who Speaks for Wolf" is a Native American story that provides a compelling case for working toward a way to value differences.[3] As the story goes, a tribe decided to move its village. According to the traditions of the tribe, young men learned to communicate with nature. At those times when the community was faced with a major choice to make, these young men were sent into the wild to learn the lessons of nature as they pertained to the tribe's question. When they returned to share their insights, the tribe gathered to hear all the information from the different sources and then make a decision, having the benefit of the broad and integrated information available to them.

In this situation, the tribe had sent the young men out to learn what nature would recommend about the tribe's move. All of the young men returned except the one who spoke for Wolf. The tribe felt pressed for time—the seasons were changing quickly that year and they felt they were in danger. They chose not to wait for him and acted on the information they had. The decision was a disaster, leading to death and disease. When the wolf boy finally caught up, he was dismayed that they had not waited for him. He told them that Wolf had given him the information they had needed to avoid danger from a tainted water source. Thanks to Wolf, he knew they should not have moved to that particular place. So the tribe gathered again to consider what to do:

> And so it was that the people devised among themselves a way of
> asking each other questions whenever a decision was to be made
> on a New Place or a New Way. [They] sought to perceive the flow
> of energy through each new possibility and how much was enough,
> and how much was too much, until at last someone would rise and
> ask the old question, to remind us of things we do not yet see clearly
> enough to remember: Tell me my brothers, tell me now my sisters,
> Who Speaks for Wolf?
> Now among a wise people they will ask what else might be
> true for them that they did not yet see. They wonder how all these
> things—seen and unseen—might affect [their] lives and the lives of
> [their] children's children's children. Then to remind us of the great

difficulties that might arise from a single omission of something we forgot to consider, they will ask the ancient question, Tell me my brothers, tell me now my sisters, Who Speaks for Wolf?[4]

As this ancient story informs us, more successful decisions are likely to be made if, when valuing different views, all views are considered. For example, in hundreds of training simulations, groups of people read about a situation, then rate and rank a list of proposed actions to take. After individuals rate the actions, groups discuss why each person rated actions in a certain way. If a group allows all views to be aired and discussed freely, the group ratings are usually vastly superior to the individual ratings when compared to the expert list of right actions in the right order. In groups where no discussion or debate is tolerated, many individual scores are higher than the group score and the group score is usually lower on average than those of groups that tolerated different views. This outcome illustrates the same point as the Native American story; difference can enrich the lives of all those who promote environments where differences exist and are valued.

Valuing Means...

Valuing means considering each perspective to be important in its own right and providing, through interactions, room for the expression of each perspective without disparagement. While any given perspective may play only a small part in a final decision or conclusion, there still must be room for it to be expressed. Valuing should not mean blind acceptance of another's view, but it does imply passion about the right of the other's view to be heard. A quote often attributed to Voltaire applies here: "I disagree with what you're saying, but I will defend to the death your right to say it." Valuing is to behave toward others in such a way that they feel respect. It is an interactional process that opens individuals to creative outcomes while avoiding premature conclusions.

So we begin our consideration of valuing by proposing that goodwill among individuals is a prerequisite; in its absence, no tolerance—much less the valuing of others—is possible. If present, goodwill leads to a motive for learning how to value differences.

Valuing Stages

Consider the following stages when thinking about valuing differences. Each is important and leads to the next. Interestingly, this process will help you no matter what difference is under consideration—culture, race, or psychological mind-set.

STAGE 1   Preconditions of Valuing

Approach the interaction with an assumption of goodwill and a belief that through interaction, a synergy will occur to provide a better answer or improved condition than one alone could produce. Commit to sharing observations and thoughts without fear of negative evaluation and with the expectation of critical consideration.

STAGE 2   Setting Ground Rules

Set ground rules to get clarity about the amount of time for the interaction and the intention of the discussion; make explicit the general topics of the discussion or conversation.

STAGE 3   Interchange

Spend twice as much time listening as speaking, keeping in mind that each person's perspective comes from his or her experience and personality, which are likely different from your own; constantly seek clarity by asking, paraphrasing, and questioning what you have heard and understood; check your own biases (see chapter 8 on communication) and emotional hot buttons; share thoughts and ideas in a manner consistent with your perspective, and show respect for the other person's style.

STAGE 4   Closure

Summarize understanding and use your knowledge of type preferences as a checklist: collected the facts (Sensing); considered the possibilities (Intuiting); reviewed the pros and cons (Thinking); initiated action consistent with values (Feeling); made a plan for next discussion (Judgment); and left the door open for new information and how it will be conveyed (Perception).

These stages are a kind of orderly way to communicate valuing. Beginning with an attitude of goodwill and a perspective that differences may lead to enhanced opportunities increases the chance that valuing will occur. Ground rules create a fair playing field for the interaction. Consider how differently you feel when your boss calls to set up a meeting and tells you what the meeting is about rather than simply telling you to show up. Think how differently an interaction would develop if your significant other said, "I need an hour with you to discuss buying a car," versus pulling up in the driveway in a new car and yelling, "Surprise!"

Critical Interchange

Listening and talking in ways that recognize and allow for differences in style and perspective create space to focus on the true intent and content of messages. This is an essential way to express respect and valuing to another person. Keep in mind that valuing is what we experience in an interaction, not just what we say or what is said to us. The experience of valuing and feeling valued is tied to all of these stages and is expressed in all the ways we communicate with each other.

In chapter 8 we discussed the dimensions of communication and how psychological type is part of this effort. We looked at how types create their own biases, express their various styles, and strive to make sense of the content of messages. These issues become more vital when considering how to create an experience of valuing among people. Communication is the medium that allows the possibility of valuing to occur.

We will approach the types first by understanding in general how the individual preferences express and experience valuing. For each of the 16 types, we will examine the role type dynamics play in valuing differences.

Valuing Preferences

Given the importance of each preference to the overall functioning of each individual, it makes sense to explore valuing first by preference and then by the dynamics of the types.

As noted earlier, Extraversion and Introversion are processes by which we initiate and reflect, engage and stand back, and attend to experiences outside our skin and inside our skin. Consider this mental wiring similar to electrical wiring. Extraversion and Introversion are the charging poles of our completed circuitry, and while both are essential to normal human functioning, we seem to get our batteries charged primarily through one or the other. Those with an Extraverted preference are energized by their environment; those with an Introverted preference by what they hold inside for consideration. This dimension is so basic to the personality of the individual that the experience of valuing begins with it.

Valuing with and Through Extraversion

Extraversion wants external space for events to occur. Expansive in the outer world, Extraversion relishes an opportunity to be expressed. Many Extraverts say that thoughts are not real until they are spoken aloud. So as an elementary aspect of valuing, Extraversion requires action, movement, and experience that can be seen or heard.

Consider the child who is constantly engaged with her environment. She talks about things, plays with things, and tells you about it while she does so, thoroughly engaged in a somewhat public way with the world around her. If her preference is for Extraversion and these actions seem to motivate and excite her, she is unlikely to feel valued when her preferred behavior results in regularly being told to shut up, sit quietly, and be a big girl.

As she becomes a woman, her desire to initiate, share ideas, and engage may be contained because of the childhood message that her natural expression was unwelcome. This is regrettable on two sides: other people may never know the richness of her ideas and enthusiasms, and she does not experience the rewards of fully engaging with her environment. By contrast, had she been given a childhood where Extraversion was nurtured, she might have grown up to be expressive and active during interactions and quite comfortable talking about her ideas and seeking out new experiences.

To feel valued, Extraversion wants an opportunity to play itself out and to receive some feedback about its performance. Feedback, by definition, means a return of energy to its source; there is no judgment about it. To get this opportunity when interacting with others, those with an Extraverted preference must be clear that they want the chance to be heard. To continue getting the best from Extraversion, maintaining active engagement throughout the interaction is important, because where they start a conversational topic is not likely to be where they will end it. In general, Extraversion wants the interaction to make ideas more real and to develop them into more complete thoughts. What begins as an idea, through rich conversation, can become either an actionable plan or a disaster well avoided. For the Extraverted person, true valuing exists through interaction that encourages the development and clarity of thought.

Valuing with and Through Introversion

Introversion is a process of reflection and reception. When time is provided for a process to occur without interruption, then the value of this process has been expressed. The need for time to attend to inner-space is vital for Introversion. The amount of time needed varies by situation. Unlike Extraversion, where discussion and action lead to clarity, stillness leads to clarity and focus with Introversion.

For Introverts, a question or comment may trigger a reaction that can appear to be withheld. As in an old pinball game, a ball has been released and is moving around and around until it finds the right slot for a score. Introverts are typically not willfully withholding reactions from those around them; they are "waiting for the ball to find the slot" before they can react. This quality often plays out as a difference in pace in an interaction. While Extraverts often demonstrate a fast pace, Introverts may appear not to keep up. But the appearance is deceiving. Consider the question of pace in a different arena: Introverts often prefer reading and other visual stimuli to auditory stimuli when learning or developing an understanding. Average reading speed is about 420 words per minute; average speaking speed is 75 to 100 words per minute. So while Extraversion may look fast and action-oriented, Introversion can actually process more complex information in a much shorter period of time. We all do both, and we all need both.

Besides the time and opportunity to reflect, Introversion usually relies on an economy of words. Whereas Extraversion by its nature uses many words and expressions, Introversion tends to rely on as few words as possible to get the point across; language is often carefully and selectively used. This is not to imply that every utterance is the outcome of deep thought, but it does mean that the Introvert highly values conciseness because it is wired into his or her process.

To express a valuing of Introversion, time for thought, allowances for pace, and attention to the language used are essential. A few moments may make all the difference in the quality of what is shared as well as the openness with which it is offered. Asking about the ideas shared is likely to lead to a broader understanding of the thought processes involved in reaching a particular conclusion. That said, finding the balance between expressing interest with a few well-chosen questions and bombarding the Introvert with reactions and more questions is an important part of the experience of valuing this function.

Valuing Information from the Sensing Function

To understand Sensing, the perceptive process that pays attention to the fullness of the moment, one begins with the awareness of physical realities and ends in attention to the present. By design, Sensing is the process that gives us the facts of life. Rooms are not simply painted but are a particular color. Carpets are not merely soft; they have a color and design about which we can be specific. Such attention to information that is immediate and present is the nature of Sensing.

This inclination to fully attend to the present often expresses itself in behaviors that are specific, practical, and concrete. For example, if those with a preference for Sensing see a way to solve a problem, they often simply go and do it rather than discuss various options. Information that explains and describes is highly valued. To the Sensing function, an experience is what it is without interpretation: a movie is scenes, costumes, sequencing of action, dialogue, and music—not the epic struggle of good and evil that Intuiting, by contrast, may report it to be.

Sensing is pulled to a positive-focused awareness of events in the moment. What happens in the future is speculation that merits little attention from the

227

person with a Sensing preference, unless it can be discussed in realistic terms and is based on projections from current factual information. Grounded in the present, Sensing catalogues information as it is experienced. For this reason, there is often identification with the familiar and with things that have happened. This results in an appreciation of traditional rituals and acknowledged routes to a given outcome. Given a choice between having an agenda or simply brainstorming at a meeting, Sensing is drawn to the agenda because it will frame the experience and provide nails on which to hang facts.

We value Sensing when we show and express recognition of the facts of a situation and of the practical actions that could be taken. Being sure not to discount factual information and requests for practical direct experience are ways to value Sensing. To value it in each person, we need to celebrate the present and show appreciation for the efficiency of attending to specific information.

Conscientiousness—following through, doing exactly what you said you would do when you said you would do it—is a way of valuing Sensing. Often simple acts of attention—notes, cards, illustrations, phone calls—provide sufficient recognition of the importance of focusing on the present. The challenge is to recognize the matter-of-fact and orderly awareness of the present while encouraging independence and appreciation for the metaphorical processes of Intuiting.

Valuing Information from the Intuiting Function

To those with a Sensing preference, the mere suggestion that an idea or a possibility could be treated as real information borders on the bizarre. How can something that is not verifiable or concrete be perceived as information? Yet this is precisely what Intuiting is designed to do: take details that quickly fade to the background and bring to the foreground their patterns, possibilities, and trends.

This tendency pulls on the figurative, the associational, and the conceptual nature of an experience, situation, or circumstance. While to the Sensing function a glass has specific qualities and dimensions, to the Intuitive process it is a multiplicity of things—holder of fluid, potential weapon, piece of art. While the Intuitive is pondering the glass as a metaphor, the Sensing type is focusing on its physical properties and practical uses.

Inherent in this immediate move from current factual information to possibilities is a perceptual autonomy. The Sensing function does not desire autonomy from practical, concrete facts, but the Intuiting function insists on independence, on freedom from the worldly, material present. This independence is often marked by an inventive and unconventional way of doing things.

It is as if the Intuitive tuner uses the antennae of perception to find patterns in signals rather than a particular signal or frequency. Often theoretical with considerable verbal fluency, those with an Intuitive preference appear appreciative of the complex and abstract. This attraction usually results in very tolerant attitudes, since most things seem quite gray rather than precisely black or white.

Often valued because it produces clever ideas, Intuiting is the source of brainstorming. In environments where standard operating procedures rule the day and innovation is an unrecognized or unwelcome resource, Intuitives soon wither or leave. To value Intuitive processes, we need to invite philosophical and theoretical discussion and to tolerate idiosyncratic conversation that appears to be leading nowhere but may actually be the shortest path to a distant point.

From the outset, a degree of faith is expected from those who value Intuiting. Unlike Sensing, where information can be shown to be true or false, Intuiting requires us to make a leap from point A to point D; maybe later we will get to B and C. Valuing Intuiting means embracing thoughts of what could be while recognizing the facts of the now.

Valuing Decisions from Thinking

Thought of as "the executive function" because of its tendency to establish criteria, evaluate by pros and cons, and select a choice based on logic, the Thinking process seeks decision. Often demanding proof of an assertion, those with a Thinking preference rely on reasoned analysis to produce the best solution.

This process responds to competence verifiable by logical demonstration. For example, those who prefer Thinking often report that acknowledging their competency in addressing a problem is more important than recognizing their effort to contribute. So important is this to the Thinking function that a well-thought-out criticism that leads to improvement in performance is highly valued.

The Thinking function is the mind's way of seeking an impartial standard by which to judge experience. Hopelessly subjective, both the Thinking and the Feeling processes rely on personal, internal abilities; the Thinking function in each of us is the voice seeking orderly, reasonable, logical sense of our experience. Those with Thinking as a preference value endurance, achievement, autonomy, and a vigorous mental approach to problem-solving.

One way to value this function is to create an interaction that promotes the independence needed to aggressively pursue answers to questions. To allow the critique of experience and thought is to provide room for the Thinking function to naturally express itself. When someone seems critical, questioning, and analytical, it may help those around him or her to recognize that from the Thinking perspective these are ways to express a valuing of the experience or object being critiqued. When Thinking types don't value a thing, they don't waste their precious time and talent trying to make it better. Only when they no longer care does the analysis stop.

This is often a difficult part of interacting with those whose preference is for Thinking: their critique can push people away though their intent is to cement a commitment to solving problems. It does no good to argue that your feelings are hurt in an interaction where the focus is on action that was taken. When the Thinking function is engaged, personal emotions are annoying distractions from the pursuit of logical choices. So to honor Thinking, focus on the problem. Make any request to discuss how the decision is being made and its effect on you at a later date. The simple desire of the Thinking function is to have an elegant and efficient analysis. Like well-made crystal, which is clear, bright, and pure, the Thinking process seeks answers that are clear, precise, and complete.

Valuing Decisions from Feeling

Because the word *feeling* is used in so many contexts, this decision-making function can be difficult to describe and understand. We use the word to describe emotion, physical sensation, and opinion: we feel love, we feel velvet and find it soft, we feel that one option is better than another. All these meanings are facets of the Judgment function.

The Feeling function of decision-making is grounded in human connections. At its root are values for well-being and avoidance of causing harm. This may show up in nurturing behavior, affiliative behavior, or idealistic commitment to a vision of human welfare.

Unlike the Thinking function, which often can be mapped as a sequential, orderly analysis almost anyone can follow, the Feeling function is charted more like a fractal in chaos theory. The Feeling function assumes that there are answers in the patterns of relationships. As in chaos theory, in which strange attractors pull and push on molecules to create patterns, the Feeling function pushes and pulls information to find the pattern as it affects human beings. This force begins with an affirmation of existence and builds the values and patterns around it like the layers of nacre an oyster secretes to create a pearl.

This affirmation expresses itself in a tender, accepting, and accommodating network of behaviors. Often expressing appreciation for the contribution of others or for the creator of an object or of a situation, those who prefer Feeling behave in ways that affirm the importance of a contribution. A key ingredient of their underlying working assumptions is that both sides can win in a situation regardless of the problem. The Feeling function carries on a private wager: that trusting your reactions, connections to values, and patterns of relationships will produce a superior result.

These pearls of judgment may have no sequential logic; rather, they should be seen for their inherent value before being analyzed for the price and measure of quality that may be imposed. To value the Feeling function, we should recognize the contribution, note the expression of commitment, identify the value of the relationship, and invite an empathetic assessment of the situation, problem, or issue.

When directed at a contribution a Feeling type has made, the critical analysis so naturally offered by the Thinking preference can be experienced as disrespect, and those with a preference for the Feeling function find little to affirm their decision-making. Told to make a logical argument, they are often forced to ignore what they consider most important in order to find a logical pathway to express their views. We show value for this function in conversation when we focus on values, human relationships, and what the larger impact on individuals could be. We can give it equal value in decision-making by providing time for those preferring the Feeling function to articulate their views of how a situation will affect the quality of life.

Valuing Orientations for Moving Through the Day: Judgment and Perception

We have noted throughout this book that Myers developed a new dimension in psychological type that helps identify the use of the mental functions in the Extraverted and Introverted attitudes. These orientations are called Judgment and Perception: the first pushes toward decision, the other toward new information.

Because of the general nature of this habit of mind, Myers was able to describe those who prefer Judgment in the outer world as desiring closure, structure, and order, and those who prefer Perception in the outer world as seeking spontaneity and more information.

These qualities are generally obvious when dealing with another person. They are noticeable almost immediately, and because of that they are often the first factors used in valuing another's work style, interpersonal reactions, and managing an environment.

Decisive, orderly individuals feel valued when they know there will be a beginning, middle, and end to a discussion. They want a plan of action, or at least a plan to make a plan. Valuing Judgment means saying a kind of interpersonal "yes" to the notion of reaching an eventual conclusion.

But go-with-the-flow individuals often plunge ahead without promise of immediate closure, preferring the unexpected and relishing the freedom to change. They want to know that decisions can be revisited and reopened. They seek comfort in knowing that people will be flexible in decisions. Often operating ad hoc, adding new information as it comes along, individuals with the Perceiving preference feel valued when time is provided to simply wander around, both intellectually and physically.

Dimensions of Valuing for Each of the 16 Types

The view of individual preferences above is a first pass at the ways and means of valuing from a psychological type perspective. But even though preferences provide clues, taken singly they cannot paint the picture with the same richness and complexity offered by considering the dynamics of the types; the complete picture should help us find better ways to express the value we feel for others that is so urgently needed in human relationships.

As noted over and over in this book, people most often give to others what they themselves most want. We assume that what makes sense to us is best for all, and we don't consider options that others may actually appreciate more. When we want people to feel our respect and know that we value them, we typically behave toward them as we wish they would behave toward us. But each type has certain conditions under which they feel valued; each type expresses valuing in discrete ways. To value other types, we must learn these ways and grow in whichever of our personal dimensions need attention. If type only leads us to recognize our own qualities and to identify how we differ from others without pulling us into new arenas of growth, then the model serves merely a self-centered need. Truly understanding type can help us genuinely value others, and this is the condition necessary to create community, whether in a single interaction or over many years. We often say the Golden Rule is to treat others as we want to be treated; yet the Platinum Rule is to treat others as they want to be treated. To live that rule is hard work as it requires getting a handle on the other person's needs and wants, while respecting our own.

Table 25 takes note of three important factors about valuing: how each of the 16 types experiences being valued, how each expresses valuing toward other types, and what lesson each needs to learn in order to value others according to their needs.

To genuinely value human differences so that everyone benefits, we need to first recognize that differences are a matter of fact. Differences simply exist; it is nature's way. The next task is to tolerate differences. Finally, with maturity,

TABLE 25
TYPE PATTERNS IN APPLYING THE "PLATINUM RULE"

ISTJ	
Introverted Sensing with Extraverted Thinking	
Experiences valuing when	Order, structure, and logical analysis are evident
Expresses valuing by	Organizing, detailing, and analyzing a situation
Most needs to learn that	Those who are questioning and value-oriented are providing a structure and analysis worthy of attention

TABLE 25
TYPE PATTERNS IN APPLYING THE "PLATINUM RULE" *(Continued)*

ISFJ

Introverted Sensing with Extraverted Feeling

Experiences valuing when	Careful, observant attention to others is evident
Expresses valuing by	Showing thoughtfulness with bringing order and making sure people are comfortable
Most needs to learn that	Those who are analytical and open-ended are showing a kind of caring

INFJ

Introverted Intuiting with Extraverted Feeling

Experiences valuing when	Ideas for helping others are given validity in discussion, and plans are made to implement ideas
Expresses valuing by	Acting on information about caring for others' needs
Most needs to learn that	Soliciting other ideas may serve practical purposes; doing is as valuable as pondering

INTJ

Introverted Intuiting with Extraverted Thinking

Experiences valuing when	Logical arguments provide a sufficient analysis to explain pros/cons and future courses of action
Expresses valuing by	Analyzing situations and providing a logical description of what has happened and what is likely to happen
Most needs to learn that	A logical analysis may not be useful in various situations; accommodating behavior may be more effective in changing people's minds

ISTP

Introverted Thinking with Extraverted Sensing

Experiences valuing when	Simple, practical actions are based on accurate information and a logical discussion
Expresses valuing by	Focusing on current experiences and providing a model to explain in concrete terms what has occurred
Most needs to learn that	People bring in personal histories and expectations that have nothing to do with the moment and that affect decisions made and actions taken

TABLE 25
TYPE PATTERNS IN APPLYING THE "PLATINUM RULE" *(Continued)*

INTP

Introverted Thinking with Extraverted Intuiting

Experiences valuing when	Models and frameworks are discussed as being possible
Expresses valuing by	Giving you attention to make your case and explain your situation
Most needs to learn that	Self-disclosure is an important aspect of relationships

---

ISFP

Introverted Feeling with Extraverted Sensing

Experiences valuing when	Personal, hands-on assistance is provided
Expresses valuing by	Gently encouraging others to act on some topic and then quietly going about doing what they believe needs to be done
Most needs to learn that	Neither gentleness nor beliefs alter the way some people act and reason out situations; being tough and questioning can be very helpful

---

INFP

Introverted Feeling with Extraverted Intuiting

Experiences valuing when	Efforts are recognized as being offerings of personal meaning
Expresses valuing by	Writing notes, making phone calls, sending symbolic gifts
Most needs to learn that	Specific, logical, and critical analysis is very valuable and important to solving problems

---

ESTP

Extraverted Sensing with Introverted Thinking

Experiences valuing when	Experiences affirm their competencies and abilities
Expresses valuing by	Involving others in activities and supporting appropriate challenges
Most needs to learn that	Quiet reflection is often a challenge and provides insights that cannot be gleaned from doing

---

ESFP

Extraverted Sensing with Introverted Feeling

Experiences valuing when	Actively involved in people-related events; offering to assist and being given the opportunity to do so

TABLE 25

TYPE PATTERNS IN APPLYING THE "PLATINUM RULE" *(Continued)*

Expresses valuing by	Inviting others to share in some activity, meal, or conversation about current personal situations
Most needs to learn that	Not being included does not indicate dislike or disregard; some people function best alone

ENFP

Extraverted Intuiting with Introverted Feeling

Experiences valuing when	Opportunities to share ideas and to openly reveal values and commitments are provided
Expresses valuing by	Offering various ideas and strategies for addressing a situation; sending mementos of experiences and conversations
Most needs to learn that	Tough, critical business rules for making decisions are ways of improving others' situations

ENTP

Extraverted Intuiting with Introverted Thinking

Experiences valuing when	Questioning is encouraged and ideas are debated
Expresses valuing by	Showing a keen verbal interest in conversations
Most needs to learn that	Patient unfolding of information may provide more useful information than answers to questions

ESTJ

Extraverted Thinking with Introverted Sensing

Experiences valuing when	Logical reasons for certain actions are acknowledged and supported
Expresses valuing by	Providing a detailed account of an experience
Most needs to learn that	Vision and relationships that are articulated and reinforced may be more useful at times than facts, details, and logic

ENTJ

Extraverted Thinking with Introverted Intuiting

Experiences valuing when	Ideas are critiqued and suggestions are provided
Expresses valuing by	Offering new perspectives and more global views
Most needs to learn that	Emotional warmth and interpersonal concern are the grease of relationships that eventually enable ideas to become realities

TABLE 25
TYPE PATTERNS IN APPLYING THE "PLATINUM RULE" *(Continued)*

ESFJ	
Extraverted Feeling with Introverted Sensing	
Experiences valuing when	Demonstrative caretaking behavior is evident
Expresses valuing by	Sympathizing with others and acting on beliefs about a situation
Most needs to learn that	Clarifying a theory or model and focusing on global issues may provide an important basis for relationships

ENFJ	
Extraverted Feeling with Introverted Intuiting	
Experiences valuing when	Ideas that are shared are recognized and noted in conversation
Expresses valuing by	Seeking opportunities to discuss situations and to check out perceptions of events
Most needs to learn that	It is important to get the facts straight and to make sure ideals are presented in a logical fashion

we must learn to embrace the contrast and approach differences not just with tolerance but with goodwill.

To reach such a state of maturity, it helps to understand that the sources of these differences are basic human patterns of Perception and Judgment. Once these patterns are recognized and the behavioral expressions understood, we each have an opportunity to follow a process of valuing that leads to mutual respect and reciprocal contributions to human well-being.

Psychological type gives us a pathway to explore human differences. Type theory assumes that all of the mental operations—Extraversion, Introversion, Sensing, Intuiting, Thinking, and Feeling—are of equal value, and that they each play an equal role in our ability to adapt and adjust to our daily challenges. Think of it as a theory of mental equity. More important, the management of differences is first and foremost a matter of individual psychology, and psychological type offers some insights about the way our minds work.

Isabel Briggs Myers wrote, "It is not too much to hope that wider and deeper understanding of the gifts of diversity may eventually reduce the misuse and non-use of those gifts. It should lessen the waste of potential, the loss of opportunity, and the number of dropouts and delinquents. It may even help with the prevention of mental illness. Whatever the circumstances of your life, whatever your personal ties, work, and responsibilities, the understanding of type can make your perceptions clearer, your judgments sounder, and your life closer to your heart's desire."[5]

Recognizing those gifts, acknowledging their role and natural expressions, and making a place for them in your conversations and relationships promises to provide bridges between differences and invites a celebration of the value in human diversity.

What's Up, Pops?

EXPLORING TYPE AND GENERATIONAL DIFFERENCES

Gerhard, age 33, works hard to connect with his team. After six months as team leader, he feels the relationships among his team members simply aren't where they need to be. Gerhard has been with the company for three years, and he is both the youngest member of the team by age and by tenure with the company. He is at least 10 years behind the other team members in the organization: Zoe, 47, Johnny, 55, Barry, 59, and Tracy, 62. Each has between 13 and 18 years of experience with the company, and the four have worked together on a number of projects over the years. When the team leader position opened up, everyone expected Tracy to be selected because of her knowledge of the product and her experience in the organization. A relatively new company president and newly appointed vice presidents had different ideas. Though they discussed the value of experience and knowledge, every appointment they'd made in the last year had been an individual in his thirties with the least seniority in his department. The mood of the team is best described as annoyed and mildly angry. Many feel that their hard work built the company's top-selling products, and now they are being pushed aside.

On a typical Monday, Gerhard makes a point of visiting each team member and asking about the project as his way to get connected. The team members, however, hear his questioning as doubting their work. A typical conversation begins with Gerhard walking into a cubicle or office with the cheery opener, "What's up, Pops?" On one particular day, Barry decided to let Gerhard know exactly what he thought of the question. He said, "That question is one of the most disrespectful and condescending things ever said to me in my entire career."

On the surface, the communication problem seems to have very little to do with type: everyone on the team prefers ESTJ. Gerhard thought he was being friendly, but Barry experienced the message as rubbing his nose in the fact that a man 26 years his junior was now his "superior." We could make a very good argument that Gerhard needs to learn a few things about emotional intelligence and, in turn, that the older team members could learn from Gerhard about taking initiative to reach out across generations. Gerhard's term "Pops" is related to the affection he feels for the older members of his family, on whom he depends for guidance and support. As is true for many ESTJ individuals, reliance on tried-and-true methods produces a stability and persistence that is comforting. According to one 45-year-old GenXer who tends to mistrust institutions, there is additional energy in trusting those who are immediate and comforting.

The longevity of today's workforce often means, as in the case of Gerhard and his team, that there are three or four generations trying to work together successfully. Some would point to the family farm or business as an example of how this has worked for eons, but only a small subset of our society has had that experience. In today's office, the shifting demographics are new and are a function of the birthrates of the past 60 years. Enhancements in social and developmental research have led to a consensus of opinion on the characteristics of the generationally diverse workforce. These various analyses, which include studies dating from a hundred years ago as well as those conducted in the past several years, identify trends in perspectives and attitudes among different generations. As a quick reminder, consider the following summary of generational characters, and keep in mind that the birth years are estimations of when shifts in social attitudes or events marked an emerging perspective. Some researchers select different dates as the markers of generational differences; a great deal depends on their assumptions about social influences on the generation. All researchers agree on the names and general characteristics as follows:

- **Boomers, born 1943 to 1960,** were raised in a post–World War II climate that encouraged bold optimism. This resulted in a generation of individuals willing to work for the best, to explore personal limits (e.g., drugs, sexual risk taking), and to work tirelessly for both personal achievement and social change. Much to their dismay, their work ethic and declining economic prosperity feel misaligned, and this only serves to underscore their ideals as a source of identity.
- **GenXers, born 1961 to 1981,** were raised in a time when social upheaval—the murder of public officials, divorce rates, mothers going to work, and rapid application of science (e.g., a man on the moon)—produced a generation that distrusts institutions and seems driven by an entrepreneurial pragmatism that is fueled by the self-reliance of survivors.
- **Millennials, born 1982 to 1995,** were raised in an environment where focusing on children, using technology, creating a better life through

work–life balance, and establishing a stable and relatively risk-free life produced a generation that insists on personal attention, collaboration (as a way to keep everyone "in the loop"), and the authority of the crowd (e.g., social networking, big brands).

- **Generation Z, born 1996–2010,** are being raised in an environment where safety has become a primary topic and the focus on "baby" is at an all-time high. Already expressing their views at six years of age, they are true digital natives. If the behavior of the generation now arriving at school is an indication of what is to come, they expect to be entertained and challenged, given maximum freedom, and that what's coming will be "electronic." New car commercials capture this perfectly: each kid in her safety seat has a headset to use while watching the show of her choice on her individual LCD screen. Some researchers report they are overwhelmingly visually engaged. They will experiment with Google glass, nano-computing, 3-D printing, and driverless cars. If the pattern holds to that of previous generations raised after a generation of low risk-takers, they will be individualists in pursuit of expression.

- **Generation Alpha, born 2011 to the present,** are raised in the most technologically advanced society and global dynamic in history. Developing countries have cell phones with access to Wi-Fi even when they don't have sanitary living conditions. In social and political life, they are growing up in an age of social division and economic segregation that is evident to all due to worldwide reporting. How all of these factors will affect their outlook and general orientation is to emerge in the coming years.

We must be careful, however, to remember that generational patterns have as many variations as there are individuals in an age group. In general, it is believed that the attitudes of a given generation begin to become "stable" around the ages of 11 to 14, and are largely influenced by public events. Those who witnessed the 9/11 attacks when they were 11 years old experienced a different emotional event than did the 50-year-olds watching the same horror unfold. It is easy to imagine that the event generated fear and a sense of instability, which could lead to a generation that is, on the whole, very careful to avoid conflict and to accommodate others.[1]

In recent years, studies about generational differences have revealed some interesting trends. When asked to rate key values, all generations placed the values in essentially the same order of priority. However, closer study of the data shows that different generations define those values very differently. For example, 50-year-olds and 30-year-olds both rate "family" at the top of the list; yet that rating means something very different for each group.

Important to our exploration of generational issues and type is the evidence that core type patterns do not change from generation to generation, though the focus of that pattern may change considerably—ISTJs at age 20 and those at age 50 share many common qualities in terms of mind-set, approach to work, communication patterns, and relationship issues. The context and content of the messages vary generationally, but the structure and style of delivery do not.

It seems fair to say that type accentuates generational perspectives. In other words, a good many 20-year-olds today share the same general take on the world, their collective expectations and hopes, and their interpretation of values. The way they express these, however, varies by type. Consider the 22-year-old INTJ who has analyzed volumes of data on the environment and puts her energy into dealing with systemic environmental waste. The way she sees and talks about these problems sounds very much like the 50-year-old INTJ woman who has analyzed reams of investment information and is putting energy into financially sound policies for her business. They share the same passion for systemic and strategic perspectives but direct that focus toward topics that are more generationally influenced.

As a way to capture some of these trends, the hallmarks of the current generations are captured in Table 26, sorted by type expressions of the mental functions (ST, SF, NF, NT). A core "want" and a primary focus are listed for each type across the generations.[2]

These patterns provide some helpful insight when developing ways to respond to those whose generational life experiences are so different. When we consider that the meaning of messages between individuals resides in the receiver of the message, understanding how meaning is affected by generational frames of reference can be quite useful. For example, Gerhard—a GenXer—feels that everyone is a free agent and that all you have to do is be competent and you'll thrive, so be fearless and go forth! This drive for competence and achievement is magnified by his ESTJ preferences. Barry—a Boomer—believes that appropriate social behavior reflects respect for others. Gerhard's question, "What's up, Pops?" strikes Barry as stemming from a failure to recognize that Barry has paid his dues. Barry expects others to appreciate his experience. Given their common typology, their delivery of their messages is experienced by the world as definitive and forceful.

In a sense, generational categories are a form of typology, though they are socially driven rather than determined by individual psychology; yet we know that categories cheat us out of subtlety and distract us from investing the time it takes to understand variations among and between patterns. At one level, it is absurd to attempt to group generations into categories.[3] Yet the evidence is clear that groups of people who experience key public events between the ages of 10 and 14 begin to develop shared attitudes that they carry with them all their

Table 26

CORE WANTS AND FOCUS FROM THE GENERATIONS AS EXPRESSED THROUGH THE COGNITIVE FUNCTIONS

	STs (Sensing + Thinking)	SFs (Sensing + Feeling)	NFs (Intuiting + Feeling)	NTs (Intuiting + Thinking)
Boomers (1943–1960)—protected by parents, challenge the conventional, workaholics, believe in the power of groups	• Want agreement on the "rules" • Rely on logical options	• Want mutual shared effort • Rely on relationships in groups	• Want agreement on the ideal • Rely on congruence of action to task	• Want systemic approach • Rely on a drive for greater competency
GenXers (1961–1981)—distrust institutions, married late, free agents, self-reliant, thrive on being fearless	• Want "personal" contract • Rely on debating with others to clarify position	• Want individual relationships • Rely on personal attention to others	• Want individual opportunity for making "meaning" • Rely on personal mission	• Want personal strategic plan • Rely on individual performance goals
Millennials (1982–1995)—want teamwork, conventional schedules, politically savvy, thrive on affirmation	• Want to measure mutual commitments • Rely on standard operating procedures	• Want a sense of common community • Rely on networks and role clarity	• Want community based on common mission • Rely on personal sense of congruence	• Want a comprehensive approach • Rely on reciprocal high standards among work and personal relationships
Z (1996–2010—protective parenting, expect to be catered to, live 24/7 in world of technology, prefer immediate answers, self-disclosing	• Appear to expect others to "follow" the set rules • Want technology to make it easy	• Appear to expect supportive relationships with little, if any, disagreement • Want others to make it easy to "do" what is required	• Appear to feel that whatever they choose to do is inherently acceptable • Want freedom for imaginative exploration	• Appear to feel that they can find an answer to any challenge • Want recognition for each accomplishment
Alpha (2011–present)—technology is omnipresent, access to information and social/economic segregation apparent worldwide	• Drawn to the efficiency of technology • Expect immediate results in all things	• Attracted to greater social conformity of immediate group • Becomes more traditional in orientation than previous two generations	• Attracted to mission-oriented activities • Demand space and opportunity for creative expression	• Driven to specific sets of expertise; earlier attraction to professionalism • Uses technology for varied experiences and skill improvement

lives. The 9/11 attack has had a different impact on the GenXer and Millennial generations than it did on the Boomers. The assassination of John F. Kennedy jolted the Boomers into a new awareness about the power of a collective response in protest, which has influenced them throughout their lives. School shootings, church and synagogue shootings, and other public violent events dramatically affect Gen Z and Alpha perspectives on the nature of risk and how to thrive.

As we mentioned, when different generational groups are asked to rate a values list, family, honesty, achievement, and happiness are rated highly by every group. Millennials place peace and equality much lower on the list than Boomers do. However, when we talk with representatives from the different generations, we hear very different pragmatic meanings for the value ratings. For example, Boomers put family first, which results in working harder and longer to secure "their happiness." Millennials report that they make sure to go home at five o'clock to be with family so that special attention is paid and "quality time secures their happiness."[4] Perhaps a harbinger of future priorities, Generation Z is the first to put world peace on the bottom of the list of values. This illustrates a key point presented throughout the book—whether we are exploring patterns through generational perspectives or personality type, the meaning isn't really known until an individual tells you her story. *Patterns can provide clues or create prisons in the way we think about and react to others.*

Once we recognize these patterns, we naturally ask, "So what?" As with all models or methods to identify trends and patterns in perspectives and behaviors, the hope is that we will use that information to make more effective choices when dealing with others. The lessons of emotional intelligence and communication covered in chapters 6 and 8 are relevant to our response to these personal differences. To pretend these patterns do not merit reflection and action is folly to the individual who wants to enrich relationships at work and in the community.

For every type, there are dimensions of the type patterns that can aid our interactions across generations. We will examine the four dimensions that are most useful and that provide the most practical answer to the "So what?" question: achievement orientation, resilience, well-being/stress management, and the use of psychological energy. The urge to achieve and establish effective relationships is a common thread through the generations. Being resilient and managing stress reflect patterns in dealing with the demands of your generational perspective. And though the meaning of experiences varies by generation, the use of psychological energy does not.

The situation with which this chapter began illustrates the importance of using the common ground that type brings rather than focusing on the potential divisiveness that generational differences can bring. Gerhard wisely reached out for help to address the underlying issues that were keeping the group from becoming a team. Through team development activities, the group found common ground in their type similarities—especially around a shared desire to achieve—as a basis for building understanding.

Regardless of the generations at work (or at home, for that matter), the desire to achieve takes many forms, all of which are valuable and vary by type. These different pursuits challenge our resilience, well-being, and energy. When working with individuals on the job or in a community activity, keep in mind that these type patterns are likely evident and strikingly similar regardless of generational differences. Table 27 provides a summary of typological patterns across these dimensions. We encourage you to use these bullets in conversation when generational issues churn negative behavior and you need a bridge over troubled waters.[5]

Table 27
PATTERNS OF THE TYPES RELATED TO KEY ASPECTS ACROSS GENERATIONS

ISTJ	Introverted Sensing with Extraverted Thinking
Achievement	• Drive to do well within clearly defined structure; work the plan • Adapt current realities to future goals
Resilience	• Efficient use of resources is an important strategy • Self-sufficient and persistent in seeking goals
Well-Being and Stress Management	• Well-being related to task achievement; feel "good" when systematic effort yields results; optimistic about the future • Access analytical frameworks and physical exercise as coping resources
Energy	• Show commitment toward others by completing tasks • Due to focus on precision in doing work, often believe that the successful completion of a task is its own feedback • Forceful in making things happen

ISTP	Introverted Thinking with Extraverted Sensing
Achievement	• Reach goals best when general expectations are clear and there is openness for multiple ways to achieve outcomes • Increases with respect of efficiency and decreases with too much process
Resilience	• Confident in lessons of experience and methods for approaching problems • Persistence increases as situations can be broken into pragmatic units
Well-Being and Stress Management	• Physically active and health conscious • Rely on analysis and active pragmatic problem-solving as coping resources

Table 27

PATTERNS OF THE TYPES RELATED TO KEY ASPECTS ACROSS GENERATIONS *(Continued)*

Energy	• Sporadic show of intensity; lively and responsive on most occasions • Like feedback about performance and are less engaged with relationship and emotional concerns

ISFJ	**Introverted Sensing with Extraverted Feeling**
Achievement	• Oriented to achieve within clearly defined structures and well-defined roles • Often seek a collaborative effort with a select few to achieve goals
Resilience	• Keep "nose to the grindstone" to get results • Persistent in seeking practical goals • Industrious in working the plan in service to others
Well-Being and Stress Management	• Coping resources primarily include networks and interpersonal relationships • Use physical activity as a stress reliever • Have some self-doubts that are addressed through clarifying direction of efforts
Energy	• Effort increases as task or situation indicates task definition and clarity • Commitment toward others through service • Assertive of feelings to a select group of people

ISFP	**Introverted Feeling with Extraverted Sensing**
Achievement	• Drive to do well within structure, and are organized for concrete rewards for independent action, initiative • Industriously work the plan
Resilience	• Efficient use of resources in seeking goals • Related to sense of service and levels of support in a setting
Well-Being and Stress Management	• Optimistic about future and choices that are available • Coping resources include creating extended reflection time and using small networks of individuals
Energy	• Gentle and often nondescript social display of energy; however, expend considerable energy finding practical solutions and concrete methods for addressing a situation • Show commitment toward others through "doing"

INFJ	**Introverted Intuiting with Extraverted Feeling**
Achievement	• Drive to do well through independent action, initiative in using gifts to help others • Methodical about realizing vision of how things could be

Table 27
PATTERNS OF THE TYPES RELATED TO KEY ASPECTS ACROSS GENERATIONS *(Continued)*

Resilience	• Determined use of resources to reach goals • Self-sufficient and strong willed around values
Well-Being and Stress Management	• Use quiet time to rejuvenate and seek to connect within select relationships as coping resources • Have few doubts about capabilities to respond to presenting challenges
Energy	• Moderate display of energy in social settings; easygoing in small groups • Likely to be energized in small groups and one-to-one conversations

INFP	Introverted Feeling with Extraverted Intuiting
Achievement	• Drive to do well within wide boundaries that promote independent action and initiative, and in settings that are comfortable with an emergent style • Increases as activity is related to personal mission and is oriented toward imaginative methods for reaching objectives
Resilience	• Persistence related to focus on mission and values • Bounce back from setbacks with renewed focus on mission and values
Well-Being and Stress Management	• Develop a supportive but select social network to support efforts • Optimistic about the future; access ideas, reframe through writing, and seek select individuals as coping resources; trust the whole of a situation
Energy	• Expend extensive energy on activities and relationships related to mission and ideals • Show commitment toward others through caring and help-oriented behaviors

INTJ	Introverted Intuiting with Extraverted Thinking
Achievement	• Among the most independent-minded individuals, driven to do well with independent action and initiative • See structures as tools for achievement not an end in themselves
Resilience	• Self-sufficient and persistent in realizing vision and frameworks • Persist even against objections if they believe their logic is solid
Well-Being and Stress Management	• Access cognitive frameworks as a coping resource; make time to plan • Achieve balance through reflection and analysis of situations

Table 27
PATTERNS OF THE TYPES RELATED TO KEY ASPECTS ACROSS GENERATIONS *(Continued)*

Energy	• Assertive of perspective and ideas to address pressing problems • Expert performance by self or others is energizing
INTP	**Introverted Thinking with Extraverted Intuiting**
Achievement	• Driven to independently excel at analyzing and theorizing • Seek out principles and underlying structures in any problem
Resilience	• Relentless effort in analyzing data and processes in service to a treasured competency or framework • Self-sufficient and persistent in seeking goals
Well-Being and Stress Management	• Feel good when using abilities; analyze before responding • Use ideas, frameworks, and dialogue with select others as coping resources
Energy	• Show commitment toward theories and problem-solving through critique • Seek to build rapport as good listeners • Enjoy and actively seek feedback on performance
ESTP	**Extraverted Sensing with Introverted Thinking**
Achievement	• Drive to do well through independent action, initiative • Increases with autonomy and opportunity for hands-on action
Resilience	• Efficient use of resources, which are applied to reaching goals • Persistent and assertive in the face of barriers
Well-Being and Stress Management	• Enjoy good physical condition using senses for enjoyment • Cope with stress through physical activity and analytical resources
Energy	• Quick to take action and take charge of situations • Show commitment to solving emergencies or pressing problems
ESTJ	**Extraverted Thinking with Introverted Sensing**
Achievement	• Drive to do well within clearly defined structure • Take initiative in areas of "tried and tested" competencies
Resilience	• Persistent and rarely discouraged in seeking well-defined goals • Rely on discipline to get through challenges
Well-Being and Stress Management	• Often in good physical condition due to attention to exercise • Coping resources are exercise, analysis, and social networks
Energy	• Commitment toward task achievement through "doing" is abundantly evident • Seek feedback to enhance performance

Table 27

PATTERNS OF THE TYPES RELATED TO KEY ASPECTS ACROSS GENERATIONS *(Continued)*

ESFP	Extraverted Sensing with Introverted Feeling
Achievement	• Enjoy structure and organization equally well with taking independent initiative • Increases with elevation in interpersonal comfort and interpersonal activities
Resilience	• Self-sufficient and efficient use of resources • Persistent in seeking service-oriented goals
Well-Being and Stress Management	• Often in good physical condition and focused on well-being and health • Coping resources include extensive social networks and physical activity
Energy	• Lively and gregarious, often easygoing and socially at ease • Show commitment toward others through "doing"

ESFJ	Extraverted Feeling with Introverted Sensing
Achievement	• Driven to attend to individual needs and to follow through on commitments • Excel in settings with roles that are clearly defined and organized
Resilience	• Increases with comfort and clarity of roles • Persistent in providing practical, hands-on assistance
Well-Being and Stress Management	• Have few self-doubts or worries; often in good physical condition • Rely on exercise, physical activity, and social support networks as coping resources
Energy	• Spend considerable energy in keeping people informed and attending to their needs • Show commitment toward others through "doing" and promoting harmony

ENFP	Extraverted Intuiting with Introverted Feeling
Achievement	• See structures and rules as mere temporary boundaries and guidelines within which independent action is initiated • Driven to create and express new ideas and innovations
Resilience	• Resourceful when confronted with challenges • Persistent in supporting others and honoring personal values
Well-Being and Stress Management	• Manage stressors by enlisting friends, colleagues, and associates in idea generation and good-natured support • Coping resources include taking new perspectives on situations and using social networks

Table 27
PATTERNS OF THE TYPES RELATED TO KEY ASPECTS ACROSS GENERATIONS *(Continued)*

Energy	• Energetic, innovative problem solver whose enthusiasm increases with participation • Show commitment toward processes that promote innovation, not necessarily the concrete actions to realize a new solution

ENFJ	**Extraverted Feeling with Introverted Intuiting**
Achievement	• Driven to do well in an environment that allows creative and innovative action • Independent-minded but equally committed to honoring the structure, defined criteria, and "rules" of performance in an organization
Resilience	• Resourceful and well informed; actively build networks as resources • Persistent regardless of barriers to achieve goals around ideals and values
Well-Being and Stress Management	• Rely on social networks, which are usually extensive when dealing with stress • Cope by working through issues and identifying lessons learned when dealing with others; reflect on causes, relationships, and reframing situations
Energy	• Reasonably dominant in social situations, often willing to take on responsibilities to help group achieve goals • Actively seek feedback about interpersonal processes; enjoy change

ENTP	**Extraverted Intuiting with Introverted Thinking**
Achievement	• Independent action and initiative in new situations • Driven to be cutting edge and competent at new challenges
Resilience	• Persistent in seeking goals as long as challenge produces new opportunities • Bounce back quickly from setbacks
Well-Being and Stress Management	• Due to general confidence in abilities, are optimistic about future • Coping resources include relying on innovative ideas, analysis of situations, and social networks; have attitude that "talking it out" is best; break stressors into smaller tasks
Energy	• Actively engaged in challenges and in whatever grabs attention • Assertively seek performance-based feedback

Table 27
PATTERNS OF THE TYPES RELATED TO KEY ASPECTS ACROSS GENERATIONS *(Continued)*

ENTJ	Extraverted Thinking with Introverted Intuiting
Achievement	• Drive to do well through independent action and initiative • See organizational structures as tools for reaching objectives
Resilience	• Assertively resourceful and persistent at efforts when implementing a plan • Don't get discouraged easily and enjoy self-sufficiency, especially when dealing with resistance
Well-Being and Stress Management	• Use analysis and conceptual frameworks as coping resources • Rely on seeing things in new ways as a coping strategy • Develop sufficient network support when faced with challenges
Energy	• High energy for analyzing and conceptual perspective-taking • Show commitment to achieving tasks, not necessarily toward others • Actively seek feedback to enhance performance

Continental Divides?

USING TYPE TO REACH ACROSS CULTURAL BOUNDARIES

Our biology makes us family. Our cultural psychology often makes us enemies. As impossible as it may seem in an age when instant communication shows images of our common humanity and the shared sources of our strife, we still seem to focus on our differences. The differences that matter most and create the largest schisms are essentially psychological—the beliefs, experiences, and deep cultural perspectives that frame our passions. From the appearance of things, we fight each other more these days because of our cultural differences than our physical ones. Interestingly, when individuals who've lived in several cultures learn type, they discover that the personality elements that help them understand differences within their culture also help communicate a commonality across cultures. Extraversion is the same process, though the appearance of it may vary. For example, one Japanese workshop participant commented that "you can always identify Extraverts and Introverts in our culture. An Extravert looks at your feet and an Introvert looks at his own."

According to various demographic reports, the large cities of the world bring together within their borders a mix of races, cultures, and ethnicities that was unimaginable a hundred years ago. Air travel makes movement among the continents easy, and now international trade and communication mean that individuals from different places have the opportunity and the challenge to continuously work and live together. The oceans that separate continents—and cultures—are euphemistically referred to as "ponds" because we can fly over them so easily now. And no matter where we go, whether next door or across the world, we are presented with the same human condition: individuals making their way through life the best way they can within the context of their worldview and personality pattern. The point made in our chapter on generational differences bears repeating here: patterns can provide clues or create prisons in the way we think about and react to others.

Everyone tries to solve the puzzle of survival, use their time and energy to best advantage, and address the challenges of daily life with the resources available to them. Each culture creates a set of "rules" on how to approach and use these resources. Rules for how to consider and use time, master the environment, and relate to others develop over eons in human communities. These rules are so deeply embedded in our development that most people rarely contemplate the unwritten rules that guide them. For example, in some cultures time is seen as a sequential unfolding, while in others the current "event" is the marker rather than the clock.[1]

Lessons within each culture are taught to each member of the community. The underlying purpose of rules in any society is to create structures for living and working in harmony with the cycles of life. These lessons frame nuanced views as to what "natural resources" are. Do we see ourselves as individuals seeking to achieve personal fulfillment or as members of a collective unit within which our positions or relations to each other are determined at birth? Enculturation is a powerful force; it encourages one culture to look at their shoes as a sign of respect and another to shake hands while looking you straight in the eye. These issues—complex and worthy of much study—are well beyond the scope of this book. We encourage you to become a student of any culture you plan to visit or to work within so that you can be the best guest. Our goal here is to understand how the phenomenon of psychological type is common across cultures and how to use the insights of type for interacting effectively with individuals from different cultures.

Crossing all boundaries of cultural experience is the individual human psychological architecture, which is the same no matter where we go. The experience of anger is the same biological event for every human being, but the triggers for anger vary by culture and by personality. Evidence shows that, though our skin color and other superficial features may vary, our bodies all work the same. Like our bodies, our psyches are basically alike. Psychological type is a framework for understanding the operational functions of the human psyche across the globe. In other words, as suggested in chapter 1, Extraversion as a process of feeding a stimulus-hungry mind is much the same in Beijing as it is in New York City or the Philippines, though the outward behavior may look very different. Context is key.

Many years ago, Roger was running a psychological type development workshop in London, England, and a group of ENTPs were meeting to discuss the key qualities of their type. At the top of the list were the words "noisy and demanding questioners." That verbal description sounds familiar to anyone who knows type and has seen more than two ENTPs in the same room. By American standards, though, the group was barely audible and extraordinarily polite; what they considered noisy and demanding was unrecognizable through an American lens on behavior. The other Londoners in the room confirmed their description indicating they were among the loudest in the room. And that is the point. They were noisy and demanding in the context of their cultural experience, and their colleagues in the room verified that perception of them.

This cultural variation underscores why it is so very problematic to tightly associate behavior with type patterns. Given that type is based on the use of psychological energies (e.g., sensing details, intuiting patterns), behavioral expressions take different forms given the culture in which an individual is raised. It is best to consider the core of the processes and, through active questioning and exploration, help identify the expressions of the type in a given culture with those who know it best. For the sake of clarification, Table 28 provides some comparisons across cultures. Elements noted as constants by various researchers have been selected, and the information reflects a key factor that permeates the culture. For example, time horizon affects how relationships are approached and business decisions are made—the longer the horizon, the less urgent the business decision.

These quick reference points should reaffirm the crucial importance of becoming a student of the culture you plan to visit. Perceptions of time, the relative importance of status and gender in relationships, the role of religion, attitudes toward nature, subtleties in body language, and the role of emotion or affection are factors about which volumes have been written and are still being written in an effort to understand the dominant cultures in the world. Our purpose here is to give some simple clues that allow an understanding of the "rules" of culture deeply embedded in the way individuals approach one another.

In a recent meeting of managers from an international manufacturing corporation, the following behaviors occurred:

- Upon entering the room, the American department manager proceeded to walk around and shake everyone's hand.
- The American manager started asking about the personal lives of the participants and began telling stories about his family and his experiences in the business.
- The manager wanted to personalize his connections, so he learned the first names of all those attending the meeting and used them repeatedly.
- No mention was made of those in the room who had more experience than the American manager and no recognition was made of various family connections or long-term service to the company. The manager wanted an egalitarian team and didn't want to imply any sort of special status.

255

Table 28[2]
SELECTED ASPECTS AND PERSPECTIVES OF FOUR CULTURES

Mexico	China	India	Egypt
• Moderate time horizon	• Long-term time horizon	• Family background is very important	• Family background is important
• Preserve people's feelings—thus good manners	• Emphasis on mutual connections	• Relatively short time horizon	• Don't try to control nature
• Live in present	• Nature "is"	• Some efforts to control nature may be worthwhile	• Islamic beliefs guide public and private life
• Respect for history, past	• Business relationship is seen as a friendship that knows no time urgency		• Five daily prayers govern the rhythm of the day
• Nature is God's creation		• Rules of interaction between men and women are sensitive	
• Social competence is as important as technical competence			• Physical closeness (such as breathing on another while talking) is common
	• Sensitive to national slights	• Avoid use of first names as a sign of respect	
• Respect and recognition are important	• Signal of business interest is caliber/status of individual assigned to work with you	• Hinduism dominates the culture and relationships	• Patriarchal culture
• Work is not inherently redeeming			• Time is flexible
			• Communication must show harmony and agreement
• Body language "read" as more crucial than spoken language	• Saving face is crucial; decisions are not made in public	• With 16 official languages, it is easy to "misread" communication	
• Decisions are centralized in organizations		• Displays of affection are inappropriate	• Connections are most important to gain access to decision makers

The first behavior mentioned annoyed the Mexicans, Indians, and Chinese in the room. The second behavior deeply offended the Chinese. Addressing participants by their first names annoyed the Indians to the point of distraction, and the failure to acknowledge family connections and long-term relationships to the business irritated just about everyone. In other words, this American manager didn't do his homework, and by behaving in ways he had been encouraged to do in the United States, he managed to generate an undercurrent of agitation and ill will. This manager happened to be an ENFJ and the high-energy personalization natural to this type magnified the offense.

If we are wise, we will study carefully the culture in which we are going to work or connect with others and give focused attention to how our typological patterns work for or unintentionally against the grain of that culture. Being aware of type processes highlights a basic set of issues that you should be attuned to:

- Do you communicate a sense of immediacy and urgency? (Se)
- Do you systematize and attempt to verify information being shared in the moment? (Si)
- Do you show expressive energy to brainstorm and share ideas? (Ne)
- Do you attend to various patterns and, thus, create scenarios for possible action? (Ni)
- Do you provide critical pluses and minuses of the situation before you? (Ti)
- Do you analyze, looking for an underlying model or theory to explain things? (Ti)
- Do you show considerable attention to the comfort of others? (Fe)
- Do you carefully link behaviors with symbols and ideals in a situation? (Fi)

Each of these behaviors is likely to be evident in various degrees in any given interaction. Depending upon the cultural context, these behaviors can be extremely productive or quite offensive. We know that these natural expressions of the core aspects of type are evident worldwide, and it is also apparent that some cultures encourage certain processes over others. Expressions that some cultures celebrate, others push against. For example, the demonstrated sense of immediacy and urgency so natural to Extraverted Sensing types would be seen as crude and disrespectful in one culture and praised in another. These core expressions remind us that wherever we go, we take our preferences with us. By being more attuned to them, we might be more inclined to make mindful choices that attend to the cultural context we're working within. Keep those insights as a kind of checklist for your behavior.

Another helpful aspect of type, when managing different cultures, is the fact that if we reduce type to bare preferences, we can quickly assess the environment in which we work with others from different countries. We can evaluate the way energy is used (Extraversion and Introversion), information is attended to (Sensing and Intuiting), decisions are made (Thinking and Feeling), and people go about doing their daily tasks (Judging and Perceiving). All of this information provides us with clues about how people like to live together. The shorthand of type gives you a useful tool for identifying ways to fit in and communicate your regard for the culture in which you find yourself.

All this being said, knowing type and how it can moderate our behavior in cross-cultural settings is no substitute for learning about the cultural differences around us. It is important to keep in mind the following checklist of items to consider when living with or working with those from another culture. Become extra sensitive to reading others' reactions to behavior, and do your homework on the following:

- How decisions are made
- How time is managed and perceived
- How accountability is determined
- How affiliation works within the group
- Which qualifications are important for others to know
- Body language "rules" of the culture (for example, scratching your ear in one culture is as offensive as extending your middle finger in another)
- How well uncertainty is tolerated
- How success is determined
- How roles are defined and viewed
- How status is granted
- How gender and generational differences affect interactions (for example, making an effort to shake the hand of a woman in some cultures would bring the conversation to an abrupt end)
- How to show respect, regard, and appreciation

TYPE AS MODERATING FACTOR

Our type can serve to moderate our behavior in such matters as those outlined above. The aspects of our type patterns most relevant to our cross-cultural interactions are *flexibility, social skill,* and *tolerance.* Flexibility means being able to shift behavior as the situation requires. Social skill is about our primary interpersonal actions and style. Tolerance reflects how open we are to differences. Surely it comes as no surprise that these are expressed differently by the 16 types. Table 29 provides the expressions of these qualities across the types. While flexibility, social skill, and tolerance are important in any relationship, they come in especially handy when dealing with cross-cultural interactions.

Every effort has been made to strip away the Western lens on the bullet descriptors, though at some level that is impossible given the heritage of the authors. We propose that you consider the behavior bullets as trends that apply across cultures, and realize that in some cultures the qualities are magnified and in others they are less intense; nonetheless, the implied quality is evident. For example, ISTJs increase in their flexibility when the plan for what's next is clear. In some cultures that plan is driven by time and task, and in other cultures it is driven by selected experiences. And keep in mind that what is ambiguous for an ISTJ in the United States may be the conventional state of affairs and therefore not a source of distress for ISTJs elsewhere.

Type is the magnifier of cultural variation and the trends are best viewed with "soft eyes"—the meaning is to be fully discovered within the context of the culture.

Table 29[3]

KEY ASPECTS OF THE TYPES AFFECTING CULTURAL EXPRESSIONS

ISTJ	Introverted Sensing with Extraverted Thinking
Flexibility	Like structure, order, and consistency
	Enjoy the feeling of efficiency in getting things done
	Often not tolerant of ambiguity or change without a thorough plan
Social Skill	Selective with efforts to initiate and build relationships
	Social but not gregarious; dealing with others needs to serve a purpose
	Build trust by abiding by social conventions
Tolerance	Demonstrate patience with others' beliefs and actions
	Fair-minded during discontent, conflict

ISFJ	Introverted Sensing with Extraverted Feeling
Flexibility	Make changes by adapting current strategies to achieve goals
	Enjoy well-defined and clearly purposeful and realistic change
	Do not like surprises and unpredictability
Social Skill	Reticent and not outgoing, enjoying one-to-one interaction
	While pleasant to be with, may be seen as socially ill at ease
	Proficient with building relationships over time and experience
Tolerance	Demonstrate moderate patience with others' beliefs and values
	Slow to engage in conflict
	Decreases as uncertainty increases

INFJ	Introverted Intuiting with Extraverted Feeling
Flexibility	Enjoy new experiences and variety
	Adaptable with changes and clever with imaginative solutions
Social Skill	Moderately inclusive of others but warmly responsive whenever others initiate
	Build relationships deliberately and cautiously, given the emotional intensity and effort involved

Table 29[3]

KEY ASPECTS OF THE TYPES AFFECTING CULTURAL EXPRESSIONS *(Continued)*

Tolerance	Nonjudgmental and trusting of others
	Often diplomatic and patient with others' beliefs and values

INTJ	**Introverted Intuiting with Extraverted Thinking**
Flexibility	Open to new ideas and enjoy innovation; earnestly promote autonomy
	Adaptable when there is good reason to be
Social Skill	Selectively inclusive of others and while outgoing, not gregarious
	Enjoy others who are perceived as competent and forthright
Tolerance	Demonstrate patience with others' ideas and perspectives
	Communicate respect for justice, fair-mindedness, and commitment to principles during discontent, conflict

ISTP	**Introverted Thinking with Extraverted Sensing**
Flexibility	Adaptable as long as the situation fits within a "working theory" of how people should behave
	Reasonably willing to explore new experiences
Social Skill	Social but not gregarious; easily entertaining to a selected audience
	Drive for efficiency often seems detached and impersonal
Tolerance	Adaptable and willing to explore new situations
	Less patient with emotionally related matters

INTP	**Introverted Thinking with Extraverted Intuiting**
Flexibility	Open to a wide range of behaviors until prized frameworks are challenged
	Increases with imaginative and innovative opportunities to address complex problems
Social Skill	Socially adept at discussing important principles, ideas, or scientific methods
	Highly selective about investing emotional energy to build relationships
Tolerance	Demonstrate patience with others' perspectives if logically and rationally presented
	Fair-minded and open to debate about ideas and possibilities

ISFP	**Introverted Feeling with Extraverted Sensing**
Flexibility	Like change and variety that are experiential in nature
	Enjoy freedom to work independently of others

Table 29[3]

KEY ASPECTS OF THE TYPES AFFECTING CULTURAL EXPRESSIONS *(Continued)*

Social Skill	Highly selective about building relationships with individuals
	Calm and "laid-back" style often communicates enjoyment with others
Tolerance	Wide range of openness about different views, beliefs, and values
	Highly concerned with promoting independence for self and others

INFP	**Introverted Feeling with Extraverted Intuiting**
Flexibility	Like change, variety, and degrees of ambiguity
	Adaptable, quick on feet, and resourceful when changes are required
Social Skill	Selective about social engagements; appear social in small groups but not gregarious; use humor to build rapport
	Build relationships carefully while being reserved and studious about others' motivations and intentions
Tolerance	Demonstrate patience with a wide range of others' beliefs and values
	Communicate regard during discontent, conflict

ESTP	**Extraverted Sensing with Introverted Thinking**
Flexibility	Adaptable and responsive to change, excited by variety
	Enjoy the moment; open to experience
Social Skill	Proficient with social relationships; socially at ease
	Self-assured; communicate enjoyment with others; responsive
Tolerance	Demonstrate patience with others' beliefs and attitudes
	Fair-minded but impatient with drawn-out analysis or processes designed to explore psychological meaning

ESFP	**Extraverted Sensing with Introverted Feeling**
Flexibility	Enjoy traditions and are open to change that serves a practical purpose of helping others
	Willing to engage and enjoy those individuals who are very different
Social Skill	Proficient with building relationships; self-assured qualities
	communicate enjoyment to others
	Very responsive in building rapport with others
Tolerance	Demonstrate patience with others' beliefs and values; fair-minded
	Communicate respect during discontent, conflict

Table 29[3]

KEY ASPECTS OF THE TYPES AFFECTING CULTURAL EXPRESSIONS *(Continued)*

ENFP	Extraverted Intuiting with Introverted Feeling
Flexibility	Immensely enjoy variety and exploring new possibilities
	Enjoy ambiguity and are open to whatever emerges as long as personal values are respected
Social Skill	Outgoing, gregarious, and activity-oriented but not concerned with making a particular impression
	Proficient at building relationships and socially at ease
Tolerance	Demonstrate openness to new ideas and others' perspectives as long as their values are not insulted
	Typically avoid conflict as a way to promote harmony and social comfort

ENTP	Extraverted Intuiting with Introverted Thinking
Flexibility	Enjoy variety, ambiguity, and the challenge of change
	Naturally inclined to rapid pace of response and resourcefulness
Social Skill	Self-assured and confident in communicating with others
	Responsive and engaging on many topics; personally disclose easily
Tolerance	Demonstrate patience with others' beliefs and values
	Conflict situations tend to initiate a competitive rather than cooperative response

ESFJ	Extraverted Feeling with Introverted Sensing
Flexibility	Pursue change that is planned and focused on improving support for self and others
	New experiences need to fit within a working structure or system to be valued
Social Skill	Proficient at building relationships and socially at ease
	Communicate enjoyment with others by being responsive and trusting
Tolerance	Reasonably patient with others' beliefs and values
	Actively communicate respect during discontent, conflict

ENFJ	Extraverted Feeling with Introverted Intuiting
Flexibility	Like change and variety as long as the plan being implemented is directed toward agreed-upon mission
	Enjoy being quick on their feet and adjust according to pressing demands of a situation

Table 29[3]
KEY ASPECTS OF THE TYPES AFFECTING CULTURAL EXPRESSIONS *(Continued)*

Social Skill	Socially at ease and very self-assured in communicating enjoyment to others
	Quick to build trust and engage numerous people in social settings
Tolerance	Process-oriented as a way to demonstrate patience with others' beliefs and values
	Communicate respect and regard of others during discontent, conflict
ESTJ	**Extraverted Thinking with Introverted Sensing**
Flexibility	Feel change is to be managed through rational frameworks
	Prefer predictability and adaptive, step-by-step adjustments to change
Social Skill	Self-assured and responsive, communicate enjoyment to others
	Build trust through reliability and dependability
Tolerance	Fair-minded and open to new ideas within defined parameters
	Communicate respect during discontent and conflict, but often use a competitive strategy to resolve differences
ENTJ	**Extraverted Thinking with Introverted Intuiting**
Flexibility	Enjoy variety and are often clever at finding innovative solutions
	Open to a range of experiences and often adjust to changes quickly
Social Skill	Outgoing and socially gregarious
	Create numerous power-oriented social networks
	Proficient with building task-oriented relationships; socially at ease
Tolerance	Demonstrate patience with others' beliefs and values if these seem orderly and subject to reasoned analysis
	Fair-minded; communicates respect of others during discontent, conflict
	Impatient with the pace of most other individuals

Human differences can be a source of great joy and mutual benefit. Regrettably, there are those for whom any difference leads to the judgment that one is better than the other and, at the extreme, that there is no room for the other. It is astonishing that so little effort is made to reach across boundaries in an age when people around the world are aware that continued life on this planet is contingent on embracing diversity and learning to work collaboratively. There may be no more important human agenda than the mutual appreciation of differences, so that we can focus our energies on preserving life.

Psychological type offers a way to reflect on those qualities that are most likely useful for enhancing cross-cultural relationships. There are some aspects of behavior that appear to facilitate mutual understanding across cultural boundaries. Flexibility, social skill, and tolerance are among the chief aspects of behavior that enable us to reach across cultural divides. Understanding how these are likely to show up—though colored by cultural expressions—can help create an interpersonal space for finding common ground.

A Beginning: Psychological Type Opens Pathways or Limits Possibilities

"Life is the hyphen between matter and spirit."[1]

—Augustus William Hare and Julius Charles Hare

This section challenges users of type to put type in the context of life and to remember that type is about inspiring us to reach toward more fulfilling lives.

12 **Follow the Evidence: A Quick Look at the Science of Type**

informs what science says about personality patterns and measurement. There are rules to guide us when evaluating truthfulness in assessments.

13 **Beyond Patterns and Types**

invites us to place type within the context of modern life and its daily demands.

14 **Knowledge Purchased**

reminds us of our uniqueness and importance of claiming our individual voice.

Follow the Evidence: A Quick Look at the Science of Type

With millions of websites reporting on the importance of knowing and using psychological type or indicating that the theory and all associated assessments are snake oil, how do you decide what is reasonable, credible, and useful? You should care about the issue of credibility of psychological type as a theory and associated assessments for three reasons:

1. decisions you might make based on various models *could create more harm* than benefit in your life and in the lives of those whom you care about;
2. resources in terms of money and time could be *wasted and misused*;
3. as a *discerning and intelligent individual,* you should care about the truth or approximations of it.

So far, one of our best strategies to evaluate claims about human behavior is the use of scientific methods.

In its purest form, science is self-correcting thought. We rely on science to constantly improve research and analysis to enhance our lives—every aspect of our lives is impacted by scientific findings. What we eat, what medicines we take, the machines we drive or use for our livelihoods, and much more in our daily lives are by-products of some scientist who kept collecting data and testing hypotheses. And serious scientists will tell us that, "based on available evidence, the following [*proposition*] is a solid working hypothesis." Notice, there is no statement of absolute proof or declaration that something else is or isn't true; the statement is that the evidence we have collected at the moment leans toward a particular hypothesis as being reliable. And it seems on a regular basis, recent studies reveal that old studies on various medicines or foods require revision in our thinking, which is no less true in the science of human behavior. As the ways of measuring evidence improves, so does the analysis; thus, perspectives change or shift accordingly.

Studies of human behavior are among the most perplexing of all of the sciences. While we can use principles of chemical interactions and electron weights to provide working knowledge of how the physical sciences work, we have no such exactness when it comes to human behavior. Even the prized neuroscientists of our age have to caution that given available evidence of how the neocortex operates, some behaviors are likely and probable. Even with some of the most sophisticated measurement tools available, neuroscientists are left with very basic linkages in neocortex activity and behavior. As things get more complex, all predictions get very questionable. Notice—no absolutes. In recent years archeologists have had to update all of their understanding about when humans started doing various things like domesticating animals and intentionally gardening because our ability to both discover and test new artifacts (like human bones or sites of human activity) has dramatically changed. All of these forms of inquiry are looking at concrete, highly accepted notions of what is real (e.g., electrons, chemical reactions, best carbon-based estimations); how much difficulty emerges when considering the sources and outcomes of human behavior?

We are left with some hard and tough questions when considering reported evidence on human behavior. How were the data collected? What tools were used in collecting the data? How were the data analyzed? What moderating conditions impact the data? How stable are the data—repeatable, dependable, consistent? What are the sources of the data and are these the best sources for analyzing the question under consideration? How were (cultural- and cognitive-based) biases neutralized in the data collection and data analysis and in the reporting of both? These questions only scratch the surface. And while the typical consumer of assessments may feel ill-equipped to ask and understand, with a little effort anyone can begin to evaluate the assertions made about an assessment or underlying theory of behavior. But you have to want to understand and put in some work to show it.

To help with all of these issues of data collection and analysis, professionals with expertise have created standards for evaluating the merits of claims on human behavior. Ways and methods of measuring and analyzing have become codified and are intended to provide a basic set of parameters that enable reasonable researchers to collect and examine data intended to provide insight and useful information to improve our understanding of human behavior and how to enhance our lives. And just as you might read the ingredients on a label of food you are considering consuming, you should find out about the available evidence of an assessment you are being exposed to.

When someone with credentials declares that a model or theory or measurement tool is completely discredited, the trained professional is claiming that all of the standards applied to the scientific study of human behavior have not been met regarding the model or inventory under question, and that no reasonable researcher will find pursuing further studies on the "discredited" theory or measurement tool of any use. In fact, to continue exploring behavior based on such models is a waste of time. This declaration should be your first clue that something is not quite right for the simple reason that true scientific inquiry does not throw away decades of data nor is eager to be so absolute about what the data mean. A serious scientist is more likely to say that the "available evidence" indicates that there are more factors involved or that the model doesn't seem to accommodate other variables so further study is needed.

Yet repeatedly over the last 50 years, individuals have felt compelled to declare Carl Jung's theory of psychological types and measurements of the model (e.g., MBTI, Pearman Personality Integrator, etc.) as discredited, and they usually declare the following as the basis of their conclusions:

- Jung had no scientific basis for any of his theories, and no credible effort to replicate his observations have been made.
- Psychological type assessment tools are not reliable and have no basis for claiming validity.
- The most popular of the type assessments, the MBTI, was developed by novices in assessment creation and testing. Thus, the lack of expertise renders the work useless.
- Other tools have more accepted scientific standards than the MBTI and more helpful tools for predicting behavior.
- Self-report tools cannot reveal the true nature of behavior.

To consider the merits of their arguments, we need to look at the available evidence.

Jung, Type, and Science

Jung used the phrase "psychological types" to encourage thinking about a kind of mind-set that permeated the way individuals approach life. His focus was on the psychology of the individual and how it gets distorted through one-sidedness and how the distortion negatively affects an individual's life. Only when the individual can see the nature of his or her psychology and the mechanism directing it can the individual take action to be freer of it. Being free means being aware, evaluating probable outcomes, considering options, and choosing a path more consistent with your unique character with clearer perceptions about who you are and sounder judgments about how you want to live your life.

Jung used a metaphorical framework to describe everyday behaviors. He was not interested in a simplified understanding of personality in this theory; rather, Jung wanted to provide a way to understand how people used psychological energy. He was an early writer on cognitive style. He simply observed that some people get energized by engaging in their world and others energized by reflecting on their world. Jung noticed that some people generally focus on one form of information and the exclusion of another. He noticed that some people relied on a logical approach to taking action and others wanted to reach for an ideal in their choices. He noted several times that his framing of psychological types was a metaphorical way to describe complex processes.

Throughout his life, he said that his theory was intended to help individuals understand how they make decisions, how these get distorted, and why it is important to both understand and flex to different ways of seeing and acting. His list of perceiving and decision oriented mental resources provides a check-list for what to add to our approach to things. For example, if you constantly rely on discrete information, you miss the pattern, and the pattern or connections in information will enrich decisions about the situation at hand.

To declare that Jung's observations are somehow in error is to deny observations from your daily life. Listed below are everyday examples of the eight functions Jung defined (and noted in parenthesis). All of these tendencies are readily evident.

Perceiving Mental Resources
- Focusing in the moment, scanning of the environment (Extraverted Sensing)
- Verifying information, getting multiple forms of confirming data (Introverted Sensing)
- Imagining and seeing scenarios and possibilities (Introverted Intuiting)
- Expressively linking data, pointing out patterns, potentials or predictions (Extraverted Intuiting)

Decision-Oriented Mental Resources
- Articulating the pros and cons of options, logical analysis (Extraverted Thinking)
- Thinking through underlying principles and models (Introverted Thinking)
- Demonstrating action to be inclusive, building rapport (Extraverted Feeling)
- Internalizing alignment of actions, choices, and ideals (Introverted Feeling)

Jung did not claim that he covered all of the behaviors or explained all of the mechanisms at work in human behavior. He simply proposed that all of us have a kind of mental committee in our head that likes to direct our attention and our approach to life in predictable ways. Our "psychological" type is simply the mind-set that generally shows up as we go about our daily life. In multiple forums, Jung noted that individuals oscillate among using these various kinds of mental resources as life demands us to accentuate a particular kind of information or decision-related approach. Current-day support for Jung's propositions is coming from the neuroscience labs of Dario Nardi, PhD, who has found, just as Jung predicted, patterns in neuro-pathways influence what we see and act on. While this is not definitive, it is profoundly substantive evidence in the use of the whole brain, but with certain accentuated patterns. Nardi goes to great lengths to present how individuals use all of their mental networks and do so with higher degrees of energy on some, less on others, and how these uses align with Jung's definitions of mental resources.[1]

While Jung hasn't been shown to be right about all things in his propositions about human psychology, he put forth a variety of hypotheses that have contemporary support. As just noted, neocortex electrical patterns reveal the types Jung predicted. The role of dreams in crystalizing memory and helping create a narrative essential to sanity has been shown repeatedly, which Jung noted was important for human functioning. Jung articulated a principle of subject-object relations in human development before there was a cogent theory on the matter. Essentially, subject-object relations go like this: if you are angry and you act out of that anger, your psychology is essentially subject to the anger. If you identify the anger, ask what the anger is about, and consider how you can use that energy productively, the anger is the object of your awareness and intentional choice. Jung noted that we are governed by our unconscious workings, and neurosciences have pointed out that 99 percent of what we think we do, our unconscious decided for us before we even consciously thought about it. For a discredited thinker, Jung is doing pretty well 90 years later.

Two Measurement Strategies

Tools that have been developed to help others "get at Jung's model" have come in various forms. One form, the MBTI, seeks to inform the person taking the tool what his or her prevailing patterns are in the kind of information one is attracted to and strategy used in decision-making. Another form, the Pearman Personality Integrator, seeks to inform the individual taking the tool that all eight mental resources are available in various degrees and various conditions, and the challenge is to learn how to flex among these resources in an intentional way. Both of these tools have applied the accepted parameters for measuring reliability and validity, and the studies are readily available for review. Still, another form is the use of a multi-rater such as Type 360, where individuals rate type-related behaviors so that observational data can be compared and analyzed to affirm the use of type and its eight functions. And as a critical point for all consumers of assessments, only those assessments where a manual or a technical guide is readily available should be worth your time. The MBTI, Pearman, and Type 360 assessments have extensive manuals that review how items were selected, how items were tested, and how scales were tested and scored. Further, these manuals cover how efforts to establish reliability and validity were accomplished. So when you question someone about the "science behind an assessment," you want to know about reliability, validity, and evidence of utility.

Consistency

Reliability is measured by looking at evidence that there is consistency in outcomes from one time to another when an individual takes the tool or when an individual responds consistently to items of a given scale. The idea is that if an assessment tool is stable, then the results are going to be the same from one administration of the tool to another. Or if it is reliable, the questions that are intended to measure an attribute (e.g., Extraversion) get similar responses. Critics of the MBTI argue that the tool is not reliable because some of the results shift from time to time for an individual. With other assessment tools, similar claims are made if the scores appear to be different over time for the same person. There is no known assessment tool that has perfect reliability; in short, there is always some variation in results from one assessment event to another. The question is whether the variation in result seems reasonable. Both the MBTI and Pearman have shown consistent results over time and within the scales themselves, with typical variations. And if someone is going to criticize that the results vary and, therefore, the assessment is in question, all 3,400 published tools are of no use because they all show variation. One can argue that the assessment developers need to enhance the reliability, but you can't claim that the tools are unreliable because of slight variations from time to time. For the science-minded, accepted correlation coefficients of methods for reliability go from .70 to .98, which is in the range of acceptable to outstanding. The MBTI and Pearman have coefficients of reliability as high or higher than the most popular and respected personality tools in the industry. And if you don't believe it, look at the respective manuals.

Is It Real?

Validity can only be estimated. If an assessment claims that Extraversion and Introversion are forms of mental energy that have certain attributes, there should be independent evidence that these attributes exist and align with the assessment results. For example, if you scored for Extraversion, is there evidence that you get energized when engaged—physical movement—within your environment and with others around you? How much of this kind of data do we need to believe that Extraversion might be a real thing? At what point do we feel the assessment is valid? Is it valid only if 100 percent of the time, when a person scores for Extraversion or Introversion, their behavior conforms to the predicted attributes? Again, this would be an impossible standard for any and all assessments. The best we can do is engage in ongoing studies to look at the alignment of assessment results to other measures or observations of behavior.

Once again, we are confronted with the question, "What is the point of convergence between results and other measures or observations that enables us to feel comfortable that the assessment is doing what it claims to do?" For the science-minded, accepted correlation coefficients of methods for validity go from .20 to .80. You might wonder why low correlations are accepted, and the simple answer is that among standards created over the years, the lowest reasonable correlation (.20) indicates that enough is going on to be noteworthy. If the correlations are too high (.80), a reasonable question emerges as to why two assessments may be needed. In other words, you want some relationship between concepts and differences to reveal how the concepts are similar and different. The MBTI and Pearman have scale correlations with multiple tools and observations that provide credible evidence that the tools are measuring what they intend. In the case of the MBTI, a relatively recent revision of the tool used the most powerful statistical model known to assessment: Item Response Theory. Without getting into the details of this very rich psychometric approach, simply know that no other tool in the history of personality assessment has ever used the method and its results continue to be unparalleled.

Error?

No doubt you have observed that the standards for the measurement of reliability seem much higher than for validity, and you may wonder why this is so. The simple reason is the recognition of the amount of error that occurs in measuring human behavior. If we are comparing an instrument against itself, we expect a high correlation. When we add another kind of tool or observation, the opportunity for scoring distortions, or error, to occur dramatically increases. And by *error*, we simply mean that whatever the reported score, it varies from the "true" score by some degree. The variance is due to factors like timing, experiences, mood, instructions provided while taking a tool, or making observations that are different, and many other reasons a score may not be the "true" score. Fortunately, we can calculate error and obviously want to have as little error as possible. Bottom line: there are standards that can be applied to determine if you should pay attention, and any credible test and assessment publisher has those data available. With regard to the MBTI or the Pearman, all standards are surpassed and, if compared with similar tools, are as good as or better than many. Follow the data!

The Briggs and Myers Problem

From the initial criticisms to the most recent, critics want to quickly discredit the MBTI and, therefore, psychological type by claiming that the mother-daughter team that created the initial MBTI assessment were novices and had no real background to do what they did. Some apologists have noted that plenty of advances in thought were provided by the novice who had a passion about something that drove their developing expertise (such as Bill Gates and Steve Jobs). These are unnecessary arguments for the simple reason that in 1995 and in 2018 the MBTI was reconstructed by a team of PhD and EdD specialists using contemporary statistical models. Interestingly, not a single critic of the MBTI since 1995 has mentioned the new form and how it was created and the statistical modeling that was used to create it. While the novice criticism might seem relevant pre-1995, it is no longer a "dog that will hunt" when arguing against the worth of the MBTI. The MBTI and other tools (like the Pearman) have been developed using accepted scientific models and methods. It is reasonable to criticize the sampling method, to question if the best statistical tools were used, and so forth, but all other claims about the weakness being based on novice creation are simply void of any value. For the science-minded, the 1995 revision of the MBTI used an American census–based sampling to analyze items and scales using a powerful model referred to as Item Response Theory (as noted above). Considered the most powerful statistical method for creating an assessment, it has very complex statistical formulas for showing the strength and completeness of items and scales. In 2018, the MBTI underwent a global sampling across 27 countries and a latent factor model was used. Again, with both methods, Myers's inventory survives and has become more robust.

The second criticism of Myers's work is that it really isn't based on Jung's theory of psychological types, and the tool is a derivative of his system. There are many deeply committed Jungian analysts who would loudly claim that Jung's name needs to be separated from the MBTI because they feel it is off the mark of Jung's thinking. There are very statistic-minded researchers who claim that Jung's material is irrelevant to the value and strength of type assessments. And this issue of the degree to which various assessments are closer to what Jung had intended is extremely complex and nuanced and well beyond the purpose of this chapter. Our view is that Briggs and Myers included a good deal of what Jung intended and missed some other aspects of his model. The Pearman was explicitly designed to provide coverage of all of Jung's eight functions and to incorporate current, modern assessment realities in measurement. The Pearman, unlike the MBTI, is directly focused on the natural and demonstrated use of the eight functions (Extraverted Thinking, Introverted Sensing, etc.) and how to flex among these functions. From its inception, the development, and testing, a panel of psychometricians, social scientists, and psychologists worked with the author (Pearman) to make sure the tool was scientifically sound.

Better Options

There is no doubt that a large number of traditional psychologists—practicing and experimental psychologists—like trait-based models of measuring human behavior. This fits with their training and is aligned with some of the intellectual biases in the field. When they write books reporting on assessment scores and patterns, they often feel compelled to note that the tool they are using has superior qualities in measuring and estimating reliability and validity. It is quite common for such reports or books to claim, "better reliability and validity than the popular MBTI, which has been discredited." One of the most popular models today is the "big five traits" that are measured by multiple tools. The five traits are Extroversion, Originality, Accommodation, Conscientiousness, and Neuroticism. Scores are reported on a standard scale from 10 to 100, with the assumption that high scores in all but Neuroticism produces a more effective personality. No surprise that in multiple studies, measures of psychological type show high correlations as such: Extraversion: Extroversion, Intuition: Originality, Feeling: Accommodation, and Judging: Conscientiousness. Much is made in traditional psychological circles that the lack of measuring Neuroticism on the part of psychological type–based tools is a serious deficit. As a point of history, Myers actually had a fifth factor she called the Comfort-Discomfort factor, which had seven subscales.

First, if you compare the statistical reports of reliability and estimates of validity, you will find these big five tools and type-based tools are about the same. So no one assessment is superior to the other in these terms. You can hold up the statistical reports side by side and come to the same conclusion.

Second, the issue about the absence of Neuroticism is important for several reasons. The measures of psychological type are interested in how a person uses his or her mind rather than assessing degrees of normalcy in behavior or even measures of socially desirable behavior. Psychological type is about mind-set and not about behavior per se, and to compare it with tools that have a different purpose is unreasonable. Trait measurements assume degrees or magnitude of traits while psychological type tools assume a preference among psychological tensions and various categories. Whereas trait measurements want to tell you "how much" you are, psychological type tools want to show you where you invest psychological energy over other possibilities. The dichotomous frame of type hides a profound paradox. The goal of the dichotomy is to find the anchor points in a complex mosaic about human beings rather than an end point for categorization or precise measurement. For example, a trait-based tool expects that most people will score in the middle of a range for Extroversion while psychological type tools report that between Introversion and Extraversion you spend more mental energy in one over the other, and the other is accessible with effort. This difference isn't simply an apples and oranges comparison. It is a complex-versus-complicated way of seeing human behavior.

It is often said that human behavior is complicated. But traditional psychology wants to use specific methods to break the behavior into units, measure it, and piece it together like an engineer would do in solving an architectural issue. This has its purposes. Psychological type sees human behavior as complex, meaning that the dynamics are such that you can't really break it apart to understand it. Type assumes that behavior is the by-product of lots of interacting variables and it is best to see these in terms of competing tensions within the human psyche. The "whole" is really greater than the sum of the parts, from the perspective of psychological type. Type is how an individual uses various psychological energies rather than the presence and expression of any given trait. It isn't reasonable to declare one as superior over the other when their purposes and foundations are qualitatively different. We can debate the relative merits of each and how each can be used. But when the type code is treated as a category of measurement (ISTJ versus ISTP versus ISFJ, etc.), distinctive statistical differences emerge indicating that the whole (i.e., ISTJ) has a quality unlike the others.

You will note the differences in spelling of *Extroversion* and *Extraversion* in the material above. Simply put, Extroversion (trait frame) is essentially looking at socially oriented behavior and degrees of sociability that an individual demonstrates. Extraversion (psychological type frame) is an assumption of how mental energy is used and stimulated, which may or may not show in sociability.

Self-Report as Useless

If you are asked to solve a puzzle problem as part of an assessment of problem-solving skill, you are providing data about yourself through performing. If you are asked to identify how good you are at problem-solving, you are giving a self-report. Let's say on solving the actual puzzle you scored a 2 but your self-report was a 5. Which is correct?

All self-report tools and assessments need to be careful in how data are reported for the simple reason that there is substantial data that self-reported behaviors may not reflect what a person actually does or what is observed by others. For example, you might say on a scale of 1 (not true, rarely show) to 5 (absolutely true, show always) that you are a 5 regarding being empathetic and friendly. Yet when a researcher asks 20 people who know you how empathetic and friendly they find you, the respondents may say something completely different—they average a 2.5. Who is right? What is unassailable is that self-reported results reveal what individuals think about themselves. This internal idealized image of self is often the guide for how an individual thinks of what and why choices are made. It is the internal baseline by which an individual constructs a belief about self. Insofar as this self-image is captured by assessments, it is a worthy discussion for deepening personal insight into who you think you are and how you think you want to be. But reporting a self-report result as definitive as a description of what you actually do is questionable. In the example above, if you gave yourself a 5 on empathy, then the reasonable report is that you *see yourself as highly empathetic* rather than "you are highly empathetic."

We can find plenty of evidence that how we report ourselves is often confirmed by other evidence; however, there is plenty of evidence that how we report ourselves is not how we behave and caters to a self-serving bias of what we find acceptable. Because the evidence is compelling in either direction, it is vital that you get additional information and observations from others whenever you are considering the results of a self-report tool. Just because you believe you are more analytical than most doesn't mean others experience you that way. This only becomes important if that perception affects your choices and your interactions. In many cases, multi-rater data helps address any differences if individuals from many frames of reference see the same thing. At that point, the difference between what you think and how you are can be a rich line of inquiry.

One of the ongoing instructions to professionals who interpret self-report tools is to remind the individual that they answered the questions and the results indicate how they see themselves as part of the journey of self-awareness. Go past that point and you are no longer giving or receiving an interpretation that has evidence to support it. And this part of the journey has it rewards. A study, soon to be published on type360.com, had several hundred individuals verify their four-letter type code and asked raters to rate how often and effective their behaviors are. The results are quite robust. For example, four-letter codes in which Extraverted Thinking has been self-reported have a high correlation (.94) with the ratings of several hundred raters. The results are similar with the other seven psychological type functions. It would seem that knowing your self well leads to effectiveness and personal authenticity, since there is alignment with how you see yourself and how others see you.

Discredited?

To determine if an assessment is discredited, look for:

- A standard manual or technical guide that provides information on how the instrument was developed and by whom.
- An underlying model of the assessment which explains a theory on which the tool is based or the nature of the basic research which drove the creation of the tool. Note that the absence of an underlying explanation for how an assessment got to be the way it is should be an alarm regarding tool credibility.
- Specific measurements of reliability such as internal self-report consistency and over-time consistency. Reports of various samples showing that people who took the tool were consistent in their answers and, when given a second time after a number of weeks or months, they got similar results. For example, if they reported Extraversion as an attribute, did the individuals in a study select most of the extraverted questions, and did they repeat that selection after a period of time?
- Reports of estimations of validity in which the assessment results were correlated with other tools, observations, lab experiments, etc. For example, if individuals in the sample selected Extraversion, did the results correlate with other measures of extraversion or behaviors associated with extraversion?
- Reports providing evidence of the utility of the assessment showing how it was used and the outcomes of using the tool. For example, did teachers discover that extraverted kids approach their studies differently than introverted kids? Do extraverted managers share information more frequently than introverted managers?

All assessment tools and associated underlying models can be declared discredited if the parameters and standards are made impossible to achieve. There are no models or measurements of human behavior that can be perfect in all cases and in all uses. The question is, do the assessments under study meet or surpass widely accepted standards? In the case of psychological type, as assessed by the MBTI or Pearman, it is the baseline that the tools meet or surpass all measurement standards. Neither the model nor the tools are discredited when you apply the widely accepted standards of test development and use. Rest easy. These tools are useful and helpful in personal development and enable individuals to reflect on how to make their lives more fulfilling.

This book reports on a great deal of data collected over decades that has consistently shown how psychological types get expressed in multiple conditions and contexts. Every effort has been made to provide evidence-based information, and when absent, to make note of it. It is our belief that paying attention to evidenced-based patterns provides information to aid in understanding oneself and others. There is abundant evidence that the patterns are real and have significant consequences in individuals' lives. Whether or not a particular assessment score is accurate is entirely up for discussion and, in the hands of a trained and capable coach, counselor, guide, facilitator, or therapist, the meaning of scores can take on new depths.

No one has claimed that the theory of psychological types or associated assessment tools are flawless; they pass the standards of legitimacy created by science-oriented professional panels and are worthy of consideration. In one sense, if the theory or the assessment tools help individuals understand themselves in meaningful ways, and it promotes a deeper understanding of self and others, having scientific support only underscores the value of the self-exploration invited by the theory and tools.

Beyond Patterns and Types

BEING TRUE TO OURSELVES

When naturalist Merlin Tuttle learned in 1986 of a plan to exterminate a million freetail bats that had taken up residence under an Austin, Texas, overpass, he launched a no-holds-barred campaign to educate nearby residents about the importance and value of bats. Tuttle proved to officials and many citizens that bats were not only benign but essential to the local economy because of the millions of insects they consume that otherwise would either destroy local farm produce or necessitate the use of costly and harmful insecticides. He further demonstrated that insect infestations could reduce tourism.[1]

As a result, evening picnickers in Austin today take up posts close to the overpass to watch the bats' nightly emergence from under the bridge, cheering them on as nature's heroes. Tuttle was driven by the belief that if people understood the true nature of the bat and its importance to them, they would change their behavior. He was right. Through education and awareness, the situation was turned on its head, and the once-feared bats are now celebrated.

If people's attitudes and behavior toward bats can change, perhaps the way they interact with others of their own species can, too. Understanding psychological type can help. We believe that healthy tolerance and acceptance at home, at work, and in the world are worthwhile goals, and that making even one small adjustment in your interactions—simply asking other people what they really mean before reacting to them based on your own assumption—will have made this book worthwhile. As should be obvious by now, we think of type as a powerful tool for creating understanding one-to-one and for creating a broader, more conducive environment for goodwill to spread globally.

Our Journey

Before writing this book, we wondered, "What do we know for certain about behavior and psychological type?" Many stories, anecdotes, and casual observations about type exist, but we wanted empirical data, not speculation. While anecdotes serve a purpose, we wanted to explore observed behaviors that are expressions of type, rather than stories about type. Besides remaining true to the data, we wanted to remain true to Carl Jung's theory of psychological type. As we traveled down this path, two things became increasingly clear.

First was the alarming realization that psychological type as conceived by Carl Jung and Isabel Myers, as well as many of the individuals who are exposed to it, is being grossly abused by some popular applications of the theory through the improper use of the Myers-Briggs Type Indicator instrument. Too many individuals come away from their exposure to the MBTI thinking that their results are better or worse than others, or that type necessarily causes behavior. Jung wrote many letters after the publication of his book demanding that his professional colleagues stop using his theory to label and categorize people in absolute ways. Such notions are directly contrary to the most fundamental tenets of type theory, which state firmly that no type is inherently more worthy than another and that preferences do not cause behavior. Preferences are prime movers of behavior, but the actual expression of behavior is contingent on a large set of factors. It's an abuse of type theory to use it to excuse unacceptable behavior ("You can't expect me to be prompt, that's not my type"); to explain poor performance ("I guess we made a mistake putting that person in the repossession department"); to blame others ("If you'd kept your head out of the clouds and paid attention to the details we wouldn't be in this mess"); to project onto others' motivations ("Folks of your type are only concerned with the bottom line!"); and to predict individual competencies ("I only hire secretaries of a certain type").

Our second realization was that while there are many empirical data points to support type theory and to explore behaviors, the complexity and richness of human experience make the exploration messy. Many of those who have fallen into the murky waters mentioned above do so out of a desire for type and type inventories to produce a neat and orderly framework of mutually exclusive types that they can use to explain and predict human behavior. The reality is, of course, that neither the theory nor an inventory was designed for such a thing. Jung himself said, "The purpose of a psychological typology is not to classify human beings into types. This in itself would be pretty pointless."[2] So, after we waded into the messiness and complexity, our journey of research and reflection led us to the many levels and applications of type explored in this book. We hope you have found each level rich with new insights about yourself and others that move you one step closer not only to understanding differences among people but toward valuing those differences.

Life Is the Text; Type Is the Subtext

Life is the text: how we live it, revel in it, destroy it, and play out our individual stories is where the true value of type resides. As one subtext among many, psychological type gives us directions through life that we can, if we choose, ignore or keep in the background. Indeed, it is difficult to take such personal topics seriously when wars abound, people are starving, earthquakes and floods ravage countries, economies are in shambles, and governments around the world are struggling to address the problems of their people. Yet if we can improve our ability to work with others, we can contribute to the improvement of everyone.

If we can teach children, young adults, and colleagues by example to communicate more effectively, develop more completely, and truly value others, we contribute to the welfare of us all. The lessons of type can help us achieve these goals if we will learn them and use them.

After leading thousands of individuals through seminars on psychological type, we are confident that many people learned for the first time that the way their minds work is normal, healthy, and, as we say in the Southern United States, "Just fiiiine!" Many have said, "If only I had known about this before, I would have done things differently," meaning they would have managed difficult situations more effectively, more humanely, than they did. Sadly, we are equally convinced that for most people the insight stops after the introduction. They learn about preferences and various type dynamics, and then fail to use them to their potential. Rare is the situation where individuals really work through the meaning of these basic concepts, and rarer still is the application of the concepts so that they actually change behavior.

Throughout this book we have argued that type is a very powerful model that explains the structure of our mental processes: we Perceive and we Judge, we Extravert and we Introvert, and we live in particular ways that create patterns. Like a watermark in fine stationery, type is embedded in the fabric of our personalities. Our challenge is to remember to look for differences as part of our efforts to communicate with, motivate, and express our value for others. Finding dignity in our own type enables us to develop our strengths and navigate the obstacles and opportunities of adulthood. Once we have been given the gift of understanding what type offers, it becomes our responsibility to recognize the importance and contributions of all people who see the world differently from us—those whose stationery bears a different but equally exquisite watermark.

Type is in the background, never the foreground, of human relations. Ultimately, the text written over the watermark tells the story. The story is made up of experiences, traits and tendencies, situational factors, and a host of forces, most of which we cannot readily access through conversation. But when we know to look beyond the text to the watermark, we may begin to understand the preferred expressions, the limitations of perception, and the needs such limitations engender.

At a minimum, psychological type provides models for two very important insights into human nature. First, it is a model for understanding human differences that provides hypotheses about people different from ourselves and that doesn't value one type over another. Second, it is a model that provides basic questions to help us solve problems in any situation or interaction.

As a constructive model of human differences, type demonstrates that whenever we are involved in an interaction, there are several forces at work that both aid and hinder communication. For example, type informs us that some people need to talk out the issues and steps they see in order to gain clarity, while others simply tell what they have concluded. Type suggests that, when making decisions, some of us rely on facts and others on possibilities; an analytical decision is as important as a choice made in tune with a network of associations. The only thing that ultimately matters is what response is appropriate, productive, and constructive in a given situation. In short, type allows us to understand differences, which invites us to consider another set of questions before jumping to conclusions.

Consider the outgoing parent who comes to understand that his or her careful, cautious, and contained child is not afraid of challenges but goes about them differently. When the parent not only understands the difference but acts in ways to affirm rather than change the child's style, the most important lesson of type has been learned. The teacher who knows that some kids need to connect with an overall plan before they complete a problem or task, and whose teaching style reflects that knowledge, has learned the power of type in motivating others. The boss who begins to recognize that employees are motivated by different things and interactions, and who behaves differently as a result, has started to understand the practical usefulness of type. Things that differ are not necessarily better or worse than one another; the dogwood and the cherry are different trees, but both flower and are beautiful in the spring.

Even if we reject type as an explanation of human differences and a template of mental functions, we can still take from it a few helpful questions applicable to home or work:

- To get work done and achieve a successful conclusion, do the people involved need an environment that provides regular stimulation and an openness to brainstorming and dialogue? To solve a problem, is regular access to information and feedback needed to increase the chances of making a good decision?

- Do you or those around you find clarity in situations by detaching from surroundings and working through information in your head before sharing it? In problem-solving, have you allowed enough time between exposure to information and required response for you and others to give your best effort?
- Are all the facts, as best they can be known and described, on the table? In problem-solving, do you gather the hard and concrete data to give you the facts and current trends required to inform your decision?
- Have you considered being persuaded by future outcomes and potential results rather than current trends? In problem-solving, do you examine the patterns in the data and strive to consider the largest, most global view?
- Have you delineated the pros and cons, weighed the alternatives by standard criteria, and measured the relative value of all the variables?
- Does your decision-making take into account the effect of the ultimate decision on people, the probable long-term effects on their relationships, and the way it reflects on the values and connections you hold most dear?
- Have you set the deadline, the goal, and the direction for your current activity?
- Have you provided opportunities to reopen a question, to reexamine a decision, and to pursue additional related information?

Ask each of these questions when you are working on a problem and you will find that you leave no stone unturned. Good, clean questions cut through the fog and can give each of us a way to address the most complex problems.

Our earnest hope is that people retain their uniqueness and their special expressions of personality even while they recognize and honor the common bridges among all normal individuals regardless of nationality, race, gender, or any of the myriad other boundaries we place between us. We believe that psychological type is an important bridge that provides an opportunity to move us individually and collectively forward in human relations. For many people, those bridges have been closed off far too long, creating unconscious barriers to understanding and development. In the fast-changing, rapidly shrinking world now often known as the global village, type is a gift. It is the language that can open the doors between and among us so long as we honor its richness and complexity, which are a reflection of the wonder and uniqueness of us all.

Jung once said, based on his experience, "people are incapable of understanding and accepting any point of view other than their own . . . forbearance, tolerance, and goodwill may help build a bridge over the chasm which lack of understanding opens between man and man."[3] We hope that we have given you ample evidence and motivation to find goodwill and tolerance within you, not just so you may understand others but so that you value them, honor them, and thank them for enriching your life. For in the end, a person's type is less important than how we treat one another, how we listen, and how we offer encouragement and show appreciation. Type merely gives us the impetus to recognize that there are differences worth paying attention to; this is the true gift and responsibility it leaves behind. Applying the wisdom that comes from understanding personality type moves us closer to using our gifts and embracing the talents of those around us to build a more tolerant and understanding global community.

CHAPTER

Knowledge Purchased

THE PRICE OF UNDERSTANDING

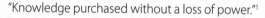

"Knowledge purchased without a loss of power."[1]

—William Wordsworth, *The Prelude: Book V*

Life is a series of exchanges. It begins when sperm and ovum exchange their solitary existences for a union; the genes join, creating an exchange of energy, ions, and electrons. We exchange the air in our lungs for new air. We exchange our time for money and status. We exchange our life activity for one sort of perceived benefit or another. Our last exchange, our last breath, our last known expenditure occurs when we die. Between the first exchange and the last, there is a constant flow, a continual give and take that makes up life. Exchange means a relationship between two or more agents that share a currency—air, water, time, money. Perhaps our most precious expression of ourselves is the way we live our lives recognizing that our lives are a series of exchanges—constantly trading something of ourselves to gain something else. At its best, the exchange, the relationship, is conscious and purposeful.

In modern times many people choose to gain knowledge through an exchange of time, activity, and sometimes cash. Most often our purpose in seeking out learning opportunities is to enhance our abilities to perform and produce, or simply to increase our satisfaction levels. When we choose to learn about ourselves, we are shown information about what our behavior looks like to other people and how our behavior and ideas affect those around us. Sometimes we may not like what we discover; other times we are elated. When we choose to participate in the exchange, we purchase knowledge about ourselves with our energy, our time, and our attention.

From the perspective of psychological type, when individuals learn, for example, that a preference for Introversion may incline them to wait before responding to a stimulus, they have gained this information at the cost of time and money for the materials and interpreter's fee. In addition, if they believe the information is accurate, they are presented with the knowledge that their behavior may affect others in unintended ways. For example, they may also discover that there are people who experience that "pause before responding" behavior as untrustworthy. People with an Introverted preference who learn of this can respond in several ways. They can decide this outcome is undesirable and seek to make a change; or they may say, "Tough! I can't change, so why worry about it?" They might even become very upset and distressed by the news. If, however, they begin to use their new knowledge as an excuse for behavior ("You can't expect an Introvert to do that!"), to blame others ("Just like a darned Extravert to misinterpret my behavior"), or to analyze others' behaviors, then a great deal has been exchanged for this newfound knowledge; namely, the Introvert will have given up approaching people openly, directly, freely, and without judgment, in exchange for the label of "Introvert." Even worse, the Introvert may have chosen to use a model or a system to forfeit personal responsibility for behavior. In such a case, the price of self-knowledge is far too high; it leads to destructive ends and an ultimate loss of personal power.

But the currency you use can also be exchanged for a constructive way to think about human expressions and behaviors. If, for example, our Introverted friend from the example above decides not to change, it is with the full awareness that the behavior has consequences. But perhaps the Introvert decides to inform others about his typical process. Armed with the new knowledge that Introversion is a typical process of looking in before looking out, he may come to realize that a simple comment to a coworker like, "That's an interesting idea. Could I have some time to think about it before I give you my opinion?" can aid others in understanding his inward-looking behavior. This knowledge of one's own type can be used to gain the space and grace needed to interact successfully.

Similarly, the Extravert who learns to preface her verbal brainstorming with "I'm just thinking out loud—don't write anything in stone until we're done!" gains similar space and grace to utilize her preference most effectively. There are examples for every dimension and every whole type, but these two illustrate the point. In these examples, the knowledge purchased surpasses the price because the personal power gained in terms of increased effectiveness in communication and relationships is virtually immeasurable.

The basics of psychological type are easy to learn and appear simple. The downside of that simplicity is that it leads some to quickly type other people, other behaviors, and other groups. This has led, regrettably, to the great overuse of type to label, pigeonhole, or limit people, effectively creating barriers to understanding rather than eliminating them. Thousands have exchanged their personal power and responsibility to grow in awareness and understanding for a rigid model of personality.

This is in direct opposition to what Jung intended. Perhaps more tragic are the individuals who reject type completely because it suggests that self-awareness is an important end, or because they deny having habits and patterns of mind. Those who exchange understanding in favor of pigeonholing, excuses, or blaming are like butterflies in a collector's net; their intellectual growth has ceased. Those who reject the whole concept are like happy caterpillars who don't want to think about growing into butterflies. Both are equally ill served by exposure to type. They are stuck, limited, and closed.

In *The Prelude,* Wordsworth was concerned with the experience of learning and living without sacrificing personal strength, personal wisdom, and individuality.[2] To learn, to gain knowledge without losing personal power, is to discover that one has an ability to perform certain kinds of magic without becoming enslaved by that very ability. If individuals have learned that life is filled with trickery and greed, and in response give up hope for satisfying relationships, they have gained knowledge at the price of personal power. Some individuals go to a psychologist for a diagnosis that will provide them an excuse: they want to be labeled so that they no longer have responsibility for their behavior. After receiving a diagnosis, they may say, "I'm borderline XYZ, so what do you expect? I have no control over it!" If in response to that new knowledge the person gives up trying to address the problem, it might be said that the individual sacrificed power—the belief and effort to improve life—in exchange for a distorted picture of himself.

Knowledge about oneself can be life-giving, as Socrates pointed out and Plato recounted in *The Republic.* As Socrates so well demonstrated in the allegory of the cave, the realization that you may have been looking at shadows rather than the real thing can be a remarkable discovery.[3] Such an insight forces you to recognize that there may still be more to learn and that you need to be mindful of the very human tendency to settle for the status quo. Awareness of this dangerous potential increases your personal power. Discovering that you have a particular talent, for instance, may spur you to pursue other things, other ideas, other behaviors—in essence, to defy the status quo.

We hope that when people learn about type, they exchange some ideas about themselves for a new perspective. Our goal is that they gain knowledge about themselves and others that, if used correctly—with tolerance and goodwill—will lead to new insights, choices, and opportunities for growth.

Using psychological type is difficult; it can invite categorization, stereotyping, and judgmental reactions. The most common of those problems can be summarized in three broad areas: when the right of self-determination of the individual is abused or ignored; when the knowledge level of the user or presenter of type is inadequate to the task; and when type is used in a context for which it was never intended (usually the result of an incompetent user of type).[4] As with all problems, however, there are also opportunities. We will use these three issues to offer insight about appropriate applications of the type model and type instruments.

The Right of Self-Determination Interpretation Settings

When presenting type or being introduced to psychological type, it is imperative that the value of the right of self-determination is honored at each juncture of interpretation. By "right of self-determination" we mean that when anyone receives the results of a psychological type instrument or any other psychological instrument, that person is acknowledged as the expert about himself. When someone is receiving results, his years of feedback from others and reflection on his own behavior take precedence over any other interpretation. It is important while exploring type preferences to consider the role that situations play in the behavior choices a person makes. He should be encouraged to reflect on how learned behaviors, such as those from childhood (for example, always finish your work before you play), affect his judgments. He should be guided to explore how developmental stretches influence his self-evaluation. If he is in the middle of a major life transition (new spouse, new job, new baby, or the like), how does this affect his thinking? In short, type should always be presented in the context of all the other major influences on behavior, and with the explicit understanding that the individual ultimately gets to decide what is true for him and what is not.

If you are a trainer or test interpreter, designing exercises that invite individuals to explore the various spheres of influence on behavior (such as life circumstances or work expectations) will help clients become clearer about which behaviors tend to be type-related and which are the by-products of other forces. The same is true when using type for personal reflection. The point is to create an opportunity to evaluate information about behavior in all of its complexity and richness. If you were thinking about a career change, or if you help others to make career changes, you would not encourage a jump from one career to another simply because a psychological instrument suggested it; you would seek much more information—competencies required, general educational issues, work variety and pace, and the like. Likewise, when taking in information about your psychological type from an interpretation session, be sure to explore various influences on your behavior. Finally, you—the receiver of type instrument data—should determine your type preferences. Creators of psychological type instruments proclaim without hesitation that the results from their tools are working hypotheses only.[5] You are the final judge. Anyone who says differently should be treated with caution.

In the absence of a thorough examination of these multiple sources of behavior, type can be used to typecast others and to support various biases. For example, if you do not consider both those times when you express Extraversion and when you express Introversion, you may fall into the trap of either overvaluing your preference or limiting yourself. From that point on, it is easy to begin to ignore the contributions of other factors on your behavior.

Instrument Administration and Sharing of Results

Another aspect of self-determination is the taking of instruments in voluntary settings and the sharing of personal information that one decides is appropriate. The benefits of any psychological instrument will be greatly enhanced if it is taken in a voluntary setting. The results are more likely to be accurate when people are confident that the results will not be shared without their permission, and when they feel free to answer questions honestly without regard for how they think they ought to respond. Everyone has a right to have personal information kept confidential and their results shared only with permission. For example, if you take a type instrument and the presenter posts your name and type without permission, your basic right of self-determination has been violated on two counts. First, you have not said such material could be shared. Second, until you determine whether the instrument accurately determined your type preferences, any pronouncements of your type are premature and unfounded.

Knowledge of the User/Interpreter

In personality assessment, no one should fall prey to the claim that an instrument designed to understand descriptive qualities or typical patterns can predict competence, excellence, or able expression of those qualities. Regrettably, many people who are qualified to purchase type instruments by virtue of their graduate degrees are nevertheless untrained and unskilled in psychological type theory, models, and history; they are likely to treat the results of the MBTI, Pearman, or other type instruments as if they are measures of personality traits (meaning they could predict behavior), or as if they are akin to horoscopes. We heard about a "qualified" professor who presents type concepts by drawing a bell curve of normalcy on the blackboard, as if something in the theory talks about abnormal behavior! Nothing could be less accurate. Those who do not understand that healthy type development is about adaptation, flexibility, and fluidity in human responsiveness are likely to make an error by saying things like, "Introverted Thinkers always look for theoretical models." We hope you clearly understand by now that within the context of psychological type only a very poorly developed type would *always* respond in any such way. The heart of typology is recognizing the pattern within the multitude of potential behaviors. Predicting with 100 percent accuracy what the behavior of an individual will be at any given instant is the holy grail of psychological researchers but perhaps a task best left to the gods.

If material about type that you read or listen to turns into predictions, ignore it! There simply are no empirical data to support the claim that all people of any type will always or nearly always respond to certain stimuli in certain ways. Besides, it is far more rewarding to consider that types respond to situations with the mental functions required to manage them, and that such adaptation can in fact result in behaviors quite atypical of the type.

Proper Context

Presented properly, psychological type and personality type tools provide a very positive and constructive model to understand differences in the way individuals process and express information. Because a key assumption of the model is that while preferences exist within us, all the mental functions are also present and have potential within each person, it is inaccurate to make any job placement, team assignment, career advancement decision, or psychotherapeutic action based solely on type. While it is valuable to know one's type and what some typical reactions and blind spots may be in a particular situation, that knowledge is best used for developmental rather than diagnostic or managerial purposes. There is a very thin line between becoming aware of a rich model for growth and development and using that model to justify prejudices. We advise you to tread carefully.

Individuals who do not understand the dynamic nature of type tend to see it in superficial ways. To consider type as some kind of educator's horoscope or parlor game is to have a poor understanding of the Extraverted–Introverted, Perception–Judgment balancing act the psyche carries out during every moment of conscious life. If all you do is look at the surface of a lake, you will miss the remarkable life underneath. Explorers of type need to be on guard against both pro-type and anti-type zealots; neither is likely to have more than a superficial understanding of typology.

A Time and a Place for Stories

If violating self-determination is the first sign that the price of learning about type is too high, and the second sign is incompetent users of type who treat results like a predictive measure rather than a preference sorter, beware of yet another sign. Hold suspect those who place over-importance on type and type instruments, and who then present materials that rely on speculative or anecdotal material for describing type.

We all have stories that we feel are illustrative of type concepts. The issue here is those who use stories to make a "factual" statement about a type rather than identifying stories for what they are—stories that may have a kernel of illustrative material in them for some people but perhaps not for others. It is easy to get stories confused with reliable, research-based descriptors, and it is incumbent upon presenters to make it clear to their audiences which are which.

Individuals who seek to read or conduct research and continue their education are more likely to provide a full picture of type and the implications of type in individual lives. Listeners and readers of psychological type material (or any psychological writings) should be encouraged to ask presenters about their education and experience with using type, perhaps asking if their training included more than one workshop. Presenters should be willing to provide lists of their involvement and/or their research related to type.

It is time for the consumer to demand a higher standard for interpreters and presenters than simply having completed a qualifying program or a course in graduate school that enabled them to purchase psychological instruments. Without malice, individuals qualified to purchase type instruments by virtue of their education, but who have no relevant type training, are likely to go out into the workforce with their new tools and models and proceed to introduce unwitting individuals to type in ways that neither honor nor serve the recipient or the model. The unfortunate outcome of all this unintentional incompetence is that a terrible price is extracted from some who are introduced to type: they develop a serious case of hardening of the categories. Like the arterial hardening that leads to death of the heart, this hardening leads to a death of the spirit.

Innovation of Web-Based Interpretations

In recent years a number of organizations have developed web-based interpretation processes of personality type tools in lieu of an individual getting a one-on-one feedback session. These sites vary in thoroughness and complexity and provide little opportunity to ask you personal questions. This development presents a series of dilemmas, such as what to do when you have a question or misunderstand. Often these websites give as little information as possible in an effort to reduce confusion, yet that leads to a lack of richness and completeness in an interpretation. In the hands of a knowledgeable professional, type becomes a splendid framework for exploring personal growth, and that simply cannot happen with a web interface. We recommend that you seek an individual interpretation by using services like those found at leadership-innovations.com or leadership-systems.com.

Evaluating Tools

Assessment tools are being produced at a phenomenal rate. With attractive marketing flair, instruments are being presented as replacements for other tools at a vastly reduced price. The price usually reflects the quality of the science applied to the tool. When someone is pushing an instrument that is to lead to our enlightenment, we have a right to ask some key questions. As a general rule, we should apply a few essential criteria for evaluating the worth of any assessment tool:

- Access to a published technical manual
- Evidence of consistency or reliability (usually in test-retest studies)
- Evidence of validity or measuring what it claims
- Studies of how the tool is used
- Recommendations for interpreting and applying the assessment

And beyond assessment tools today, iPad applications, web-based applications, and other digital platforms include type rich information. iPad applications such as Teamosity or Careerfitosity are based on key research that lead the developers to make both an assessment and interpretation guidance available at your fingertips. It is important to know the source of the digital material and who and how the material was created.

A Wish, a Hope, and a Meditation

Throughout this book we have argued that type is a splendid model for understanding human expressions and typical patterns of responses in communication and for walking a path toward valuing those differences. We have illustrated how multilayered the type model is and how remarkable it can be as a framework for supporting individual growth and development. Our work suggests that the empirical support exists for type to be seen as a serious model of human dispositions. We are excited about the development of important type research and the growth in the use of type around the world. While our enthusiasm is sometimes tempered by the reality that for many people the price for self-discovery through learning about type has been much too high, our hope when we first wrote and published the first edition of this book in 1997 is even stronger today: that through our work and that of others you will be more able to make conscious, positive choices that use your knowledge of type to build trust and effectiveness in your relationships and bring joy to your life and thereby to the world.

Appendix A:
Measurement of Type

O ver the past 70 years, a number of assessment tools for personality or psychological type have emerged to serve different purposes and goals. The following summary is intended to provide some guidance for considering which assessment tool is most useful for you. The tools are listed in order of development.

Myers-Briggs Type Indicator®
Published by The Myers Briggs Company

Administered to millions of people since its inception, the Myers-Briggs Type Indicator (MBTI) was first released in 1962. The assessment provides a four-letter personality type with an index of voting consistency. You receive a result such as E 23, S 5, T 12, J 11, with the letter indicating a preference and number reflecting the consistency of voting. Available with facet, or subscales, the MBTI tool is designed for a quick and reliable report of type. MBTI Step I provides a code and consistency index. Step II provides the code and 20 Facet scales with consistency indexes.

Pearman Personality Integrator®

Released by a global and cross-cultural publisher, Multi-Health Systems, Inc (MHS) of Toronto, Canada, the Pearman Personality Integrator provides an index of how comfortable and how much demonstrated the eight functions are and what elements are critical to flexing within the type system. The developer wanted individuals to become aware of their use of all eight Jungian functions and how both the degree of comfort and the degree of use can sometimes work against each other, reducing overall well-being. By ascertaining ways to renew energy and gain greater flexibility, the report prompts key tactics for development consideration. Rather than a four-letter code, individuals get eight function scores to provide a full picture of the use of the mental energies Jung proposed we have access to.

Appendix B

Matrix of Type Functions Development through Work Experiences

Appendix B: Type Development through Work Experiences

(Find the intersection of the Type Function and Work Experience to identify activity that develops the function)

Activity	Introverted Sensing (Si) Clarity/Accuracy	Introverted Intuiting (Ni) Futurizing	Introverted Thinking (Ti) Analyzing	Introverted Feeling (Fi) Evaluating	Extraverted Sensing (Se) Action	Extraverted Intuiting (Ne) Abstracting	Extraverted Thinking (Te) Critiquing	Extraverted Feeling (Fe) Empathizing
Benchmark performance	☑		☑				☑	
Integrate systems across units	☑	☑	☑		☑		☑	
Lead a task force		☑				☑	☑	☑
Serve at trade show booth					☑	☑	☑	☑
Represent company on community board		☑	☑	☑		☑		☑
Mentor a new employee	☑	☑	☑	☑		☑		☑
Intentionally mend conflictual relationship		☑		☑	☑	☑		☑
Evaluate the impact of training	☑		☑				☑	
Teach a course		☑	☑				☑	

Task								
Work with a team where you have no expertise	☑		☑			☑	☑	
Manage a fix-it operation		☑		☑		☑		☑
Manage a start-up operation				☑		☑	☑	☑
Analyze customer complaints						☑		☑
Find a mentor for a specific area	☑	☑				☑	☑	
Develop a risk management plan for department		☑	☑				☑	☑
Do a competitive analysis		☑	☑			☑	☑	☑
Work with the most dissatisfied customer	☑	☑	☑					
Manage a multinational project	☑	☑	☑	☑			☑	
Lead a virtual team	☑		☑			☑	☑	☑

Appendix C

Matrix of Type Functions Development through Leisure Experiences

Appendix C: Type Development through Leisure Experiences

(Find the intersection of the Type Function and Leisure Experience to identify the activity that develops the function)

Key Quality	Introverted Sensing (Si) Clarity/Accuracy	Introverted Intuiting (Ni) Futurizing	Introverted Thinking (Ti) Analyzing	Introverted Feeling (Fi) Evaluating	Extraverted Sensing (Se) Action	Extraverted Intuiting (Ne) Abstracting	Extraverted Thinking (Te) Critiquing	Extraverted Feeling (Fe) Empathizing
30-minute focus on color, design	☑							
Acting	☑				☑			☑
Art Gallery*	☑	☑	☑	☑**		☑		☑
Bike Riding			☑		☑			
Book Club	☑		☑			☑	☑	☑
Cinema				☑		☑		☑
Concerts					☑			
Cooking			☑		☑		☑	
Dancing					☑			
Dinner party	☑	☑	☑		☑			☑
Gardening*	☑				☑			
Gym Activity	☑				☑			
Hand crafts	☑		☑		☑	☑		
Hiking	☑	☑	☑		☑			

Activity								
Horseback Riding					☑			
Investment Club	☑		☑			☑	☑	☑
Listening to music	☑	☑		☑**		☑		
Painting (art)	☑	☑	☑		☑	☑		
Photography*	☑	☑		☑**	☑			
Puzzles	☑		☑		☑	☑	☑	
Read to children					☑	☑		☑
Reading	☑	☑	☑	☑				
Road Trip	☑	☑			☑			
Sailing	☑		☑		☑			
Service activities e.g., soup kitchen				☑	☑	☑		☑
Speed Shopping					☑		☑	
Swimming	☑		☑		☑			
Tennis/Games	☑		☑		☑		☑	
Theatre		☑		☑		☑		☑
Woodworking	☑	☑	☑		☑			
Yoga	☑	☑		☑				

*No less than five minutes focusing on each object.

**Generate as many possible values and ideals reflected in the objects.

Notes

1. Nicholson, W. *Shadowlands*. New York: Plume, 1991.

Prescript

1. Myers, Isabel B. Unpublished letter read by Dr. Mary McCaulley at the International Conference of the Association for Psychological Type, 1991, Richmond, VA.

Section 1

1. Briggs, Isabel Myers. *Gifts Differing*. Palo Alto, CA: Consulting Psychologists Press, 1980, Inc., p. 7.

Chapter 1

1. Jung, Carl G. *Psychological Types*. Princeton: Princeton University Press, 1971, p. 333.
2. Myers, Isabel B., McCaulley, M., Quenk, N., and Hammer, A. *Manual: A Guide to the Development and Use of the Myers-Briggs Type Indicator*. Mountain View, CA: CPP, Inc., 1998; Majors, M. *Manual: Majors Personality Type Indicator*, Boulder, CO: Breckenridge Institute, 2007, pp. 4–11.
3. Jung, *Psychological Types*, pp. 330–405.
4. Myers, et al., *Manual: A Guide to the Development*, pp. 25–26.
5. Briggs, Isabel Myers. *Gifts Differing*. Palo Alto: Consulting Psychologists Press, 1980, Inc., pp. 69–76.
6. Ibid., pp. 17–26.
7. Storm, H. *Seven Arrows*. Toronto: Ballantine Books, Random House, 1972.
8. Wilson, M. and Languis, M. "Differences in Brain Electrical Activity Patterns Between Introverted and Extraverted Adults," *Journal of Psychological Type, 18* (1989), pp. 14–23.
9. This issue is very important. Today most American psychologists consider Introversion a form of odd behavior. As an example, see Barrick, M. R., and Mount, M. K. "The Big Five Personality Dimensions and Job Performance," *Personnel Psychology,* 1991, pp. 1–23. Even in more recent research reports, Introversion is seen as backward, neurotic, and quite unattractive. See Howard, P. and Howard J., *Manual: Workplace Big Five*. Charlotte, NC: Center for Applied Cognitive Studies, 2009.

307

10. Jung, *Psychological Types,* pp. 359–361.
11. Coon, Dennis. *Introduction to Psychology: Gateways to Mind and Behavior.* Boston: Cengage Learning,1989, pp. 256–275.
12. Jung, *Psychological Types,* pp. 368–370.
13. We have worked with a thousand teams over thirty years. These comments are the top four statements among all teams.
14. Myers and Myers, *Gifts Differing,* pp. 37–38.
15. Ibid., pp. 69–70.
16. Provost, J. *Procrastination.* Gainesville, FL: Center for the Application of Psychological Type, 1988.
17. Myers, et al., *Manual: A Guide to the Development,* pp. 35-102; Majors, *Manual: Majors Personality,* pp. 5–32.
18. Gough, H. and Thorne, A. *Portraits of Type.* Palo Alto, CA: Psychological Consultants, 1991; Mitchell, W. "A Test of Type Theory Using the TDI," *Journal of Psychological Type, 22* (1991), pp. 15–26.

Chapter 2

1. Ackerman, D. *A Natural History of the Senses.* New York: Random House, 1990, pp. 287–299.
2. Myers and Myers, *Gifts Differing,* pp. 83–116.
3. Jung, *Psychological Types,* pp. 405–407; Myers, *Introduction to Type,* pp. 8–23.
4. Myers and Myers, *Gifts Differing,* pp. 14–15.
5. Capra, F. *Tao of Physics.* Berkeley, CA: Shambala Press, 1975, pp. 5–27.
6. Jung, *Psychological Types,* pp. 175, 418–20.
7. Ibid., p. 516.
8. Intersecting research from psychological research publications such as *The Journal of Psychological Type,* articles in the database of the Center for Applications of Psychological Types.
9. Most of the time the general descriptions seem acceptable. However, there are sometimes considerable objections to the entire description.
10. Pearman, R. and Fleenor, J. "Differences in Observed and Self-Reported Qualities of Psychological Types," *Journal of Psychological Type, 39* (1996), pp. 3–17.

Section 2

1. "Ralph Waldo Emerson," Poets.org, https://poets.org/poet/ralph-waldo-emerson

Chapter 3

1. Jung, *Modern Man in Search of a Soul,* pp. 92–94.
2. Cohen, J. "Social Relationships and Health," *Journal of the American Psychological Association, 59*: 8 (2006), pp. 676–84.
3. Neff, Kristin, *Self-Compassion: The Proven Power of Being Kind to Yourself* April 19, 2011, HarperCollins Publishers.

Chapter 4

1. Von Franz, M. L. "The Inferior Function," Jung's Typology, Spring Publication, 1971, pp. 3–67; Myers and McCaulley, *Manual: A Guide to the Development and Use of the Myers-Briggs Type Indicator*, p. 18; Sharp, D. *Personality Types*. Toronto: Inner City Books, 1987, pp. 21–24; Jung, *Psychological Types*, p. 450.
2. For a full discussion of this aspect of the inferior function, see Quenk, N. *Beside Ourselves*. Mountain View, CA: CPP, Inc., 1993.
3. Jung, *Psychological Types*, p. 450.

Chapter 5

1. *The Wizard of Oz*. Victor Fleming, director. Hollywood: Metro-Goldwyn-Mayer Pictures, 1939. Based on L. Frank Baum's *The Wonderful World of Oz*, 1900.
2. Extensive work on this aspect of child development has been completed by Jerome Kagan, PhD, Harvard University Professor of Education. Review any child development research journal to follow his work.
3. Corlett, E. and Millner, N. *Navigating Midlife*. Mountain View, CA: CPP, Inc., 1993, pp. 27–47.
4. brenebrown.com/blog/2013/01/14/shame-v-guilt/
5. Brown, B., *I Thought It Was Just Me, (But It Isn't)*. New York: Gotham, 2007.
6. McCall, M., et al. *The Lessons of Experience*. New York: Macmillan, 1988, pp. 6–13.

Section 3

1. "Ready, Set, Go! 13 Quotes to Inspire You to Take Action," *SUCCESS*, https://www.success.com/ready-set-go-13-quotes-to-inspire-you-to-take-action/.

Chapter 6

1. Mayer, J., Salovey, P., Caruso, D. *MSCEIT: User's Manual*. Toronto: MHS, Ins, 2002, pp. 710.
2. Pearman, R. *Understanding Emotions*. Winston-Salem, NC: Leadership Performance Systems, Inc., 2006, pp. 10–14. Reprinted with permission.
3. Pearman, R. *Emotions and Type* blog, *typeemotions.com* (2009).
4. Pearman, R. *Understanding Emotions*. Winston-Salem, NC: Leadership Performance Systems, Inc., 2006, pp. 10–14. Reprinted with permission.
5. Brown, Brené, *Rising Strong*, Random House LLC, 2015, p. 87, Kindle.
6. Pearman, R. *Introduction to Type and Emotional Intelligence*. Mountain View, CA: CPP, Inc. Reprinted with permission.
7. Ibid.

Chapter 7

1. Pearman, R. *Using Type Effectively*. Winston-Salem, NC: Leadership Performance Systems, Inc., 2010. Reprinted with permission.

2. Pearman, R. Various career-planning workshops and presentations from 1981 to 2010. Materials based on integration of studies from multiple sources and disciplines. Illustration 1 captures a summary of key findings. This is the first publication of this integrated perspective on career planning and decision-making.

3. *DIY* by Pearman, R. and Eichinger, R. (2019) TeamTelligent Publisher.

4. *YOU* by Pearman, R., Lombardo, M, and Eichinger, R. (2006). Korn Ferry, Inc.

5. Pearman, R. (2010). Confidential study completed for a global corporation whose headquarters are in the Midwest of the United States. By legal contract, the company cannot be listed but the results are shared with permission. Sample size included the entire management staff and the analysis included all performance and development data collected by the organization. Similar research results produced Pearman, R., Lombardo, M., and Eichinger, R. *YOU: Being More Effective in Your MBTI Type*. Minneapolis: Lominger, Inc., 2006.

6. "Listening to Shame," TED Talks, https://www.ted.com/talks/brene_brown_listening_to_shame/transcript?language=en.

7. Pearman, R. *Emotions and Health*. Winston-Salem, NC: Leadership Performance Systems, Inc., 2008, pp. 4–6.

8. Brown, K., Creswell, J., and Ryan, R. Handbook of Mindfulness: Theory, Research, and Practice. New York: *The Guildford Press*, 2016.

Section 4

1. "The Apocryphal Twain: "Kindness Is Language the Deaf Can Hear," Center for Mark Twain Studies, June 1, 2017, https://marktwainstudies.com/apocryphaltwainoptimism/.

Chapter 8

1. Jung, *Psychological Types,* pp. 290–294; 457–458.

2. Jung, Carl G. *On the Nature of the Psyche*. Princeton: Princeton University Press, 1960, pp. 134–35.

3. McAleer, G. and Knode, S. "Senior Military Leaders and the MBTI," 1995 Conference Proceedings: Conscious Choices, Unconscious Forces, Association for Psychological Type, APTX, Newport Beach, CA, pp. 111–13.

4. Myers and McCaulley, et al. *Manual: A Guide to the Development and Use of the Myers-Briggs Type Indicator,* 1998, pp. 22–23.

Chapter 9

1. Pearman, R. "Diversity Denied: Type Bias in Manager Selection," paper presented at the eleventh biennial conference of the Association for Psychological Type, July 15, 1995, Kansas City, MO.

2. Jung, Carl G. *Symbols of Transformation*. Princeton: Princeton University Press, 1956, p. 440.

3. Spencer, P. U. *Who Speaks for Wolf*. Austin, TX: Tribe of Two Press, 1983.

4. Ibid., pp. 36–37.
5. Myers and Myers, *Gifts Differing,* p. 178.

Chapter 10

1. Howe, N. and Strauss, W. "The Next 20 Years: How Customer and Workforce Attitudes Will Evolve," *Harvard Business Review,* online edition, January 8, 2008, pp. 1–10.
2. Pearman, R. and Hummel-Crowe, R. *Using Type Effectively Across Generations.* Winston-Salem, NC: Leadership Performance Systems, Inc., 2010. Reprinted with permission.
3. Zemke, R., Raines, C., and Filipczak, B. *Generations at Work.* New York: AMA-COM, Inc., 2000; Bennis, W. and Thomas, R. *Geeks & Geezers.* Cambridge, MA: Harvard Business School Press, 2002.
4. Deal, J. *Retiring the Generation Gap.* San Francisco: Jossey-Bass, 2007. Similar results were discovered with data collected by Roger R. Pearman in interviews with cross-generational students when he was an assistant professor in the Calloway School of Business, Wake Forest University.
5. Pearman, R. *Introduction to Type® and Emotional Intelligence.* Mountain View, CA: CPP, Inc., 2002, pp. 22–51. Used with permission.

Chapter 11

1. Trompenaars, F. and Hampden-Turner, C. *Riding the Waves of Culture.* New York, NY: McGraw-Hill, 1998, pp. 35–142; Harris, P. and Moran, R. *Managing Cultural Differences.* London: Gulf Publishing Company, 1996, pp. 15–59; Gundling, E. *Working Globesmart.* Palo Alto, CA: Davies-Black Publishing, 2003, pp. 23–127; Ferraro, G. *Global Brains.* Charlotte, NC: Intercultural Associates, 2002, pp. 77–118.
2. Ibid.
3. Pearman, R. *Introduction to Type' and Emotional Intelligence.* Mountain View, CA: CPP, Inc., 2002, pp. 20–51. Reprinted with permission.

Section 5

1. Augustus William Hare and Julius Charles Hare, *Guesses at Truth By Two Brothers,* 1827.

Chapter 12

1. Nardi, D. *Neuroscience of Personality: Brain Savvy Insights for All Types of People.* Los Angeles: Radiance House, 2011.

Chapter 13

1. Tuttle, M. D. "North American Bats." *National Geographic, 188*: 2 (1995), pp. 36–57.

2. Jung, Carl G. *Memories, Dreams, and Reflections.* New Haven, CT: Yale University Press, 1963, pp. 207.
3. Jung, *Psychological Types,* pp. 554–55.

Chapter 14

1. Stillinger, J. *Wordsworth: Selected Poems and Preludes.* Boston: Houghton Mifflin, 1965, pp. 241–58.
2. *Ibid.*
3. Hamilton, E. and Carins, H., eds. *Plato.* Princeton: Princeton University Press, 1973, pp. 747–72.
4. Pearman, R. "Knowledge Purchased: Uses and Misuses of the MBTI." *Bulletin of Psychological Type.* Winter, 1993, pp. 2–3.
5. A statement frequently made as a summary of the type verification steps suggested in Myers and McCaulley. *Manual: A Guide to the Development and Use of the Myers-Briggs Type Indicator,* pp. 52–61.

Index

About the Authors

ROGER R. PEARMAN, EdD, is the founder of Leadership Performance Systems, Inc., which provides extensive coaching and talent development services for organizations in the United States, Europe, and Asia, and co-founder of TeamTelligent, LLC, which provides comprehensive talent management consulting and product services. Roger has served as a visiting faculty member of the Calloway School of Business, Wake Forest University. He is a Senior Adjunct Associate for the Center for Creative Leadership. As a former COO of a financial services company and president of the International Association of Psychological Type, he gained extensive practical knowledge related to the development of individuals and organizations. Roger has worked with users of personality type on every continent, which has provided a rich ground for research contributions. His research received the Myers Research Award and the McCaulley Lifetime Achievement Award. A contributor to Inc.com and Talent Management, Roger's publications include:

> *Hard Wired Leadership: Unleashing Personality for the New Millennium Leader* (1998)
> *Enhancing Leadership Effectiveness* (2000)
> *Leadership Advantage* (2001)
> *Introduction to Type® and Emotional Intelligence* (2002)
> *Using the MBTI® Tool to Enrich Emotional Intelligence* (2005)
> *Type 360™—an award-winning multi-rater instrument* (2003)
> *YOU, Being More Effective in Your MBTI® Type* (2005)
> *Understanding Emotions* (2007)
> *Emotions and Leadership and Emotions and Health* (2008)

Roger is also co-creator of these iPad Applications, which use Psychological Type:

Teamosity
Careerfitosity
Relate!

Roger completed his bachelor's and master's degrees from Wake Forest University and his doctoral degree from the University of North Carolina at Greensboro. Through his research, training, coaching, writing, and consulting services, Roger seeks to help individuals learn how to be more effective. He lives with his wife of thirty-seven years in Winston-Salem, North Carolina; adult daughter Olivia and son Luke are making their way in life using their gifts.

SARAH C. ALBRITTON, MS, is known for delivering high-impact coaching and leadership consulting to chief/senior executives and their teams in companies throughout the world. She has been an independent coach and consultant since 1991. A Certified Daring Way™ and Rising Strong™ Facilitator since 2014, she was one of only 12 Master Facilitators selected for Dr. Brené Brown's Brave Leaders Inc and is now a Certified Dare To Lead™ Facilitator. She received her formal coach training at the Center for Creative Leadership (CCL) in 1999 before coaching certifications existed! She was an adjunct faculty member at CCL for seven years in the early 2000s, where she coached senior leaders and high-profile clients.

A dynamic, highly esteemed speaker, coach, and consultant, Sarah is known for her fearless and supportive candor. Anchoring her relationships in trust, respect, and a healthy dose of humor, she uses well-grounded assessment data from 360 tools, personality assessments, and interviews to gain insight and offer challenge to inspire honest reflection and lasting strategic change. The lyric from Broadway hit *Wicked* sums it up: "Don't be offended by my frank analysis. Just think of it as personality dialysis!"

Sarah holds degrees in Economics (BA) from Wake Forest University and Educational Leadership (MS) from Florida State University. She holds many certifications in personality and leadership assessment tools, and has served on the faculty of several certification programs training other coaches in effective application and interpretation techniques.

Sarah lives in Winston-Salem, North Carolina, with her husband, Andrew LaRowe, their 14-year-old rescue-Pit, and a holiday assortment of six grown children (and partners) and five growing grandchildren who live up and down the east coast. She hopes "home" means a warm welcome, good food, loving conversation, live music, rest, and lots of laughter wherever two or more are gathered.